A HISTORY OF
Transylvania

A HISTORY OF
Transylvania

BY ȘTEFAN PASCU

UNIVERSITY OF CLUJ-NAPOCA

TRANSLATED BY

D. Robert Ladd

WAYNE STATE UNIVERSITY PRESS

DETROIT, 1982

Library of Congress Cataloging in Publication Data

Pascu, Ştefan.
  A history of Transylvania.

  Translation of: Voievodatul Transilvaniei.
  Bibliography: p.
  Includes index.
  1. Transylvania—History. I. Title.
DR280.P3713 1982   949.8′4   82-8669
ISBN 0-8143-1722-7   AACR2

Contents

Maps and Illustrations

Foreword

HERE, FOR THE FIRST TIME in English, the complete Romanian position on Transylvania is presented in all its complexity.[1] Both that position and the way in which it is presented by the Romanian side have many nuances, as the reader of this volume will soon discover, for Romanian-Magyar polemics on the Transylvanian question are no mere scholarly exercise. The stakes are high for both countries, and the issue has long aroused explosive sentiment at home and strong reaction abroad. Because today both countries are under the influence of the Soviet Union, actual armed conflict over Transylvania is improbable. Should Soviet control of its empire weaken further, the issue may well become explosive, however; for now, the war is being conducted "esoterically."

Professor Ştefan Pascu's research attainments and standing in Romanian academic circles make his book a telling shot from the Romanian side, one that will not long remain unanswered upon its publication. The writing of such a history by a single person is in itself an impressive feat: Transylvania's diverse systems of government, languages, and cultures make it even more remarkable. Though the product of a collective scholarly effort is homogenized and usually dull, one of the principal arguments for collective works is the fact that one person rarely possesses the interdisciplinary resources to do his subject justice. Pascu, the dean of Romanian historians, is one of only a handful of scholars who could even attempt such a survey single-handedly, and he has marshaled his resources, experience, passionate commitment, and historical vision to breathe life into the treatment of this topic. He is a master of the relevant languages and materials; he has produced major monographs on the most complex aspects of the medieval and modern history of the region. Along with the political-geographical narrative, his interests encompass demography and statistics and social history,[2] and he has given us the case for Transylvania in the context of an analytic and synthetic history of the region.

In 1944, at the beginning of his career, Pascu published *Istoria Transilvaniei.* That book and this one are vast in scope, beginning with Antiquity and terminating the narrative with the interwar România Mare. The pre-Romanian phase of Transylvanian history is given much greater attention in the current treatment, reflecting present Romanian historiographical emphasis on origins, while the medieval voivodate era looms larger in the earlier work. Both narratives more or less end after World War I: the movement Pascu is tracing is toward the Union of 1918—once this is achieved, the story is over; then too, from the Romanian point of view, after 1918 Transylvania as such no longer has a separate history. In 1944 Pascu was writing in a pre-socialist Transylvania rent asunder by the 1940 Vienna partition. In 1982, in a reunified Transylvania within the Romanian Socialist Republic, he applies a Marxist-Leninist paradigm. In 1944, Romanian cultural policy reflected individual bent more than official design. In 1982, cultural policy is subject to the minute scrutiny of official watchdogs. In both histories, however, we are given the history of Romania and Transylvania from the vantage point of a committed Romanian nationalist. Both works stress the unity and ethnic awareness (linguistic, cultural, and so forth) of all Romanians; the artificiality of the political boundaries which separate them; the millennial continuity and primacy of the Romanians in the region; and the gradual (perhaps inevitable) evolution of Transylvania toward the establishment of a Greater Romania in 1918 despite Great-Power opposition and interference and repeated attempts to defuse nationalist aspirations.[3] Finally, in this book we find again certain events emphasized, e.g., the reign of Michael the Brave and the revolution of Horia, which become elements of the Romanian nationalist catechism.

The book is an excellent illustration of southeast European historical scholarship and interests. The national historiography of each people—the questions raised by a nation's historians—naturally reflect its national experiences. Positivist historians used to imagine that history would somehow emerge from the accumulation of documents; it is now apparent that history emerges from the historians' inquiries.[4] In the best of all possible worlds, the historian might pursue his course along the lines dictated by his own curiosity, skill, and ability, eventually arriving at whatever approximation of the truth that these provide him. In the real world, a wide variety of factors influence the choice of questions he pursues, the shaping of those questions, the means by which they are investigated, and the argumentation that results. These factors are often further complicated by the geopolitical situation of his country (its size, the dispositions of its neighbors, etc.) and especially by the presence and intensity of national sentiment in the intellectual culture that has developed.

For the people of eastern Europe, history has an importance and significance that is astonishing to Americans. The amount of public attention devoted to historical events, research, publications, and education is extraordinary. Even more striking is the allocation of scarce resources to historical pursuits through academies, institutes, libraries, and printing houses. "Few areas are as history-minded as Central and Eastern Europe," Robert R. King notes, and explains why: "There history is perhaps the most important foundation stone of national consciousness; the past is not a subject for harmless small talk."[5] The linguistic element is probably an equally crucial factor in the raising of national consciousness, at least initially, but King's general point is perfectly correct. Thus Henry L. Roberts can write, concerning the "historical mode" of thinking about oneself in eastern Europe: "Its self-perception is, in part at least, provided by its historical awareness and a tradition of historiography, that is, the past as organized and interpreted by the historian."[6]

This observation is strikingly illustrated by Professor Pascu's work here. While the Transylvanian debate takes place on ethnic, economic, and other levels, it is on the historical front that the most ammunition is expended, the most imposing defensive bastions constructed, and the most frequent sorties made. For the eastern European, history can be something of an obsession, a "reality" based on the nation's "shared belief in a common history . . . real or imagined."[7] The dilemma arises in trying to think historically without allowing that thinking to dominate one's search for the facts and the shape of the past. Quite often this perception of a national past is expanded into a vision of present and future as well. That this occurs is indicated from time to time by an explosive response to any innocent remarks or questions that to the slightest degree intrude upon the basic themes and theses of national history as written in eastern Europe. As Roberts notes, the historian is the organizer and interpreter of the past, not merely its recorder.

The logic of this position becomes clearer if we accept the nationalist premise that the very survival or advancement of one's particular nation or national group is intimately related to maintenance of such themes and theses. The historian is therefore seen not as a purveyor of objects of antiquarian interest but rather as the guardian of the national hearth. And when such concerns are reinforced by and linked to the political interests of a totalitarian state mechanism, the combination can be particularly potent.

For the people of large and reasonably secure political entities, such as the United States, the nationalist fervor of Eastern Europeans is either mysterious or deplorable. However, when we consider what the nation means to these peoples, another perspective must be developed. Walter Sulzbach defined a nation as "a group of people which wishes to be sovereign among other peoples and therefore desires a state of its own."[8] The link between state establishment and survival and ethnic survival thereby becomes a crucial factor in shaping the ideas and concepts which dominate a national culture.[9]

This emphasis is further augmented in eastern Europe by the relatively late emergence of national consciousness and state sovereignty in the region. In western Europe, the modern centralized territorial state and the national consciousness emerged over a long period of time and more or less concurrently. This was not the case in eastern, particularly southeastern, Europe.[10] Such circumstances made for a significantly different dynamic in East and West, as Alexandru Duțu's recent comparative study of Romania and Europe[11] convincingly demonstrates.

The development of Romanian scholarship, like that of southeastern Europe in general, was heavily influenced by the significant role played by the "philosopher-patriot"[12] in the late medieval and early modern period. Scholarly writing was the vehicle for the expression of national awareness (if not for the emergence of that sentiment itself); it is noteworthy that it continues to be so into the twentieth century. Romanian historiography in the academic sense began to emerge about a century ago with the work of A. D. Xenopol (1847–1920) at the University of Iași and the new generation at the University of Bucharest in 1891, led by Ioan Bogdan (1864–1919). These were soon joined by other remarkable figures: Dimitrie Onciul (1856–1923), N. Iorga (1871–1940), Constantin Giurescu (1875–1918), and Vasile Pârvan (1882–1927).[13]

The real flourishing of the profession occurred, however, after World War I and the unification of all Romanians into a single state. Many of the first generation continued their work; they were joined by the great university schools of the inter-war era grouped around prominent journals: at Bucharest, N. Iorga's *Revista Istorică* (1915–1946) and his Institute of Universal History and C. C. Giurescu's *Revista Istorică Română* (1931–1947) and his Institute of National History;[14] at Cluj, the Institute of National History under the leadership of Ioan Lupaş and Al. Lăpedatu, with their *Anuarul Institutului de Istorie Naţională din Cluj* (1921–1945); at Iaşi, Ilie Minea's *Cercetări Istorice* (1925–1947); and at Cernăuţi, Ioan Nistor's *Codrul Cosminului* (1924–1935).

The Cluj school was conspicuous in the forefront of this development.[15] Founded concurrently with the Romanian University of Cluj after World War I, the institute at Cluj generated much first-class scholarship, especially on the Transylvanian matter. Ştefan Pascu was a product of that school and then a key member of its research and didactic cadre.[16]

The establishment of the Communist regime in Romania between 1945 and 1948 caused not only major social and political but also cultural and intellectual disruption. However, in contrast to Hungary, for example, a surprisingly large part of the Romanian cultural elite survived the changeover.[17] Romanian historical scholarship underwent a drastic "conversion" to the Marxist-Leninist model, first under Stalinist-Zhdanov conceptions, then (after 1956) under an increasingly Romanianized version of Marxist orthodoxy.[18] Ştefan Pascu was both a spokesman for the Cluj tradition and a leading member of the new Cluj school. This eventually brought him to a prominent position in Romanian historical circles as a whole (he became president of the national historical committee and a fellow of the Romanian Academy).

By happy chance, Professor Pascu's two treatments of the history of Transylvania not only provide a picture of this complex region's long and troubled history but also may be viewed as, in effect, works of summation. The 1944 study came at the end of two decades or more of pioneering work by the Cluj school. As Pompiliu Teodor perceptively points out,[19] this work really provides the student of historiography with a synthesis of the efforts (methodological and thematic) of Cluj historians between the wars. In the same way, the current work, though it does not end an era of scholarship, provides us with a synthesis of the methods, ideas, and emphases of contemporary Romanian Marxist historical scholarship.

An outstanding facet of Romanian Marxist historiography is the role it plays in the policies of the Romanian state and the Romanian Communist Party. One of the consequences of a totally integrated political system such as that of the Socialist Republic of Romania is that the closely controlled public media, which category includes the dissemination of historical analysis, often convey a variety of messages on a variety of levels. Historical studies produced in such societies not only present current scholarly understanding concerning the past but also consciously reflect the present official conceptions of that society. Though analysis of such "esoteric communications" gives rise to the much-maligned, and often absurd, findings of the Kremlinologists, it would be a serious mistake to deny that such communication exists and can be interpreted.[20] Professor Pascu's book is primarily a work of historical interpretation and synthesis and must be approached as such. However, it is also a product of a society in which public expression must be consonant with public policy, so that here we may detect trends in contemporary Romanian foreign policy, policy toward national minorities, and the political and social mobilization that the Romanian Communist Party is trying to carry out under increasingly difficult circumstances.

In Romania today, history serves both legitimating and mobilizing functions crucial to regime maintenance. The government's efforts to carry out a program of developing and utilizing the national heritage are not unique in eastern Europe, but they are unusual because of the degree to which they have been carried and because of the success with which traditional national themes have been co-opted into the service of those in power.[21] Thus it is possible for a recent article in a party journal to set forth the official line as follows: "In the conception of the Romanian Communist Party, reflected in a conspicuous manner in the thought of Comrade Nicolae Ceauşescu, the study of history occupies a major place in ideological activity, being considered not only an act of knowing the past of mankind but—beyond that, and especially—as a powerful means of political education, of the formation and development of self-consciousness, in a patriotic and revolutionary spirit, of the masses, especially the youth."[22]

Because the Romanian population subscribes to the national desiderata virtually as a matter of national defense, such pleas are not taken lightly. Patriotism, education, and Communist regime politics are combined into a whole that will brook no variation. As the president of Romania stressed not long ago, "Patriotism was, is, and will always remain a good of the nation of our people—and any deviation from revolutionary patriotism . . . conscious or unconscious, serves the interests of the enemies of the people."[23]

In the light of these nationalist sentiments, the extraordinarily high level of historical consciousness in southeastern Europe, and official policy considerations, the publication of this book in the United States is an event of no little importance, not only for what it tells us about the past of one of Europe's most interesting and historically complex areas but for what it shows us of Romanian historiography. Finally, as a work by a leading member of the Romanian cultural establishment, the book provides a useful, if indirect, view of contemporary Romanian political and cultural policy.

Paul E. Michelson
Huntington College

Notes

1. An extended essay by C. C. Giurescu, *Transylvania in the History of the Romanian People,* was published in Bucharest by Meridiane in 1968. Robert R. King (*Minorities under Communism: Nationalities as a Source of Tension among Balkan Communist States* [Cambridge, Mass., 1973], pp. 174–76) presents a review of earlier scholarly salvos on this question.
2. Typical are works on the peasant revolts (1947, 1957), the medieval voivodate (1971, 1979), Avram Iancu (1972), the Union of 1918 (1968), and even a history of the handicraft industry in medieval Transylvania (1954).
3. See Paul E. Michelson, "Unity and Continuity in Romanian History," *Canadian Review of Studies in Nationalism* 8 (1981):29–69, for further discussion.
4. See David Hackett Fischer, *Historians' Fallacies* (New York, 1970), *passim,* and J. H. Hexter, *Doing History* (Bloomington, Ind., 1971), pp. 139ff.
5. *Minorities under Communism,* p. 171.
6. *Eastern Europe: Politics, Revolution, and Diplomacy* (New York, 1970), p. 4.
7. Boyd C. Shafer, *The Faces of Nationalism* (New York, 1972), p. 18. This belief is one of ten traits which Shafer identifies as characteristic of nationalism.
8. *National Consciousness* (Washington, D.C., 1943), p. 66.
9. Whether state sovereignty is actually critical to the ethnos or ethnic consciousness decisive in achievement of sovereignty is not significant: it is the perceived link that matters.

10. King, *Minorities under Communism*, pp. 7–8.
11. *European Intellectual Movements and Modernization of Romanian Culture* (Bucharest, 1981), especially pp. 87ff. Duțu cautions us to avoid overly stressing "lateness' or the separateness of eastern and western Europe, however.
12. The term is suggested by Duțu, *ibid.*, pp. 47ff.
13. Two general treatments are Lucian Boia, *Evoluția istoriografiei române* (Bucharest, 1976), and Pompiliu Teodor, *Evoluția gîndirii istorice românești* (Cluj, 1970). I have a more specialized study under way tentatively entitled *A New Nation Looks at Its Past: The Development of Romanian Historiography, 1890–1947.*
14. See Paul E. Michelson, "The Master of Synthesis: Constantin C. Giurescu and the Coming of Age of Romanian Historiography, 1919–1947," in *Romania between East and West*, edited by Stephen Fischer-Galati and Radu R. Florescu (New York, 1982).
15. A useful retrospective is Al. Borza et al., *Institutul de Istorie Națională din Cluj-Sibiu, 1920–1945* (Sibiu, 1945).
16. See his "Metoda de muncă științifică la Institutul de Istorie Națională din Cluj-Sibiu în primul sfert de veac (1920–1945)," in *ibid.*, pp. 99–105.
17. For some, survival meant quick political footwork; others went to prison camp and were reinstated in academic posts only later. This is not to overlook or minimize the loss of numerous scholars after 1948, whose deaths were caused by the new regime.
18. This story is strikingly told by Vlad Georgescu in *Politica și istorie: Cazul comuniștilor români 1944–1977* (Munich, 1981). Also useful is Michael J. Rura's *Reinterpretation of History as a Method of Furthering Communism in Rumania* (Washington, D.C., 1961).
19. Teodor, *Sub semnul lui Clio* (Cluj, 1974), p. 6.
20. See William E. Griffith, *Communist Esoteric Communications: Explication de Texte* (Cambridge, Mass., 1967).
21. For a succinct and forthright analysis of this process, see R. V. Burks' "The Romanian National Deviation: An Accounting," *Continuity*, no. 2 (1981), pp. 63–104. See also Michelson, "Unity and Continuity." For the relationship between history and the current Romanian regime, see Robert R. King, *History of the Romanian Communist Party* (Stanford, 1980), especially pp. 1–6 and 120–34, and Georgescu, *Politica.* Pascu has written on Ceaușescu's policy vis-à-vis historiography as well: "Tovarășul Nicolae Ceaușescu și reașezarea istoriei la locul potrivit importanței sale," *Tribuna* 22, nos. 3–4 (1978):1, 14. A recent survey of Romanian policy and development that provides excellent coverage is Daniel N. Nelson, ed., *Romania in the 1980s* (Boulder, Col., 1981).
22. Ion Ardeleanu and Mircea Mușat, "Unele probleme fundamentale ale istoriei patriei, ale Partidului Comunist Român," *Anale de Istorie* 27 (1981):76, in an article expressly addressed to history teachers. The title of another recent article makes the same message clear: "Past-Present, an Indissoluable Relationship." Cf. V. Cristian, "Trecut-prezent, o relație indisolubilă," *Cronica* 16 (1981):2.
23. In a speech carried by the Party daily *Scînteia*, November 26, 1981. Compare Al. Tănase, "Patriotismul și legitimitatea națiunii în lumea contemporană," *România Literară* 15 (1982):5. On education and patriotism, see Pascu's "Educația patriotică a tineretului," *Revista Pedagogică* 15 (1966):16–25.

Note on the Translation

THIS VOLUME, the first extended history of Transylvania to be published in English, presents a synthesis of Ştefan Pascu's *Voievodatul Transilvaniei*, materials drawn from his other works, and passages written specifically for English-language publication. The translation is relatively free, but the factual and interpretive substance of Pascu's work has not been altered. The translator wishes to thank Mr. Ioan A. Popa for his help.

The most difficult problem for the translator is to find a consistent method for dealing with the numerous geographical and personal names that occur in the history of multiethnic and politically troubled Transylvania. In the few cases where Romanian place names have well-known English equivalents, the anglicized names have been used in the forms preferred in *Webster's New Geographical Dictionary* (1977), with two exceptions. Following traditional Romanian usage, *Ţara Românească* has been used to refer to the territory more familiar to English-speakers as Wallachia; likewise, the Romanian adjective *Muntenian* has been used to refer to the inhabitants, characteristics, or events in *Ţara Românească*. If no anglicized form exists, the translation uses the modern Romanian spelling.

Personal names follow essentially the same pattern. If an anglicized form is in general use, that preferred in *Webster's Biographical Dictionary* has been used. In all other cases, names are spelled according to the individual's native language. (Hungarian names, however, occur as given-family name, rather than in the usual Hungarian family-given order.)

In both the text and the Bibliography, the titles of manuscripts and printed works are cited in the original language, with Romanian and Hungarian titles translated in brackets following the first reference. Social, political, and cultural organizations have been cited in English only in textual references.

Introduction

TRANSYLVANIA, as the name is generally used, encompasses over 39,000 square miles, or slightly less than half of the area of Romania as a whole. It presents an exceptionally varied terrain, at once complex and picturesque. Bounded by the Carpathians and the Tisza Plain, the Transylvanian landscape ranges from low plains to high mountains. All those who have known it have been awed by this majestic countryside and have sought to describe it in a variety of ways. Even to the casual eye, the beauty of Transylvania—whether to the north, south, east, or west—is striking.

The Carpathian Mountains surround Transylvania like a fortress wall on the north, east, and south, with the Bihor Mountains—which the Romanians call the Munţii Apuseni, or "Western Mountains"—closing the circle. The southern Transylvanian Alps average 5,000 feet and the eastern Moldavian Carpathians around 4,000, while the western range averages under 3,000. The peaks of the Carpathians are not only hospitable, but very useful to man; the level plateaus, covered with lush alpine pastures, support herds of sheep in the summer. The philologist Ovidiu Densuşianu saw the Carpathians as friendly companions, radiating an almost classical harmony and serenity. Such hospitable splendor affords sufficient explanation for the fact that these mountains are inhabited at altitudes up to and even beyond 4,000 feet.

The Carpathians further show their generosity to man by the numerous passes which cut across their width like so many open windows. And since time immemorial, people have moved their sheep and other livestock through these passes, from Transylvania to Ţara Românească and Moldavia, in their annual migration from mountain to lowland pastures. Through them people have traveled, in groups or alone, with carts and wagons loaded with goods bound for market. Such continual comings and goings forged a powerful bond among related peoples, establishing a solid basis for the shared language and culture, the economic and political community, of the modern Romanian people.

Emerging from the mountains, one encounters the basins, those welcoming ramparts of the Carpathians, gradually stepping down from the peaks, the faithful sentinels. From north to south the great intra-Carpathian basins are strung out one after another, beginning with the northernmost Maramureş basin and leading down to the southernmost Bîrsa basin, followed, to the west, by the basins of Sibiu and Secaş. These areas all have supported human populations from times long past. The Bihor Mountains likewise are ringed by a continuous chain of basins: the Sălaj, Huedin, Turda, Alba Iulia, Zlatna, Zărand, Beiuş, and Oaş. The basins are open toward the interior, most often following the river valleys coming down from the mountains. Thus they lead one on into the Transylvanian plateau, with its irregular rolling hills, the higher Tîrnave Hills in the south and the Someş plateau in the north, and the lower and gentler Transylvanian plain in the center. Between the band of basins and the flat plain is a ring of hills, and the lowest step leads down to the wide, flat Tisza plain.

Transylvania is watered by five great rivers rising in the heart of the mountains: the Olt, Mureş, Tîrnave, Criş, and Someş. In their descent they are swelled by other rivers and streams, both placid and turbulent, which drain and nourish the broad, fertile valleys. The system looks like the veins of a leaf, with some rivers flowing west to drain Transylvania and then joining the Tisza and subsequently the Danube. Others have cut through the mighty mountains, carving narrow gorges that link the people and places north, south, and east of the Carpathians, and then flow across to the same Danube, the river that protected prehistoric men, the Dacians, the Daco-Romans, and finally the Romanians themselves.

Modern Transylvania is the creation of the indigenous Romanians and those peoples—Hungarians, Szeklers, Germans, and Serbs—who have lived alongside them and helped to shape an unusually rich and complex cultural heritage. The Romanians, a synthesis of the Dacian and Roman peoples, have always constituted an absolute majority of the Transylvanian population. The Hungarians and Szeklers, who belong to the same Turkic family

of peoples, settled in Transylvania in the eleventh and twelfth
centuries. The Germans are represented by two groups: the Saxons, whose colonies were established in the twelfth century, and
the Swabians, who came in the eighteenth. Serbs fleeing the
threat of Ottoman expansionism settled in the Banat in the fifteenth and sixteenth centuries. Each of these peoples brought its
distinctive traditions and institutions, which, taking root beside
the native culture, proved to be resistant to change. Transylvanian culture also was enriched by the uninterrupted ties between
the indigenous population and the other branches of the Romanian people inhabiting Moldavia and Țara Românească, the lands
to the south and east of the Carpathians. Transylvania was or-
ganically linked to these two territories; their economic, cultural, and institutional ties crossed artificial political boundaries, for they were based on a common ethnic foundation, a
common language and culture, and common interests. It was
not until the twentieth century, however, that international recognition of Transylvania's right to a place within a unified Romanian state was confirmed by the treaty of Trianon (1920).

In a sense, the turbulent history of Transylvania is the story of
evolution toward Great Romania, no matter which foreign
power might claim political authority over its land. All of the
area north, south, and east of the Carpathians has been inhabited
since prehistoric times by the same basic ethnic group: first the
Dacians, then the Daco-Romans, and finally their descendants,
the Romanians. Thus for millennia the whole territory has been
inhabited by people of a single background, speaking the same
dialectically undifferentiated language of Latin origin. Faced
with similar needs and similar resources, these people created a
unified culture, identical customs and traditions. A single people
came into being in Transylvania, Țara Românească, Moldavia,
and Dobruja, the result of the symbiosis and eventual fusion of
the Dacian substratum with the Roman superstratum. They
were deeply attached to their native soil, whether in the mountains or in the hills and lowlands. They took to the forests in the
face of adversity, to the plateaus and plains during more fruitful,
peaceful times; they laboriously tilled their fields and defended
them with their very lives. This great ethnic group was so tough
and resilient that the upheavals of the Age of Migration failed to
alter its structure as the wandering tribes passed through. The
ethnolinguistic unity of the Romanians, together with the continuing ties of various kinds between them and the other peoples

within their territorial boundaries, early gave birth to an active national consciousness.

From the beginning, the Romanians' Roman lineage and the Latin origin of their language formed part of their conscious identity, and as time passed this self-awareness grew sharper and more focused. This fact is seen very vividly in accounts by two Italian humanists, Poggio Bracciolini and Flavio Biondo, who wrote only two years apart, but without borrowing one another's impressions. In 1451, Bracciolini knew from hearsay that the Romanians were the descendants of Trajan's colonists, while in 1453 Biondo knew of their Roman origin from the Romanians themselves, as well as from the evidence of their language, which they prized like a jewel from Rome. Their testimony was corroborated in 1532 by Francesco della Valle, who based his observations on personal experiences, either at the Dealu monastery or in Tîrgoviște. From this and similar evidence, one can draw the irrefutable inference that the Romanian people were aware of the Roman origin of themselves and their language long before any scholarly discussion, Romanian or foreign, of the subject. Collective consciousness preceded scientific knowledge, not the reverse. This popular awareness, attested in medieval writings, later became known throughout Europe because of those writings; later still, it was taken up by sixteenth- and seventeenth-century Romanian chroniclers from two different sources: the ever-fresh awareness among the people themselves and the scholarly work to which they had been exposed at the humanistic schools where they were educated. The Romanian humanist Nicholaus Olahus, for example, also stated that the Romanians of Transylvania, Țara Românească, and Moldavia regarded themselves as a Roman colony, as proved, in particular, by words shared in Romanian and Latin. Probably more than anyone else, Olahus expressed the dual origin, popular and scholarly, of this idea.

This existence of such a collective popular identity accounts for the Romanians' strong attachment to their language, a feeling so intense that foreigners often were astonished by it. Antonio Bonfini, another Italian humanist, was amazed that the Romanians had preserved Latin amid the turmoil of so many barbarian invasions; he explained it by saying that the Romanians seemed to have fought more for the preservation of their language than for their lives.

The people's awareness was transmitted from generation to

generation, and was transformed into scholarly awareness. Scholars hoped to disseminate written work in Romanian and thus to promote it as a language of culture. This scholarly activity marked the formal beginning of the Romanian literary language, but the formation of it may be considered to have begun approximately a century before the scholarly work. It was a regular process resulting from the mixing of the local speech of northern Țara Românească and that of southern Transylvania. This admixture is first observed in the earliest written Romanian texts, which circulated on both sides of the Carpathians. Around the end of the fifteenth century, translations into Romanian were made in Maramureș; also circulated south of the Carpathians were the *Catehism* [Catechism] of Sibiu (1544), the first book ever printed in Romanian, and the *Evangheliar* [Gospel] of 1546, the first printed work in Romanian still extant. Both were the work of a scholar who had emigrated to Transylvania from Moldavia, a man known as Filip the Moldavian.

The works of Deacon Coresi, especially those printed in Romanian in Brașov, likewise played a considerable role in the formation of the literary language, while at the same time meeting spiritual needs. In the twenty-six years from 1556 to 1582, Coresi published thirty-five books, although not all of them were purely Romanian. As Coresi's books, and those of others who followed him, reached even into the most remote villages, the early literary language was propagated as well. Coresi and his successors made it more uniform, thus laying the foundation of the modern Romanian written language.

All Romanians, moreover, also observed the same customs and traditions, with only insignificant local variations. For baptisms and weddings, wakes and burials, planting and harvesting, for fixing property lines and arbitrating disputes, they kept to the age-old practices and the Romanian law, the *jus valachicum.* Judges and "wise old men" adjudicated disputes, holding court under an "old leafy tree" in front of the church, on Sundays or whenever needed. According to a learned Transylvanian Hungarian of the eighteenth century, József Benkö, the Romanian way of life was so entrenched that one would find it easier to take the club from the hand of Hercules than to dissuade the Romanians from their folkways (*Transsilvania,* 1788).

Today the people of Transylvania continue to enrich their society, struggling to develop the land, to achieve liberty and justice, progress and prosperity. The history of Transylvania is an important chapter in the chronicles of Europe. If the present volume succeeds in setting forth that chapter, then to the extent that the reader is satisfied, the author will be satisfied. *Lectori salutem!*

A HISTORY OF
Transylvania

1

Pre-Roman Transylvania

Paleolithic and Neolithic Man

WE CAN TRACE THE BEGINNINGS of the history of Transylvania back hundreds of millennia, to the early Stone Age. At that time—some 600,000 years before Christ—man in Transylvania was emerging from the ape, as in other areas of Europe and in America, Asia, and Africa. According to anthropologists, these ape-men, or hominids, lived in bands or hordes. They existed very much like forest animals, eating whatever nature provided and sheltering in caves, under cliffs, and on riverbanks; their clothing was untreated animal skins. The hominids—with the help of that spark of intelligence which placed them a step above the other animals—were somewhat more advanced in their attempt to fashion rudimentary tools. Traces of what may be called human society dating from this period have been discovered in Transylvania at Racoviţa, in the vicinity of Sibiu; these remains are much like those found in Oltenia in the Dîrjov valley.

The next stage was the organization of human groups into clans or tribes. People of this period (40,000 to 12,000 B.C.) continued to live in caves, as, for example, those of Ohabaponor and Cioclovina in Transylvania, or of Baia de Fier in Oltenia. These caves are very similar to the well-known cave of Le Moustier in France, which has given its name to the civilization of the period. But there were also dwelling sites on high plains, better protected from danger and easier to defend with stone weapons. Tools such as spearheads, knives, and scrapers also helped Upper Paleolithic man to secure food by hunting, fishing, and gathering, although the domestication of animals such as pigs and dogs had already begun. Man's most epochal discoveries, however, were the use of fire from nature and, later, the making of fire by

rubbing sticks together. In short, one may justifiably characterize man of this era as *homo sapiens*. Furthermore, this "reasoning man" began to separate himself from nature, creating images
to influence supernatural forces in the hope that those forces
could be made more benevolent through various rituals, ceremonies, and sacrifices. Belief in an afterlife began to establish itself,
as did the need to provide a tangible expression for esthetic
feelings in the form of pictures of animals and hunting scenes
painted on the walls of caves.

The term "Neolithic revolution," which recent researchers
have used to characterize the following period, refers to the
grinding and even drilling of stone, through which more effective and efficient tools and weapons were fashioned. Clothing
progressed further, thanks to the newly developed crafts of spinning and weaving. Yet another innovation which revolutionized
life was pottery making. At first pots were shaped by hand and
sun-dried; later they were fired in kilns. The significance of this
new invention is proved by the large quantities of pots that have
been discovered, which points to their wide use, especially in
cooking. Finally, with the domestication of a larger number of
animals, and with the cultivation of plants for both food and
textiles (though on a small scale, as only hoes were used for
tilling), man was transformed from a hunter and gatherer to a
producer. This permitted him some degree of freedom from the
whims of nature and assured him of a better way of life, which
in turn produced a noticeable increase in population and a rela-
tive development of society.

Because women played a leading role in the daily activities of
tilling the soil and engaging in crafts, they were assured of a
dominant role in society. Matriarchy was in full flower, as were
matrilineal clans, from whose union tribes were formed. These
tribes owned land communally, worked communally, and benefited communally from the fruits of their labors. Moreover,
through raising crops and animals, people began to feel bound to
the land they cultivated, which led to a more settled way of life.
They built dwellings in fertile river valleys and plains where
they could obtain water and tillable land, and therefore food for
themselves and for their animals. Their houses were sod huts,
built half under the ground, or above-ground structures of wood
and adobe, always with a hearth for heating and cooking.

Human settlements from the Neolithic period have been discovered throughout Transylvania. Artifacts that have been un-

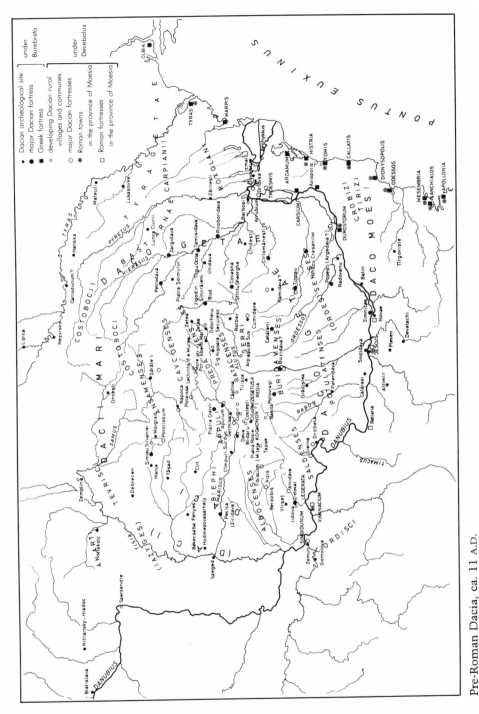

Pre-Roman Dacia, ca. 11 A.D.

3

earthed include hand-shaped ceramics of quite good quality, axes drilled for hafting, small iron objects, gold ornaments, and fired clay tablets with an archaic script. The creators of these treasures were the indigenous tribes, though there were certain influences from southeastern Europe and even Asia Minor.

The so-called Neolithic revolution was complete by the last stages of this era, which may be regarded as the transition to the Bronze Age. More and more tools and other artifacts were made of copper. Pottery was much improved, both in the quality of the raw clay and in production techniques; it was decorated with incised patterns of red, white, and black. Agriculture developed extensively, thanks to the replacement of the hoe by the plow; plows were made of wood, with a stone or deer-antler plowshare. Sheepherding also developed at this time. These economic developments increasingly emphasized male activities, and men began to play a more significant role in society. The patriarchy began to undermine the matriarchy. Burial of the dead became universal, and abstract concepts were given tangible form in fired clay figurines which symbolized fertility, fecundity, reasoning, dancing, and so forth.

Because of these advances, all aspects of society developed. Great settlements typical of this civilization have been discovered in Transylvania at Petreşti and Ariuşd. These are very similar to those in Oltenia at Gumelniţa and Coţofeni and in Moldavia at Cucuteni. The inhabitants of these settlements and the creators of these material and cultural treasures belonged to the great family of Indo-European peoples and were the forerunners of the Thracian-Geto-Dacian tribes. These tribes become much more distinct during the following Bronze and Iron Ages.

The Bronze Age

Bronze Age civilization was established throughout the Romanian territories by the efforts and intelligence of the Dacian population, the branch of the great Thracian people north of the Danube. The Thracians lived in the Carpathian-Danube-Balkan area, and were, according to Herodotus, the most numerous and powerful people after the Indians. In the opinion of Bogdan-Petriceicu Haşdeu, the learned historian and philologist of the second half of the nineteenth century, the Thracians and the Dacian

Reconstruction of the sacred enclosure at the Dacian capital of Sarmizegetusa.

Burebista, king of the Dacians (ca. 82–44 B.C.).

tribes were the ancestors of the Romanian people—that is, they constituted the ethnic substratum of Romania. It was the Dacians who, recognizing that copper was unsuitable for making durable tools and implements, first attempted to alloy it with lead or tin to produce a more resistant metal, bronze. For about a millennium (1,700 to 800 B.C.), it was bronze, in different forms and with different uses, that made this civilization superior to that of preceding eras. The Dacian culture of the Bronze Age is known from the excavation of numerous village sites, and its various forms are named after the most significant of these: the Mureş civilization (southern Transylvania), the Otomani civilization (western Transylvania), the Sighişoara civilization (central Transylvania), and the Noua civilization (southeastern Transylvania, with extensions into Muntenia).

For the most part, tools that were absolutely necessary in performing everyday tasks, such as sickles and axes, were made of bronze; so too were weapons (spearheads and arrowheads, daggers, swords, and battle-axes) and jewelry (rings, beads, buckles, and earrings). Numerous finds of bronze tools and artifacts— over 250 in Transylvania alone—constitute impressive evidence for the development in metalworking techniques. For example, 5,000 artifacts and tools of all types, with a total weight of over a ton, were found at Ocna Mureş in central Transylvania. The value of Dacian objects is also shown by the fact that they were prized far and wide—in central Europe, for instance, and on the Baltic coast. The improvements in tools and the domestication of animals brought substantial progress in agriculture, through the use of plows and wagons drawn by animals; in the clearing of forests, made possible by bronze axes; and in crafts, especially metallurgy (bronze and gold), but also in the household crafts of spinning and weaving and in pottery making, which was improved in every way. The Dacians were essentially agricultural and pastoral, which both permitted and required a continuing exchange of goods among the various tribes. Thus the way was paved for a more homogeneous intertribal society.

As society became more complex, however, social structures became more complex as well. The predominant form of community was the rural commune, characterized by mutual ownership and use of cropland, forests, pastures, and rivers, and by equal sharing of the products of community labors. With the exception of prisoners of war, who were essentially slaves, the members of the commune enjoyed freedom. Yet the social and economic role of the patriarchal family, a kinship group which included several generations descended from a common ancestor, gradually became more important. The family had the right of "usufruct"—that is, the right to cultivate and harvest for its own benefit a section of the communal lands. Moreover, it owned its own agricultural implements and animals. Thus private property began to appear alongside communal property, and with it the possibility of socioeconomic differentiation among tribal members. A thin stratum of society began to be distinguished from the mass of the population and this elite class gradually grew into a tribal aristocracy. Ultimately the appearance of private property and the beginnings of a dominant class created the desire to take over neighboring territories, which in turn generated conflict and intertribal war.

Thus economic ties, material and cultural exchanges, and common interests created the conditions for occasional cooperation, but there was also a need to defend lands and freedoms threatened by other tribes. The result under certain circumstances was the formation of true tribal federations. Delegates of the allied tribes, respecting the principle of democracy as it was understood at the time, elected representatives to lead the federation, granting them legal, economic, political, and military powers. Since one of the main motives for the creation of such federations was mutual defense, their most important function was military. The term "military democracy" is often applied to these alliances, and their leaders had a significant military role. Actual fortifications have been discovered at Sighetul Marmației, Coldău, and Mediaș.

The cultural development of Dacian society in this period is mirrored in its religious and artistic life. Nature worship led to the creation of a sun cult, and sun symbols—spirals, simple circles, and circles with spokes—have been found on a variety of objects. Sacrifices of agricultural products and of animals were offered to the sun god. Burial of the dead was replaced by cremation. Examples of Dacian art are seen in the decoration of pottery and bronze artifacts with geometric designs, spirals, stars, and, less frequently, human and animal figures.

The Iron Age

The Dacians, as they sought to make their work easier and more efficient, learned how to work and use iron. Because of its durability, iron was superior to bronze as bronze was superior to copper, and the new metal in its turn revolutionized agriculture. The iron plowshare penetrates more deeply into soil and thus makes it more productive; iron hoes similarly proved more efficient. Iron axes, saws, and picks were used for clearing forests and increasing agricultural acreage, while iron chisels, hammers, and tongs were exceptionally useful in woodworking and construction of all sorts. Ceramic work also improved, since objects could be turned on a wheel instead of shaped only by hand. This general economic development brought about a much greater flow of goods, both within tribes and among different tribes, and regardless of whether a particular tribe was a member of a federation. Direct barter increasingly was replaced by transactions using coins. The Dacians minted their own money, modeled on Greek coinage, as well as using the coins of the peoples with whom they traded. These facts provide further evidence of the development of their society, not only economically but politically as well.

The Dacians continued to live in communes; however, whereas in the Bronze Age the community was based largely on kinship, in the Iron Age it was based primarily on socioeconomic interests. The family itself was transformed: in place of the extended family, there was now a smaller, monogamous unit consisting of parents and children. Changes in the character of the commune— including the periodic parceling out of land among small families, the creation of certain political and military positions, and the extension of private property—furthered the development of a tribal aristocracy. In particular, the right to own goods and chattels was modified, but the right to land use also tended to become the right to land ownership.

Alongside the indigenous population north of the Danube, foreign peoples now began to settle. Some were from the south (Illyrians), others from the east (Scythians), and still others from the west (Celts and Bastarnae). They were influenced by the Dacians and in various spheres of activity influenced them in turn, but the cultural superiority of the Dacian tribes made it inevitable that the foreign peoples would be assimilated into the native population. However, there were also Greek colonies in Dobruja, on the Black Sea at Histria, Tomi (modern Constanţa), and Callatis; these, particularly through trade relations, had a more lasting influence.

Little by little, Dacian society made remarkable progress, and

Burebista, the king who united the Dacian people. Painting by Traian Ciucurescu.

Dacian metalwork.

it must be placed, along with the Greek and Roman societies, among the most highly developed of the time. The social structure became better fixed and resembled, although it was not identical to it, the structure of Roman society. There were two Dacian classes, with opposing interests: the wealthy nobility, known as *tarabostes* or *pileati* in contemporary sources, so called because of the type of cap they wore; and the peasantry, known as *comati*, after their long locks of hair. Unlike Greek and Roman nobles, the Dacian nobility cannot be considered slaveholders, because peasants did not become slaves, though they were obliged to perform certain services for the nobility.

Dacian society also was similar to that of the Greeks and Romans in its technological and artistic development. Architecture, as may be seen in forts all over Dacia—especially those in the Orăştie Mountains and the Sibiu Mountains in Transylvania—was equal to that of similar Greek and Roman buildings. The Dacians' advanced art is shown in such artifacts as large two-handled vessels for storing provisions, crucibles for melting precious metals, small lamps, and pottery painted with geometric designs and plant and animal figures. Further evidence is provided by bronze and silver jewelry, including rings, clasps, earrings, and belt buckles decorated with human figures, as well as silver vases such as those from the rich find at Sîncrăieni in eastern Transylvania. Agricultural implements and other tools have also been discovered in great quantity.

The Dacian religion, like that of other Iron Age peoples,was polytheistic. The most revered among the Dacian deities were Zalmoxis, the god of plant life and fertility, and Gebeleisis, the god of light. A warlike people such as the Dacians could not be without a god of war similar to the Roman Mars; they also worshiped a goddess of the moon and the forests, who was named Bendis. Dacian altars were either square or circular; the heaviest concentration of them, quite naturally, was in Transylvania near Sarmizegetusa, the most important political center. A large circular altar with andesite pillars discovered at Sarmizegetusa represents the Dacian calendar, which was based on a 360-day year divided into twelve months of thirty days each, with six-day weeks.

One can scarcely imagine a society as important as that of Dacia without a written language, and in fact vases bearing the names of persons and of Dacian tribes—in Greek and Latin char-

Dacian and Macedonian coins found at Cugir in Transylvania.

Dacian silver goblets (first century B.C. to first century A.D.) from Sîncrăieni, southern Transylvania.

acters—have been found in two widely separated sites, at Ocniţa in Oltenia and at Sarmizegetusa. Unfortunately, these inscriptions are too scanty to provide us with any detailed knowledge of the language. However, reconstructions from modern Romanian words of Dacian origin prove that the Dacians spoke a dialect of Thracian, which is a member of the great Indo-European family of languages. Experts estimate that over 160 Dacian words are preserved in Romanian; these are mostly words denoting everyday life and social relations. Among them are *moş* 'old man'; *copil* 'child'; *prunc* 'babe'; *ţarină* 'tilled land'; *zestre* 'dowry'; *brînză* 'cheese'; *zăr* 'whey'; *brad* 'fir tree'; *gorun* 'oak tree'; *mînz* 'colt'; and *mal* 'riverbank'. Many Dacian river names have also been preserved—for instance, *Donaris* (Rom. *Dunăre* 'Danube'). The discovery of the names of certain medicinal plants and medical instruments attests to the Dacians' medical skills, and apparently they also had some veterinary knowledge.

The level of Dacian society before the Roman conquest is further shown by the existence of numerous village and town sites and by a number of imposing fortresses. The most important was at the capital, Sarmizegetusa; it was surrounded by other defensive sites at Costeşti, Blidaru, Piatra Roşie, and Baniţa. Similar fortresses have also been discovered at Căpîlna in the Sebeş valley and at Tilişca in southern Transylvania, at Piatra Craivii near Alba Iulia, and at Bîtca Doamnei, in Neamţ County in Moldavia. In addition to these military sites, rather well-developed market towns have been found. Their names— Piroboridava, Argedava, Pelendava, and Ziridava, for example— leave no room for doubt about their Dacian origin, because *dava* is a Dacian word meaning "town" or "fortified settlement." Ptolemy's map also shows other Dacian settlements at the sites of modern Cluj, Alba Iulia, and Turnu-Severin.

Throughout Dacia, the tribes joined in federations covering ever-wider territories; the fortresses and towns just listed were probably political and military centers for various tribes, while Sarmizegetusa was first a political and military center for a tribal federation and later for the centralized Dacian state. One of the earliest alliances was that led by Dromichaites at the end of the fourth century B.C., whose capital was on the Argeş River; this federation even succeeded in defeating Lisimah, king of the Thracians. In the third century B.C., Oroles forged an alliance in Transylvania which later was joined by tribes from other parts of

Dacian gold jewelry found in the Hinova hoard.

Dacia. Eventually, in the first century B.C., under the leadership of Burebista, it developed into a large and powerful state. This centralized state covered a vast area, from the mountains of Slovakia to the Balkan Mountains and Olbia on the Black Sea. Its main political and military center was in the Orăștie Mountains, where the fortification system was greatly expanded, but there were also other centers beyond the Carpathians, as for instance one at Popești on the Argeș.

An inscription at Dionysiopolis characterizes Burebista as "first and foremost among the kings of Thrace," but a more complete picture is given by Strabo in *Geographia* 2.61, who says that Burebista "on coming to power among his people . . . uplifted them . . . so that in a few years he formed a powerful state and made the majority of the neighboring people subject to the Getae [Dacians]. He even succeeded in inspiring fear among the Romans." Burebista's political and military power allowed him to become involved in the civil war between Caesar and Pompey, in which he took the latter's side with the hope of extending his domain still further. However, both Burebista and Caesar were killed in 44 B.C., the victims of separate conspiracies, and war between the two great powers was thus averted.

With Burebista's death, the state he had founded diminished somewhat, but it maintained itself within Transylvania. It was there, in A.D. 87, that Decebalus succeeded in reestablishing a Dacian state that encompassed all of the territories inhabited by Dacian tribes. He completed the system of fortifications in the Orăștie Mountains and reorganized and equipped the army. These measures were certainly necessary. The Romans, having conquered the Balkan Peninsula, were showing an interest in conquest and expansion north of the Danube. Decebalus was preparing for confrontation with the greatest power of the day, the Roman Empire. His character, as it is sketched by the Roman historian Dio Cassius in *Historia romana* 67.61, seems to have been well suited to such an audacious action. The Dacian king was "skilled in war, bold in action . . . [and] brave in battle." Decebalus's courage and skill—and, of course, the courage and skill of the Dacian people themselves—brought them two victories over the Romans.

Even later, in defeat, the king knew how to win the peace. In return for acknowledging the authority of the Roman Empire, he obtained both the money and craftsmen he needed to build more fortified encampments and the military training cadres he needed to organize his army more efficiently for yet another confrontation with the Romans. Discovering Decebalus's intentions, Trajan waged two difficult campaigns against him (A.D. 101–2 and A.D. 105–6). He succeeded in crushing the Dacian resistance, and conquered Dacia was reorganized as a Roman province.

2

Roman Rule and Daco-Roman Civilization

Political, Economic, and Military Organization

WITH TRAJAN'S CONQUEST, most of Dacia came under Roman rule. The conquered territories included what is now the Banat, Transylvania except the northwestern section, Oltenia, Muntenia, Dobruja, and southern Moldavia; these areas were integrated into the Roman Empire as the peripheral provinces of Dacia and Lower Moesia. Trajan organized Dacia as an imperial province, with the capital at what was then called both Ulpia Traiana and Sarmizegetusa. The preservation of the old name of the capital of Burebista and Decebalus, thus combined with the name of the conquering emperor, signified both continuity and a new rule. As an imperial province, Dacia was directly subordinate to the emperor, who was represented by a governor chosen from the Senate and given the title *legatus Augusti propraetore.*

In the interests of better organization and defense, Dacia was divided in 119 into two provinces, Dacia Inferior or Lower Dacia (Oltenia and southern Transylvania), with the capital at Drobeta (modern Turnu-Severin), and Dacia Superior or Upper Dacia (the rest of conquered Transylvania and the Banat), with the capital at Ulpia Traiana-Sarmizegetusa. The former was governed by a Roman knight known as *procurator Augusti*, while the latter was under the control of a senator designated *legatus Augusti propraetore.* Under Marcus Aurelius, for much the same reasons, the Dacian provinces were again reorganized, creating three: Malvensis, with its capital at Malva (modern Celei), covering the Banat and Oltenia; Apulensis, with its capital at Apulum (modern Alba Iulia), taking in southern and central Transylvania; and Porolissensis, with its capital originally at Napoca (modern Cluj) and later at Porolissum (modern Moigrad), covering the upper part of Transylvania.

Two principal problems occupied the Romans after the conquest of Dacia and Moesia: first, defending the provinces against invasion by outside peoples and insurrection by the Dacians; and second, achieving the most profitable economic and administrative organization. The first problem was solved by bringing in roughly 40,000 soldiers, or about 10 percent of the total imperial army. These legions, together with auxiliary infantry troops (*cohortes*) and cavalry troops (*alae*), were stationed in camps near the towns of Apulum, Potaissa (modern Turda), Porolissum, Micia (modern Vețel), and Tibiscum (modern Jupa), all of which were in Transylvania or the Banat, and at other camps in Lower Dacia and Moesia. The problem of economic and administrative organization was solved through the cooperation of the Dacian population and of the colonists—peasants, craftsmen, miners, merchants, landowners, officials, and veterans—that the Romans imported from all over the empire.

Agricultural development was achieved primarily through the work of the Dacian peasants, who continued to live in rural communes. The peasants remained free, though they did have a number of obligations to the state and even to the leaders of the commune. In other words, there was some socioeconomic differentiation among members of the commune, but without slavery. There was also some private ownership of land taken from the communes by the Dacian upper class and by the Roman colonists. No one created a large estate, however, except for a very few Roman aristocrats. Such properties, where Dacians or Roman colonists worked with slaves, have been discovered at Hobița in southern Transylvania and at Ciumăfaia in central Transylvania. Large palacelike residences for landowners are equally rare.

There were more significant changes in mining. The underground riches of Dacia—especially Transylvanian gold and silver—were major incentives for the Roman conquest. The new rulers were eager to exploit these resources as profitably as possible, and the gold and silver mines were declared state property. Mining specialists were brought in from other provinces, and particularly from Illyria, where mining was better developed. The miners entered into a kind of contract with the state in its capacity as owner of the mines. These contracts were written on wax tablets, of which a large number have been

Decebalus, king of the Dacians (A.D. 87–106.)

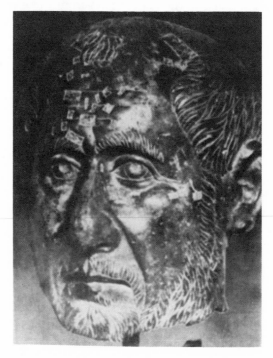

The Roman emperor Trajan. Bronze head found at Sarmizegetusa-
Ulpia Traiană.

found in the Bihor Mountains, where the richest gold- and silver-mining operations were located. There were mines at Alburnus Maior (modern Roşia), Abruttus (modern Abrud), and Ampellum (modern Zlatna), which was also the headquarters of the mining administration. Around Hunedoara were copper mines (at Micia) and iron mines (at Ghelar and Teliuc). Finally, the salt mines at Salinae (modern Ocna Mureş), Cedonia (Ocna Sibiului), and elsewhere were also known and exploited in Roman times. Both miners and various kinds of craftsmen were organized into associations called *collegiae.* The most important were those of the blacksmiths (which included carpenters, bricklayers, and probably potters as well), the textile workers, the masons, and certain others.

The *collegiae* in the strictest sense of the word were especially developed in towns. As settlements grew, many military legion headquarters and administrative and cultural centers were granted the status of municipalities and colonies. In order to facilitate commerce among the burgeoning towns, villages, and mining centers, as well as to serve the needs of the army, the Romans built a network of remarkably fine roads, some of which are still in use today. One such started from the Danube at Lederata in the Banat, passed through Tibiscum, Ulpia Traiana-Sarmizegetusa, and Potaissa to Napoca, at which point it split, one branch leading north as far as Porolissum and the other south to Apulum. Another principal road, the Via Alutana, also started at the Danube and went up the Olt valley as far as southern Transylvania.

Superior organization could not help but have significant effects on cultural and religious life, especially since Roman culture had penetrated Dacia even before the actual conquest. With the ground thus prepared, the economic union and cultural coexistence brought about by Roman rule had a considerable effect on Dacian culture. There was a noticeable rise in literacy, and Dacian religious beliefs were infused with Roman deities, creeds, and customs. Progress was made in sciences such as astronomy and medicine. These and other effects eventually produced a thoroughly mixed Daco-Roman civilization.

The Romanization of Dacia

During the greatest expansion of the Roman Empire, in the era of Augustus and Trajan, Roman influences were felt throughout most of Europe, from the Atlantic to the Black Sea, from the Mediterranean to the British Isles, from North Africa to the Middle East. To be sure, it is only to be expected that there were differences in the degree of influence over such a wide area. The geographic location, pre-Roman cultural tradition, receptivity to Roman culture and language, length of exposure to Romanizing influences, and the interest or lack of interest of the Romans themselves in leaving their mark all affected the Romanization of any given people. Yet even with such explainable differences, we find traces of Roman culture everywhere.

The term "Romanization" has two fundamental meanings as it is commonly used in modern scholarship: first, the colonization of a conquered territory by Roman or Latin-speaking settlers; and second, the assimilation of the native population of all or most of the conquered territory and the establishment of the Latin language and of the Roman provincial way of life, including Roman customs, culture, and mentality (forma mentis). Romanization in the first sense does not necessarily imply a long-lasting or deeply rooted effect, but in the second sense it indicates that the subject people adopted the essential elements of Roman civilization. Thus, in order to analyze the importance of the Roman conquest of any given indigenous population, we need to know to what extent the people adopted the conquerors' language, thought, and culture; how durable these influences were; and what significance they had for the subsequent development of the people's own language, thought, and culture. In place of general formulations and answers, we must provide concrete analyses of the specific historical conditions affecting one or another Romanized people. The effects of Roman rule can be traced, for example, in material aspects of life such as agriculture, industry, and commerce, or in changes in languages, thought, art, religion, and customs. To be sure, not all of these aspects are equally important; some are basic and others secondary, but all taken together make up the complex process of Romanization.

The "villa-based" economy introduced by the Romans made for significant changes in the life of the Dacian people—most of whom were peasants—even though the rural communes did not completely disappear. Examples of different blendings of indigenous tradition with Roman innovation can be seen in the design of houses and in objects of everyday use. For the most part, the former maintained the old Dacian tradition, while household objects, more easily replaced, were Romanized, both because Roman articles were fashionable and because in many cases they were technically and functionally superior. Romanization proceeded more quickly and radically in mining and industrial production. Romanized or largely Romanized foreign craftsmen and miners (Italians, Illyrians, and Middle Easterners), well organized in *collegiae*, were able to produce more goods of better quality. Both colonists and natives came to prefer their products or products of Roman workmanship and style imported from other imperial centers and provinces. Gradually—first in the heavily Romanized areas and later in more outlying regions—indigenous craftsmen also adopted the foreign models, although the old, indigenous pre-Roman forms did not totally disappear. Many Thracian, Celtic, and Illyrian models survived and coexisted with the Roman forms, even influencing them to some extent.

This peaceful coexistence between Roman and native forms can be observed in place names, dress, customs and manners, and language as well. Latin inscriptions—roughly 3,500 of them, an impressive number considering the extent of the Roman provinces—maintained both Roman and native names for generations. The bas-reliefs on Trajan's Column show pre-Roman local dress. Funeral rites still preserved some pre-Roman traditions, which suggests that certain customs could not be easily or suddenly abandoned. The tradition of burial mounds coexisted for a time with certain types of tomb images and religious monuments. Roman deities, however, such as Jupiter, Diana, Venus, and Mithras, "the Invincible Sun"—brought by the Romans from the East—became more and more prevalent as time passed, especially east of the border between Novicum and Pannonia.

Given the Romans' great organizational ability, Romanization of politcal–administrative institutions and of the names for such institutions proceeded rapidly, first in the urban centers (municipalities and colonies) and then in the rural areas (farms and estates). The army must have afforded one of the most receptive fields for Romanizing influences. As Roman and non-Roman imperial citizens were integrated in the legions and auxiliary troops, non-Romans found themselves in a new environment from which, in effect, there was no way home. The army's role in furthering Romanization was even greater in that elements from all social strata were recruited into combat forces and peacekeeping and border units. The long period of military service,

Battles between the Dacians and the Romans. Bas-reliefs on Trajan's Column, Rome.

the fact that Latin was the language of the army, and the particular Roman style of military organization and command led to the Romanization of all soldiers, no matter what their ethnic group or social background. Furthermore, by the time soldiers had completed their service and become veterans, they were Romanized, and thus contributed in turn to Romanizing others. In those provinces such as Illyria and Dacia, where the army was strong and played an important role as "protector of the empire," its Romanizing role was greater than in the Gallo-Germanic and Hispano-Italic provinces in the west.

The ultimate consequence of the Romanization of the Dacians was the formation of a new people, the Romanian people. While this was a prolonged process, spread out over a wide area, it was not uniform over the whole Danube-Carpathian region. For one thing, there was a broad difference between the territory effectively controlled by the Romans, which included the greater part of Transylvania, Muntenia, Oltenia, Dobruja, and lower Moldavia, and the regions that were merely under strong Roman influence, which included northern Transylvania and the northern part of Moldavia. But the degree of Romanization differed even within these two areas. The process was fastest and most thorough in the section along the Danube—dotted with towns, rural settlements, and military installations for legions and auxiliary troops—and in areas with urban and military concentrations in the interior. Regions where rural life predominated were affected less, but by no means untouched.

In order to provide a clearer, more exact understanding of the Romanization of Dacia, it is necessary to repeat a well-known general fact: the Dacian population north of the Danube was subject to Roman influence long before the beginning of Roman rule. Roman manufactured goods, coins (later copied by the Dacians themselves), construction techniques, and merchants and builders were present north of the Danube roughly two centuries before the Roman conquest. Thus the ground was prepared for the smooth, rapid acceptance of Roman culture, technology, and customs, and of the Latin language.

Since colonization and military presence formed the basis of Romanization, we should look at their role more closely. Colonization was encouraged and to some extent organized, primarily by Trajan, but by subsequent emperors as well. There can be no doubt that colonization proceeded rapidly. Visions of Dacian riches attracted great numbers of colonists, and creating a strongly Romanized region north of the Danube was a deliberate imperial policy. Proof of this policy is seen in the presence of a large army of legions and auxiliary troops in the first decade following the conquest; the construction of a vast network of roads; the creation of many nonmilitary settlements; and the early existence of towns. It is documented also by Eutropius in his *Breviarium ab urbe condita* (8.6.2), who tells us, "Once Trajan had conquered Dacia, he transported vast numbers of people there from the entire Roman world, to found cities and till the soil." Eutropius further notes (8.2.2) that Hadrian, at the beginning of his reign, intended to withdraw from Dacia, but he gave up the idea after his friends advised him not to surrender so many Roman citizens to the barbarians.

In any case, the total military and civilian population that migrated to Dacia was certainly very large. As in other frontier regions, there were a great many troops; three legions and numerous auxiliary units, or about 55,000 to 60,000 men, were sent there, and in addition were their families, who lived in towns or in settlements near the camps. The total probably was roughly 77,000 to 84,000 soldiers and dependents. Moreover, there were many administrative officials, merchants, craftsmen, and slaves. The number of towns (*municipia* and *coloniae*, including four subject to *ius Italicum*) rose to eleven, and rather large numbers of rural settlements (*vici* and *pagi*) were founded, as well as spas and estates. Thus, even in Trajan's time, the influx must have reached 500,000, which represents an increase of something like 50 percent over the preconquest population.

It is important to emphasize that the overwhelming majority of the newcomers to Dacian lands were Latin-speakers, lived according to Roman customs, and actively spread Roman culture among the original inhabitants. From inscriptions on stone or wax and military and other documents, it can be inferred that a large number of the colonists came from long-Romanized regions such as Hispania, Gallia, Dalmatia, Upper Moesia, and even Italy itself. Many inscriptions attest to the presence of families of Italic origin in the towns; apparently there also were farmers, merchants, and craftsmen of Italic ancestry in rural areas. Some three-quarters of the personal names in inscriptions prove to be Roman or show Roman influence. Inscriptions and the deities worshiped in urban centers and in the gold-mining regions of the Bihor Mountains prove that Dacia was also colonized by various eastern peoples and immigrants from areas of

Greek language and culture, but these people also spoke Latin. Moreover, with rare exceptions their inscriptions, both public and private, were in Latin as well. Of the roughly 3,500 inscriptions known from Oltenia, Transylvania, and the Banat, only about 30 are in Greek, and a mere 4 in Palmyrene Aramaic—with a Latin parallel text. It is generally known and acknowledged that the realities of life made Latin the common language for all the inhabitants of the provinces, both in public life and in the private dealings of individuals.

The "Romanness" of Dacia strikes us everywhere. We see it in the layout and internal organization of towns, in the design of public buildings and private houses, in the adoption of gods from the Roman pantheon and the religious organization of communities, in traditions and fashions in the arts, and in the form of the legal system. Nor should it be forgotten that there was an *ordo Augustalium*, a social, political, and religious institution, in Ulpia Traiana-Sarmizegetusa; the capital was also the site of the Council of the Three Dacias (*concilium trium Daciarum*), which celebrated the cult of the empire. In a word, Dacia was fully integrated into the Roman Empire, even though there still persisted local peculiarities which can be explained by Dacia's geographic location and the social and ethnic makeup of its population.

The Dacians did not live in isolation during the period of Roman rule, but took an active part in the economic and military life of their land. The native population found it necessary to adopt the new language, customs, and institutions in order to participate. Romanization also was furthered by mixed marriages, by army recruiting, and by the granting of Roman citizenship to freedmen in the provinces in A.D. 212, during the reign of Caracalla. The Roman authorities' insistence that the indigenous population be integrated with Roman society corresponded to the Dacians' own wishes.

In the countryside, the natives either lived separately in traditional settlements of wooden huts or sod houses with storage cellars, or together with the colonists. Their agricultural implements and other tools, household objects, pottery, and jewelry are best described as Daco-Roman, although specifically Dacian characteristics are especially pronounced in pottery. At least a few coins have been found throughout the province, both as isolated pieces and in hoards. Even in the countryside, Roman workmanship and Roman influence on Dacian styles is seen in

25

stone inscriptions, statuary, clay lamps, and in luxury items and installations like frescoes, plumbing, and central heating. Dacian religious life, with the exception of funeral rites and customs, also changed markedly. For the most part the natives continued the later Dacian method of cremation, placing the remains in urns in flat tombs or directly into a simple grave. However, they did borrow from the Roman colonists a few customs of a broadly Roman-provincial type unknown to them before the conquest: tombs with a burnt grave and a coin for Charon, the ferryman for the dead, are definitely attested on Dacian territory from provincial times. Furthermore, the well-known phenomenon of *interpretatio Romana*—the worshiping of non-Roman deities under Roman names—certainly occurred in Dacia as in other provinces. All in all, we may say that the indigenous population was thoroughly assimilated, linguistically and otherwise, during the 170 years of Roman rule. It had become Daco-Roman.

After Aurelian's withdrawal of the army and the provincial administration in 271–74, the Romanization of the territories north of the Danube did not cease, instead continuing in new forms through the sixth century. Romanizing influences continued to be felt in the large-scale propagation of Christianity through the medium of Latin; in the continuing economic and cultural ties between the Daco-Romans and the Roman territories south of the Danube; in the maintenance of economic life based on the Roman monetary system; and in the return of Roman-Byzantine rule north of the Danube under Constantine the Great and Justinian, which saw the Banat and most of Oltenia and Muntenia once again incorporated into the empire. In fact, the left bank of the Danube was never totally abandoned by the Romans after Aurelian; from the Banat to southern Moldavia, important bridgeheads were maintained north of the river, primarily for strategic military purposes, but also with the goal of preserving economic and cultural ties with Trajan's Dacia.

Most of the territory now inhabited by the Romanian people was included in the Roman provinces of Dacia, Moesia, and Scythia, but powerful Roman influences also were felt in the northern parts of Transylvania and Moldavia which remained outside the empire. Romanization began in those regions as well during Roman rule and continued after it. To understand this process more thoroughly, one must remember that the boundary of Roman rule and the fortifications that marked it were neither completely fixed nor impenetrable. On the contrary, there was unrestricted passage from one side to the other. Moreover, there was a brief period during which the Romans dominated certain areas rather far beyond the empire's more permanent limits. Trajan himself had planned to incorporate northern Transylvania into the empire, and the numerous Roman coins and artifacts discovered there attest to more than mere influence. A decisive example is Komorova, near Cernăuţi, where a large settlement has been discovered, with above-ground dwellings, public buildings of stone and brick, large quantities of glass and pottery, and Roman coins, all of which date from the second, third, or fourth centuries A.D. Romanian and Soviet researchers have concluded that such finds can only be explained by assuming a period of effective Roman rule. Other articles of Roman workmanship also have been discovered elsewhere in upper Moldavia, providing further proof of temporary Roman incursion and lasting Roman influence even there.

The Romanization of these territories intensified under Constantine the Great and Justinian; as elsewhere, the propagation of Christianity in the fourth to sixth centuries was an important factor. Although they either never were part of the Roman Empire or were so only briefly, these areas were nevertheless subject to cultural and linguistic Romanization for some four centuries. Moreover, in the centuries after Aurelian's withdrawal, when there were no Roman borders, Romanization spread far past the old boundaries of the former province, gradually assimilating the free Dacians as well. The largest group of these, the Carps, thus disappear from history through the same process that affected their cousins in the empire. Nor should we ignore the fact that, according to Gallienus-Aurelian (Aurelius Victor, *De Caesaribus*, 22–23), some of the free Dacians from the east and west of what is now modern Romania penetrated former Roman Dacia, where they in their turn eventually were assimilated into the local Romanized group.

However, Romanization did not mean the disappearance of the Dacian population, either as an ethnic element or as a cultural influence. Dacian survivals are proved more and more convincingly by ongoing archeological research. Dacian military units were formed during Trajan's reign and maintained by his successors; a cohort of Dacians was active in Britannia. Dacian personal names are recorded in Latin inscriptions, and the names of places and rivers of course constitute still further evidence. Dacian material culture also is increasingly attested by archeological research. Today over one hundred settlements are known in Transylvania alone where traces of the Dacian culture of the second and third centuries A.D. have been found. Recent investigations have also unearthed many more of the rural communes where the Dacian population continued to live. Of the more important ones we may cite Caşolţ and Slimnic in southern Transylvania and Lechinţa de Mureş, Obreja, and Noşlac in central Transylvania; Dacian funeral installations have been discovered in these settlements and in others. Finally, archeologists have discovered many settlements where the Roman and Dacian cultures coexisted in perfect harmony.

Thus it was that the new Daco-Roman ethnic synthesis began to take shape. At the end of this long process of fusion, a new people would appear on the stage of history: the Romanians.

Daco-Roman Civilization in the Age of Migration

The withdrawal of the Roman army and administration from the province of Dacia did not mean that the Daco-Romans abandoned their lands. That Daco-Roman civilization north of the Danube survived the so-called Age of Migration, the vast movement of nomadic tribesmen that occurred during the fourth to seventh centuries A.D., is indisputable. In the first place, a people would not so readily abandon lands in which they had lived for millennia; there is no historical evidence that an entire people has ever left its home in the face of invasion. Second, the newcomers would have prevented any such mass evacuation, because they needed Dacian material and military support. Third, the Romans did not, as is commonly argued, withdraw primarily because of the pressure of migrating peoples, but rather for strategic reasons, the Danube being a more defensible imperial border. Several decades elapsed between the Roman withdrawal and the first settlement by the first wave of migrating peoples, the Goths. Fourth, the territories south of the Danube were neither more peaceful nor safer than those to the north. And fifth, the Romans considered the Germanic tribes living on former imperial lands to be military and political allies (foederati).

These facts are fully confirmed by evidence from written sources, legal records, and archeological, linguistic, and ethnographic research. For example, in the fourth century new walls were constructed to fortify an old palace at Sarmizegetusa, the city's stone entrance gates were built, and the amphitheater was transformed into a virtual fortress. The people of this former capital of Roman Dacia, far from abandoning their city, were taking measures to defend themselves against the migrating tribes. Similarly, the Daco-Roman population remained in the former Roman capitals of Apulum, Napoca, and Porolissum. Daco-Roman tombs from the fourth century have been discovered in the ruins of the Roman baths and various other Roman buildings at Apulum. These tombs contain vases and jewelry that are unquestionably of Roman workmanship, being virtually identical to those found in Lower Moesia and Pannonia. The Roman character of these finds has been confirmed by numerous other discoveries in various other parts of Roman Dacia. Red pottery of Roman style continued to be manufactured at various locations in central Transylvania; these have been dated by metal objects and coins from the third and fourth centuries. Daco-Roman rural settlements have been discovered at Bratei and Brîncovenești, and at sites further north, among them Cluj-Mănăștur and Suatu. In other areas, the Daco-Romans, forced by the migrating tribes to abandon their earlier fortified settlements, rebuilt in more mountainous areas, as, for example, those discovered at Proștea Mică and Cetatea de Baltă in central and eastern Transylvania.

Daco-Roman funeral pyres, and Roman coins minted in the late third and fourth centuries, after Aurelian's withdrawal, have been discovered at several Transylvanian sites, including one near Cluj and one at Tîrgu Mureș. Two Roman pottery kilns dating from the fourth century have also been found near Cluj. Moreover, other finds include a variety of third- and fourth-century Christian monuments and other artifacts: coffins with the sign of the cross at Cluj and Zlatna; lamps and vases with crosses at Alba Iulia, Dej, and Moigrad; and a devotional cross with Latin inscriptions and a Christian monogram at Biertan. Jewelry decorated with Christian symbols has been unearthed in numerous locations in central Transylvania, including Biertan, Feisa, Alba Iulia, Turda, and Vețel, as well as further to the north and northeast, at Bologa, Sic, Moigrad, and elsewhere. All these objects were either made locally or imported for the Christian population, which would have to have been the Daco-Romans, since the Goths, the first migrating tribe to pass through the region, were at the time neither Latin-speaking nor Christian.

Excavating the walls of Roman Napoca.

The first of the *foederati* to coexist with the Daco-Romans were the Germanic Visigoths, who entered the area from the north and tended to depend upon the indigenous population for the necessities of life. Recent research points to the conclusion that the Visigoths were never very numerous and occupied a rather restricted area. They mixed little with the local population, being content merely to collect tribute, usually in the form of agricultural products. In their brief century on Dacian soil, the Visigoths left traces primarily of their material culture, such as the great find at Sîntana de Mureş in central Transylvania and the burial grounds at Spanţov and Tîrgşor, south of the Carpathians on the Muntenian plain. The Visigoths' stay north of the Danube came to an end in the last third of the fourth century, when most of them, following defeats by the Huns, moved south of that river; the small minority that remained was assimilated by the indigenous population.

The Huns, a Turanian people, established their main settlements in Pannonia, and in Transylvania their presence was felt primarily as regular raids by marauding bands. Under the leadership of Attila, these people of the steppes brought despotic rule to a vast area, but their nomadic way of life meant that their domination was short-lived. Since they were not an agricultural people, like the Visigoths they forced local populations to pay tribute in farm produce. A few troves of artifacts from the first half of the fifth century, discovered in the Cluj vicinity at Apahida and Someşeni, and in the northeast at Cepari, remain from the Huns' raids and incursions into Transylvania.

Yet another Germanic tribe, the Ostrogoths, descended on the territory north of the Danube in the fifth century, while the area was still under the control of the Huns. Evidence of their stopover is the treasure found at Pietroasa, in the southeast corner of the Moldavian Carpathians—the so-called Hen with the Golden Chicks. There are also a few tombs of Ostrogoth princes, containing many artifacts, at Apahida.

Hun domination, such as it was, came to an end in the middle of the fifth century, following severe defeats at the hands of the Gepids, another Germanic tribe. Yet not even the Gepids ever effectively ruled Transylvania; their center of power was in southern Pannonia, in the region of the Danube, Tisza, and Sava rivers. Those who did get to Transylvania lived alongside the local population, either separately or in the same settlements. Such coexistence is proved by the mixture of Daco-Roman and

Gepid artifacts found at Moreşti and Porumbenii Mici, in central and eastern Transylvania. Since their principal livelihood was raising cattle, the Gepids forced the local population to pay only a modest tax in agricultural products.

Sometime after the middle of the sixth century, the Gepids were defeated by the Avars, a people of the steppes, in alliance with another Germanic tribe, the Langobards. Like the Huns and the Gepids, the Avars had their headquarters in Pannonia, where there were extensive plains and rich pastureland for their animals. The presence of Avar tribes or of Avar elements in Transylvania is attested by the tomb of a silversmith discovered at Felanc, near Arad, and by other tombs found at Teiuş in central Transylvania. Like the earlier peoples, the Avars collected agricultural tribute. Their domination finally came to a disastrous end when they were defeated by the Franks in the last decade of the eighth century; they had already lost their place in the Danube-Carpathian region to Slavic tribes during the seventh century. The first wave of Slavs north of the Danube moved on after a short stay and settled on the Balkan Peninsula. Those few who did remain were assimilated.

As archeological research continues, new proofs of the nature of Daco-Roman civilization come to light. Roman coins of the fourth and fifth centuries, the great majority of bronze and a few of silver, have been discovered throughout the area. Bronze money reflects the humble socioeconomic status of its Daco-Roman users; the migrating peoples used only gold and silver coins. A more significant proof is furnished by the hoards of coins discovered at several Transylvanian sites: at Sarmigezetusa; in the Banat at Orşova and Răcăjdia; at Hunedoara; near Tîrgu Mureş; in the northeast near Dej, and in other places. The coins in these treasure troves are from the third and fourth centuries. These discoveries are complemented by others from the fourth and fifth centuries, which confirm that Latin was the language of the Daco-Roman population, both at home and in public life. On a silver ring discovered at Veţel, we find the inscription *Quartine vivas* ("Long life to you, Quartinus"); on the devotional cross found at Biertan is inscribed *Ego Zenovius votum posui* ("I, Zenovius, brought this offering"); still other Latin inscriptions were found on a brick unearthed at Gornea in the Banat and on the bottom of a vessel at Porolissum. The Daco-Roman population also passed on through the ages the most important Latin words and concepts pertaining to religious life: *creştin* (Lat. *christianus*

Funeral stela from Căşei.

Wax tablet from the gold mines at Alburnus Maior (Roşia).

'Christian'); *cruce* (Lat. *crux* 'cross'); *Dumnezeu* (Lat. *Dominus Deus* 'Lord God'); *înger* (Lat. *angelus* 'angel'); *biserica* (Lat. *basilica* 'church'). The last of these is maintained only in Romanian and the Rhaeto-Romance dialects spoken by a small group in Switzerland; the name for a house of worship in all other neo-Latin languages derives from a Greek word, *ecclesia* (Ital. *chiesa;* Fr. *église;* Span. *iglesia;* Port. *igreja*). In Albanian, too, the word for church (*chesa*) been borrowed from Greek; this would also be the case in Romanian if the Daco-Romans had actually retreated south to the Balkan Peninsula.

The continuity of tradition and population is further seen in the socioeconomic and political organization of Daco-Roman society. The native population had continued to live in communes under the Romans, and after the withdrawal these communes experienced a substantial revival. On the other hand, the Daco-Roman towns continued to flourish for about a century, but then declined into rural or semiurban settlements as they deteriorated under successive waves of migrating peoples. Thus the Daco-Romans were chiefly an agricultural people, and only to a much lesser extent craftsmen and miners. These village residents owned, worked, and profited from their land in common. They chose leaders known as judges, who had both legal and administrative powers; the judges were assisted by so-called wise old men, who had the same powers. Again we see proof of the continuity of the Daco-Roman civilization north of the Danube, for Romanian *jude* 'judge' is derived from Latin *judex,* and Romanian *oameni buni și bătrîni,* roughly 'wise old men', has its origins in Latin *homines boni et veterani.*

Meanwhile, relations with the Byzantine Empire had a positive influence on the inhabitants of Dacian lands, as the Roman Empire in general, and its eastern branch in particular, continued to enjoy great prestige. Although the empire no longer had direct authority over them, the "barbarian" territories still belonged to the Roman sphere of influence. This can be seen from the political organization of village communes into groups now known as "popular Romanias;" after the term coined by the great Romanian historian Nicolae Iorga. Such groups were formed by the banding together of several neighboring villages in a river valley or small natural basin which would offer protection against the migrating peoples. The very name of these organizations reveals their Romanness and their popular character. They were considered "Romania" by the inhabitants themselves, who knew they had belonged and practically still did belong to the empire. Such organizations existed all over the territory of the former province of Dacia, although they were concentrated in the basin regions on either side of the Carpathians and in the Olt, Tîrnave, Someş, and Criş valleys. However, the organization of communes and the emergence of a ruling class were the first signs of social stratification, since the powers that the community granted to the ruling group implied their socioeconomic and political superiority and a certain degree of privilege. This development pointed down the road to a new socioeconomic era, the medieval or feudal period.

3

The Emergence of the Romanian People

BEHIND THE SCREEN, as it were, of barbarian domination the Daco-Roman population and Romanized society north of the Danube continued to evolve. The migrating peoples, content to collect material and military assistance, did not interfere in social and political life. Thus "ethnogenesis," the birth of the Romanian people, could continue on its course. The essence of this process was the synthesis of the two fundamental components, Dacian and Roman, with only slight influences attributable to relations between the indigenous and migrating populations. Throughout the fourth to sixth centuries, the Romanness of the culture was strengthened by the presence of the Byzantine Empire in certain territories north of the Danube, under the Roman emperors Constantine the Great, Valens, and Justinian. The evolution of the Romanian people and their language thus began to reach completion, and the new forms to emerge more clearly, until in the seventh and eighth centuries we see a qualitative change: the Daco-Roman population becomes the Romanian people, and their language, so-called Vulgar Latin, becomes Romanian.

These processes were similar to those that occurred on the Italian Peninsula, the Iberian Peninsula, and in Gaul, affecting primarily the Etruscans, the Italic tribes, the Iberian Celts, and the Gauls, who were also a Celtic people. In the case of the Romanians, however, the name "Roman" itself was preserved. This word survives in Greek, with a political meaning and as an adverb, and in the name of Romantsch, one of the Rhaeto-Romance dialects of the Swiss canton of Grisons, but otherwise it is preserved only in the name of the Romanian language, *limba rômană*. That is, the people who remained north of the Danube considered themselves to be Romans, even though they lived under the sway of the migrating peoples. Neither the Byzantine authorities nor the barbarian rulers prevented relations with Roman areas south of the Danube. Indeed, as we learn from the Roman writer Sextus Aurelius Victor, the reconquest of Dacia was an important item on the political agenda of the Byzantine Empire. This plan was actually carried out in considerable area north of the Danube, and Roman-Byzantine influences thus were much strengthened in the Danube-Carpathian territories. At any rate, there was reason enough for the Daco-Romans north of the Danube to consider themselves an integral part of "Romania" and for the existence of the local political organizations, the "popular Romanias." These groups also are known by the Celto-Germanic term "Wallachia," but the Romanians have never called themselves Wallachs or Vlachs, but rather *Romani* or *Români.* Likewise, they have never called their own political formation Wallachia, but Romania or Țara Românească ("Romanian country").

These "Romanias" inhabited by "Romani" were an important reality. This explains the Gothic chieftain Ataulf's decision, recounted by Orosius, to give up the idea of transforming "Romania" into "Gothia" (*Historiarum adversus paganos* 7.22.7). Temestius, another contemporary writer, wrote that a Gothic chieftain named Athanaric preferred the title *judex potentissimus,* obviously under the influence of local institutions of Roman origin. As we have noted, the assemblies of village communes led by *judices* and *homines boni et veterani* also had Roman roots; similar institutions were found in Venice and other parts of Italy (especially Sardinia), and in Gaul and Dalmatia.

The enthusiasm generated by Arianism, a Christian creed closer to the interests of the masses than orthodox Roman Catholicism, also contributed to a revitalization of Latin culture in Daco-Roman areas. This is shown, among other ways, by the fact that Bishop Wulfila used Latin when bringing his Arian-tinged Christianity to the "Goths." Since the actual Goths did not know Latin, Wulfila had to have been preaching not to them, but to the Daco-Romans. (Priscus Panites, an envoy of the Byzantine emperor to the "court of Attila," wrote that as he traveled north of the Danube he was able to communicate with the local populace, who spoke a language he called "Ausonic," a Romance language.) The Latin aspect of the church is important, since the hierarchical organization of the church institutions took on certain popular social and political characteristics. Most of the bishops in these regions in the fourth to sixth centuries were Latin-speaking, which means that their cultural outlook was also Latin.

The complex civilization of the Danube-Carpathian region found expression linguistically as Moeso-Dacian Vulgar Latin became 'româna comună'. The developing language was enriched by a few Slavic and Greek lexical elements, but its syntax and morphology was not at all affected by other languages, and the grammatical structure of modern Romanian is purely Romance. The preservation of a common language, with all its subtleties, by a people or ethnic group necessarily implies continuous and extensive communication and trade relations among the inhabitants of the area. Indeed, the material and cultural remains of the population that inhabited Dacian territory form a coherent whole, known as the Bratei Culture. Finds include ceramics, brooches, combs, and small food mills characterized by elements of indigenous Romance style, as well as ceramics, metal objects, and coins that are marked by Byzantine influence. The Bratei Culture, the creation of the Daco-Roman people, is known from finds all over Romania: at Bratei, Ciumeşti, and Moreşti in Transylvania; at Costişa and Monoaia in Moldavia; and at Ipoteşti and Stolniceşti in Oltenia and Muntenia. The fact that the culture shows only insignificant regional variations implies that the entire Romanian territory was occupied by the same Daco-Roman stock. Furthermore, the great number of sites from the third through the sixth centuries in which the material culture continues the Roman provincial tradition—about one hundred such sites have been identified so far in Transylvania alone—testifies to the wide dissemination of their way of life.

The Bratei Culture was succeeded—both chronologically and taxonomically—by another known as the Ipoteşti-Cîndeşti-Ciurelu Culture. This society, which flourished in the seventh and eighth centuries, was sedentary, rural, and evidenced some social differentiation. The principal activities were farming, animal husbandry, and a few crafts. Simple agricultural tools, household objects, and ceramics of the same local style have been found, together with various decorative items, such as bronze filigree bracelets, crosses of silver or bronze filigree, and bronze appliques. Funeral practices included both burial and cremation. The characteristics of this society confirm its evolutionary connection to the preceding Dacian and Roman provincial culture. It, too, was the creation of a Romance population, and represents the continuation of the Roman tradition with Byzantine influences.

The indigenous society influenced the culture that was brought or established by the Slavic peoples who settled in the Danube-Carpathian region beginning in the sixth century, that known as the Săratu-Monteoru-Balta Verde Culture. The resultant mingling of Romance and Slavic elements is seen almost everywhere in which remains of this culture are found: at Suceava-Şipot in Moldavia; at Ipoteşti and Cîndeşti in Muntenia; and in the Tîrnave-Someş region in Transylvania. In certain cases we may speak of a mixed culture, but the proportion is heavily weighted toward the indigenous Romanized element, especially in ceramics. Archeological discoveries also permit us a glimpse at the economic life of the indigenous population. The principal activities of the inhabitants of the Danube-Carpathian region during these troubled times were agriculture, animal husbandry, mining, and various crafts; these are attested by the discovery of large quantities of carbonized seeds, agricultural implements, and bones of large and small animals throughout the area. In these new conditions the village communes experienced a strong revival.

The Romanian word for 'village' itself—*sat*—is from Latin *fossatum* 'area surrounded by moats or ditches'; likewise, when such villages formed a "popular Romania," it was known to the common people as *ţară* 'country', from the Latin *terra*. The vast majority of agricultural terms are also of Latin origin, preserved by a people that never abandoned its fields (*ogoare*, Lat. *agri*). Thus the Daco-Romans continued to grow such crops as wheat (*grîu*, Lat. *granum*), barley (*orz*, Lat. *hordeum*), rye (*secară*, Lat. *secale*), millet (*mei*, Lat. *milium*), flax (*in*, Lat. *linum*), and hemp (*cînepa*, Lat. *cannabis*); they continued to plow (*ara*, Lat. *arare*), sow (*semăna*, Lat. *seminare*), reap (*secera*, Lat. *sicilare*), and harvest (*culege*, Lat. *colligere*). They took their grain to the mill (*moară*, Lat. *mola*) to grind (*măcina*, Lat. *molinare*) it into flour (*făina*, Lat. *farina*) from which to make bread (*pîine*, Lat. *panis*). Their agricultural work required animals (*animale*, Lat. *animalia*) such as horses (*cai*, Lat. *caballi*) and oxen (*boi*, Lat. *boves*). By raising cattle (*vaci*, Lat. *vacae*), pigs (*porci*, Lat. *porci*), sheep (*oi*, Lat. *oves*), and goats (*capre*, Lat. *caprae*), they obtained meat (*carne*, Lat. *carnem*), milk (*lapte*, Lat. *lactem*), cheese (*caş*, Lat. *caseum*), and wool (*lînă*, Lat. *lana*). They also crafted agricultural tools and household objects, such as the plow (*aratru*, Lat. *aratrum*), ax (*secure*, Lat. *securis*), sickle (*secera*, Lat. *sicilis*), and pitchfork (*furcă*, Lat. *furca*). Blacksmiths (*fierari*, Lat. *fabri*), worked with iron (*fier*, Lat. *ferrum*); potters (*olari*, Lat. *ollari*) made pots (*oale*, Lat. *ollae*); gold (*aur*, Lat. *aurum*) and silver (*argint*, Lat. *argentum*) were made into jewelry by goldsmiths (*aurari*, Lat. *aurarii*) and silversmiths (*argintari*, Lat. *argentarii*). Houses (*case*, Lat. *casae*) were made of wood (*lemn*, Lat. *lignum*), earth (*pămînt*, Lat. *pavimentum*), clay (*lut*, Lat. *lutum*), and stone (*piatră*, Lat. *petra*).

Modern scholars unanimously accept the Latinity of the Romanian language. The very fact that words designating the most important aspects of daily life are of Latin origin would be sufficient to demonstrate the truth of this idea. The modern Romanian language is a Latin tongue spoken by a people who have preserved without interruption the name of their ancestors, the Romans. The language preserves the structure of Latin and the great majority of the Latin vocabulary. Its lexical stock is overwhelmingly Latin, both qualitatively and quantitatively—that is, considering both the function and the frequency of the words. Linguistic scholars have also established another important fact, namely that the rhythm of Romanian folk poetry is the rhythm of Latin verse. A poem titled "To the Star That Has Risen" ("La Steaua care-a răsărit"), written by Mihai Eminescu, Romania's greatest poet, provides convincing evidence both of the nature of the rhythm and of the Romance character of Romanian vocabulary. Of its fifty-four words, fifty-one are Latin or formed in Romanian of Latin elements, while only three are Slavic. The face of a language and its lexical character can be judged not only by the number of words, but also by their use in the living idiom. It is impossible to form a Romanian sentence using only non-Latin words; on the other hand, an average page of a popular writer will contain 85 to 90 percent Latin as against only 10 to 15 percent non-Latin words. In folk poetry, there are whole stanzas—even whole poems—that consist only of Latin words.

Taking into account all the linguistic evidence—grammar (including morphology and syntax) and lexicon (including archaisms and foreign, especially Slavic, influence)—contemporary scholars have concluded that the Romanian people and language evolved in the strongly Romanized regions along the Lower Danube (where there were about forty Romanized, Latin-speaking towns) and in Dacia north of the Danube, where Latin was likewise spoken in towns, military camps, mining centers, and craftsmen's *collegiae*. Summarizing the formation of the Romanian people and their language, one may say that the process proper began with the Romanization of the population north of the Danube in the second to fourth centuries; at the heart of it were the two main ethnic elements, Dacian and Roman. Various migrating peoples who settled in the area added some minor features, as also was true in the case of the other neo-Latin peoples and languages. Beginning in the sixth century, the evolving Romanian culture was augmented by Slavic elements, but the Romanized culture north of the Danube was stronger than that of the Slavic population, and therefore the latter was assimilated. (On the Balkan Peninsula, on the other hand, the Slavs prevailed and in great measure submerged the Romanized culture there.)

The qualitative transformation of the Daco-Romans into Romanians, and of Vulgar Latin into the Romanian language, took place in the eighth century. The words *torna, torna fratre,* from the seventh century, are closer to Latin than to Romanian. By the end of the following century, however, the formation of the Romanian people, in all its major aspects, was complete.

4

Early Medieval Civilization

The Dawn of Feudal Society

THE CIVILIZATION of the eighth and ninth centuries in Transylvania was a direct continuation of that of the preceding period. Known as the Romanian Dridu Civilization, after the place in Țara Românească where the most extensive remains have been found, the society was created by the Romanian people and retained its original character everywhere they lived. It developed in the eighth century as the indigenous ethnic element consolidated following the assimilation of the first wave of Slavic peoples; the earliest beginnings of feudal social, political, and economic forms made their appearance at the same time. In the ninth and tenth centuries, the predominately rural earlier society evolved toward a more complex form, as certain rural settlements began to take on a more townlike character.

The first phase of the Romanian Dridu Civilization is attested by simple dwellings, built both above the ground and partly underground, cemeteries, ceramics, agricultural tools, jewelry, religious objects, and other items, the creations of a settled population of farmers, herdsmen, and craftsmen. The largest portion of these archeological remains are ceramics, which were turned on a slow wheel. The predominant form is a pot of Roman style, without handles and with a pronounced shoulder and rim; also common are colored decorative pieces with ornamentation such as fluting, incised lines, and banding. In the eighth century, gray pottery with bright markings reappeared, especially in the towns. The development of larger pottery and iron works, with a substantial production of high-quality goods, naturally implies the existence of opportunities for trade in such products.

Villages became more common in hill and plain areas; in

many cases they were constructed on the sites of fourth- or fifth-century Dacian or Roman settlements. The grouping of individual farms into large clusters proves that the population was organized into communes or local political units. These communities had earthen fortresses, as, for example, in Arad (Vladimirescu) in southwest Transylvania and in Moreşti and Dăbîca in central and northeastern Transylvania, which are similar to those at Tirgovişte in Ţara Românească and at Voineşti in Moldavia. These were military and political centers for the leaders of the communes and of communal alliances. Communal ownership and use of water, woods, pastures, and most of the cultivated fields continued, but private property rights were extended to include a small plot of arable land.

Evidence for village clusters also is seen in cemeteries, which are found all over Romania from Dobruja to Transylvania; these cemeteries contain large numbers of tombs and obviously were directly proportional to the size of settlements. In this era both cremation and burial were practiced, in a ratio of about 85 percent cremations to 15 percent burials. Many Christian objects, such as crosses, encolpions, and medallions with crosses, have been found in the graves; these were used exclusively by the indigenous population, since the migrating peoples who settled on Romanian territory were not Christian. The indigenous Christianity had a folk character, however, since Dacia had not been officially Christianized.

In this period new Slavic tribes, more numerous and better organized than those of the seventh century, settled on Romanian territory. Their influence was correspondingly more substantial, but it was felt primarily in the Romanian vocabulary. Like the Romanians, these Slavs were organized into village communes, but they settled chiefly in the plains, as they feared and avoided the hilly regions. Slavic influence thus is noticeable in the terminology used to refer to certain occupations, tools, and political institutions in the areas where the two groups coexisted, though the activities and objects themselves retained their Romanian character. The Slavs also transmitted some influences from the Bulgarian kingdom, which has been established in 686 after the Bulgars settled south of the Danube in the Byzantine Empire.

At the beginning of the tenth century, yet another foreign people, the Magyars, entered Transylvania. Their penetration of Transylvania was similar to other expeditions which these tribes

Ninth- and tenth-century artifacts discovered at Dǎbîca: pottery, beads, and silver buttons.

undertook in western Europe and Byzantine Empire after settling in Pannonia in 895–96. The Magyars, of Finno-Ugric origin, had left the region of the northern Ural Mountains around the end of the ninth century, in response to pressure from other tribes. Under the leadership of "Duke" Arpad, they settled first in Pannonia and later in the Tisza plain. They found these new territories, inhabited by Slavs, Romanians, and others, insufficient for grazing their herds, which was their principal occupation in their new home. Thus they undertook expeditions of conquest in order both to expand their pasture lands and to obtain Transylvania's underground riches—especially salt, which was an absolute necessity for themselves and their animals, but which Pannonia lacked. After they had accomplished these goals, the majority of the tribesmen withdrew from Transylvania. Only a few remained among the indigenous population, which explains why, in all of Transylvania, definite traces of the tenth-century Magyar population have been discovered only in Cluj, Biharea-Oradea, and Siclău-Arad (from the early tenth century), and at Gîmbaş and possibly at Lapodea near Aiud (later in the century). However, even these remains—tombs and artifacts—could date from the period of warfare between the Magyars and the indigenous population rather than from afterwards. It should be remembered that the tombs of a few nomadic horsemen are not enough evidence to determine who ruled a given territory.

Political Organization

By about A.D. 1000, there had been noticeable developments in all spheres of Romanian economic, social, political, demographic, and cultural life. Technological progress in agriculture, such as the improvement of farming implements and the more efficient use of draft animals, made it possible for the peasants to clear more forests and break new ground for cultivation. Improved food supplies led to an increase in population, which tended to concentrate in ever-larger settlements. Distances between inhabited areas grew smaller, communication grew easier, and political life became better organized. Circumstances thus again favored the stratification of communities and the emergence of a socioeconomically privileged group—a group that gradually developed into a communal aristocracy and later into a ruling class. From this group were chosen (freely or otherwise) community leaders, and later the heads of newly developed political institutions.

In fact, Romanian society in the ninth to eleventh centuries was marked by a considerable degree of political organization. There is evidence that communes in river valleys and natural basins all over Transylvania had formed alliances called *knezates* and *voivodates*. Knezates were smaller and less important than the voivodates, which were also popularly known as *ţări*, "countries." These alliances were headed by a judge, a *knez* (roughly, "prince"), or a *voivode* ("duke"). Descriptions of the form and nature of the political groupings can be found in written sources and are complemented by historical and archeological research.

The most important of the written sources is the chronicle known as the *Gesta Hungarorum*, the late twelfth-century work of a certain *P. magister, Belae regis notarius* (Master Peter or Paul, secretary to King Béla—probably Béla III). This chronicle is complemented and confirmed in various ways by other Magyar chronicles, including the *Legenda Maior Sancti Gerhardi*, the *Gesta Hungarorum* of Simon of Kéza, and the *Chronicon Pictum Vindobonense*. The *P. magister Gesta Hungarorum* in particular has been thoroughly studied over the last two centuries, but scholarly opinions of its historical accuracy vary widely. The most recent and best-founded conclusions, however, are that it is an incontestably valuable work, at once scholarly and literary. The author was a most learned alumnus of the University of Paris, who, though he based his own work principally on an official chronicle written in the eleventh century, also was fortunate in his capacity as notary or secretary to the king to have access to authentic primary information.

According to the *P. magister* chronicle, when the Magyar tribes invaded at the beginning of the tenth century, most of Transylvania was organized into three great voivodates (or "duchies," to translate the Latin terminology of the various sources): Crişana, under the viovode Menumorut, which stretched from the Mureş on the south to the Someş on the north, and from the Meseş Gates on the east to the Tisza on the west; the Banat, under the viovode Glad, which covered the territory from the Mureş on the north to the Danube on the south, and from the western region of the Haţeg on the east to the Tisza on the west; and Transylvania, the largest area, from the Meseş Gates in the west to the middle

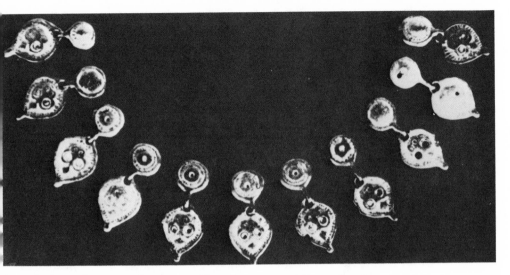

Eleventh-century bronze necklace from central Transylvania.

Mureş in the southeast and Maramureş in the northwest. This voivodate was led by the Romanian (*Blachus*) voivode Gelu, whose subjects included both Romanians and Slavs (*Blachi et Sclavi*).

These political units were certainly "countries" like the many other *ţări* into which the Romanian lands were divided at the time. Written sources mention Ţara Românilor (Bolohovanilor) and Ţara Cîmpulungului Moldovenesc in the northeast; Ţara Vrancei (or Ţara Brodnicilor) in southern Moldavia; Ţara Tigheciului (Chigheciului) in eastern Moldavia; Ţara Buzaelor in eastern Muntenia; Ţara Românească (that is, "Wallachia"); another Ţara Românească in southern Muntenia; Ţara Cîmpulungului Muscel in central Muntenia; Ţara Lovíştei, Ţara Jiurilor, Ţara Mehedinţilor, and Ţara Severinului in western Oltenia; Ţara Haţegului, Ţara Almaşului, Ţara Făgăraşului (Albului), and Ţara Bîrsei in southern Transylvania, Ţara Năsăudului in northeastern Transylvania; Ţara Oaşului, Ţara Silvaniei, and Ţara Beiuşului in northwestern Transylvania; Ţara Zarandului in southwestern Transylvania; and many others, whose sites were primarily in foothill basins and extended out into the surrounding area. There were unquestionably other *ţări* as well, but these would not have been mentioned by the chroniclers if they had nothing to do with the Magyar tribes on their expeditions in search of minerals and pastures.

The chronicles also confirm that these *ţări* were political units. Menumorut, in his negotiations with Usubu, the envoy of the Magyar leader Arpad, stated that the country (*terram*) which the Magyars wanted him to surrender of his own free will would never be ceded to anyone as long as he was alive, and that he would never hand over his country (*terram*) in the south, either out of love or out of fear. The *P. magister* chronicle itself calls the voivodate of Gelu "the country of Transylvania" (*terra Ultrasilvane*). The voivodate of the Banat is also designated a *terra.* Recent archeological excavations on the outskirts of Alba Iulia (Apulum) have also brought to light an uncommonly large Romanian necropolis dating from the eighth to ninth centuries. The semiurban settlement there was the center of another voivodate that included a vast territory on both banks of the middle Mureş River. Likewise, the latest digs have uncovered some forty settlements belonging to the voivodate of Alba, of which those at Moreşti and Blandiana were fortified. The center of the voivodate of Alba was in Alba Iulia (Alba Transilvana). Archeo-

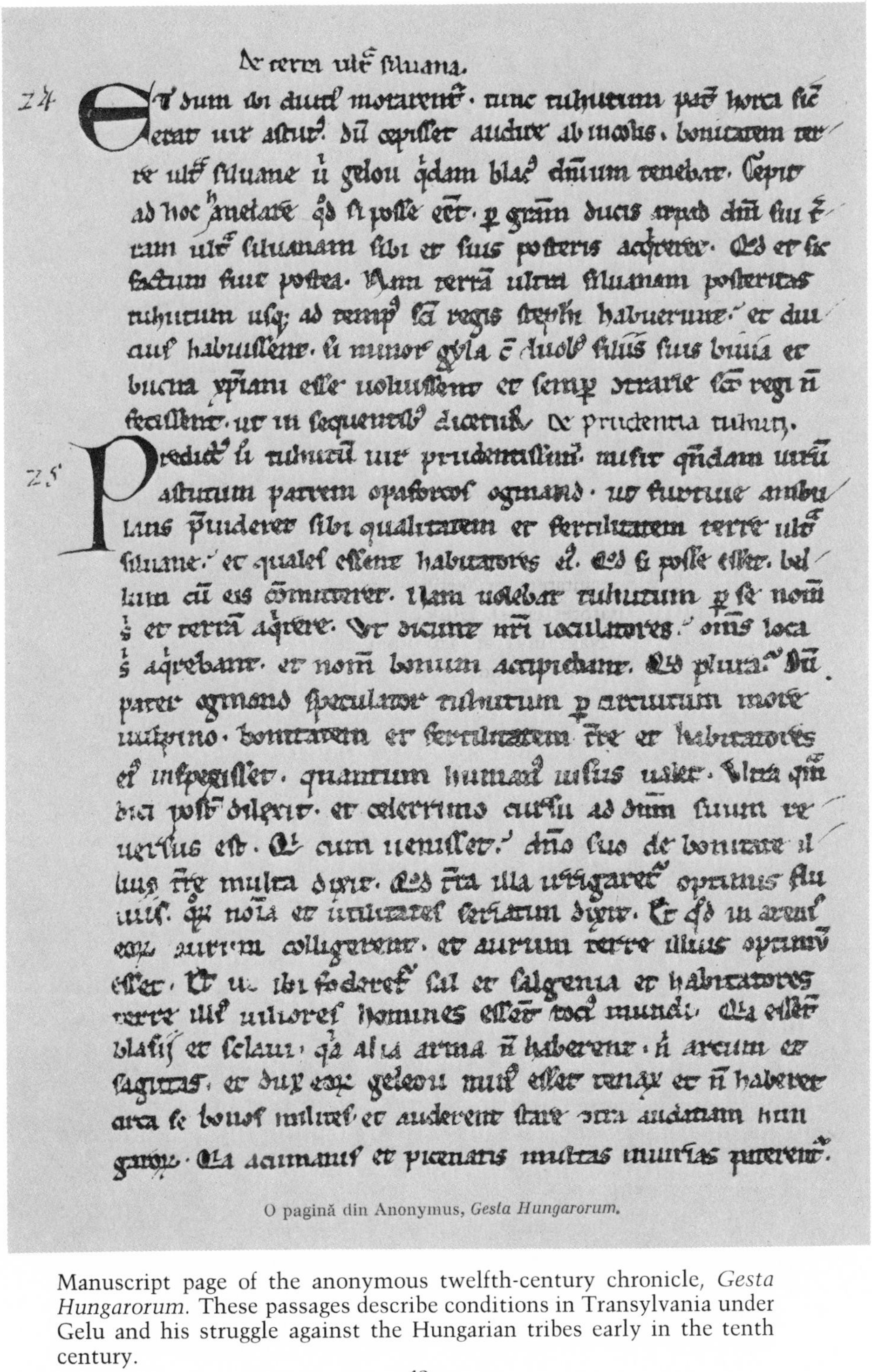

De terra ultrasiluana.

[Medieval Latin manuscript text in Gesta Hungarorum, marginal numbers 24 and 25, largely in an abbreviated twelfth-century hand.]

O pagină din Anonymus, *Gesta Hungarorum.*

Manuscript page of the anonymous twelfth-century chronicle, *Gesta Hungarorum.* These passages describe conditions in Transylvania under Gelu and his struggle against the Hungarian tribes early in the tenth century.

logical research proves that it existed as long ago as the eighth or ninth centuries; it is also mentioned in the later *Legenda Maior Sancti Stephani* and *Chronicon Posoniense.*

These countries were the result of powerful alliances of village communes. Written and archeological records permit us to paint a faithful picture of the village society and its culture. Farming and herding, for example, are attested in many ways, and we know that millet, wheat, barley, rye, peas, flax, and hemp were all grown. Typically, a large number of crops were planted in a relatively small area surrounding a village, but since the practice of rotating crops at two- or three-year intervals was unknown, soil quickly lost its fertility. Once a field stopped producing satisfactorily, it was abandoned, being reused only after having lain fallow for some time. Other areas were cleared and turned into agricultural fields. In this way a kind of rotation was achieved, in the sense that everything moved around the village site where the farming population resided.

Written sources and archeological evidence attest also to widespread stockbreeding and herding, the principal adjuncts to agriculture. The *Legenda Maior Sancti Gerhardi* tells of herds of horses belonging to the voivode of the Banat and the notables of his court; it also mentions numerous flocks of sheep and cattle cared for by herdsmen. Further proof that the people of this area were stockbreeders and herdsmen is the discovery of quantities of cattle, sheep, goat, and horse bones, shears for sheep, cowbells, and so on. The herdsmen practiced "transhumance"—the seasonal moving of flocks from one pasture region to another—but they left their families in the villages, thus maintaining their bonds to established settlements.

The people of tenth-century Transylvania knew and practiced all the crafts necessary for meeting the basic human need for clothing, shelter, and defense, as well as making household and farming tools, and even a few of what were at the time luxury items. The most important of these crafts was ironworking, attested both by tools and agricultural implements, and by the ore-processing furnaces discovered at several places in Transylvania. Next in importance was ceramics, as is proved by the wealth of local pottery that has been excavated. Weaving of cloth also was done in every household, on both vertical and horizontal looms. Finally, a few craftsmen knew the art of making jewelry; their products have been found at several sites, and they are amply displayed in the rich treasure of the court of the

Transylvanian voivode. Furthermore, the development of economic life throughout the whole country is confirmed by the discovery of Byzantine coins dating from 867 to 1025; these have been discovered in several localities in Transylvania as well as in other regions.

Socioeconomic Structures

The noticeable increase in the forces of production created the conditions for certain social changes. The principal economic characteristic of this period is that communal property coexisted with individual or individualized property, a fact that provided the basis for the transition to a society based on private property. Private ownership of real estate can only arise when lands can be used indefinitely. As long as agriculture involved field rotation, the property rights of the first person to clear a piece of land and put it to the plow were no more than a right of temporary use, lasting only until the land had to be left to lie fallow. Thus at this stage hereditary private ownership encompassed only things that could be used indefinitely: houses and the gardens around them, orchards, and livestock. Fields, pastures, woods, and watercourses continued to be owned collectively. The distribution of "shares" or "lots" was done by the "community"—that is, by a general assembly of the village people, probably under the direction of the wise old men and of the village chiefs, the judges and knezi.

The communal ownership of land also explains the collective nature of civic responsibilities. Taxes were set by the entire community and then apportioned among its members by the wise old men. The community was also collectively responsible for protecting its members from robbery and murder; for helping to find and apprehend wrongdoers, and for imposing punishments for crimes committed within its jurisdiction. Through its judges and wise old men, the commune also was the forum for resolving disputes between individual members.

However, social stratification in the communes is confirmed by contemporary written sources from all over Transylvania. For example, the anonymous notary of King Béla III describes the chieftains of the Romanian groups in Crişana, the Banat, and Transylvania proper. In his accounts of the battles they fought against the Magyar tribes in the early tenth century, these voivodes are presented as powerful feudal lords, controlling a kind of military aristocracy, and through them substantial troops of cavalry and infantry. These lords accumulated substantial wealth in the towns where they resided, while their subjects, the common people, lived in poverty. The poor owed military and other obligations to the local political rulers and the military aristocracy; moreover, they suffered from repeated attacks by the Pechenegs, an Asiatic tribe.

Valuable information on the social situation in the Banat is contained in the *Legenda Maior Sancti Gerhardi*. Because of its links to the Bulgar state and the Byzantine Empire, society in the Banat was somewhat further developed than in the rest of Transylvania, but there were no fundamental distinctions. The saint's life makes it apparent that these areas of the Banat and Crișana were fairly far down the road to feudalism by the beginning of the eleventh century. There was a military aristocracy around the voivode and his court; these noblemen (*nobiles*), as the *Legenda* calls them, owned the herds and flocks which were looked after by herdsmen (*pastores*) dependent on, and to a certain extent enslaved by, them. The *nobiles*, since they enjoyed the support of the political rulers, were able to usurp the lands of the village communes and turn them into their own estates (*allodia*, in the words of the *Legenda*). These they worked with the help of their subjects, some of whom lived in the courts (*curiae*) of the new rulers. The author of the *Legenda* uses twelfth-century terminology in his description of these earlier conditions, but there still can be no doubt that social stratification existed, and that there were feudal lords who controlled both persons and lands.

When several village communes formed a local political organization, or *knezate*, they chose a knez from among the ablest judges or wise old men in the several villages. The knez exercised powers similar to those of the judges, but extending over the entire knezate. The leader of a large or strong knezate thus had considerable authority.

Owing to political, economic, and military necessity—not to mention the desire of certain knezi for expansion—there subsequently arose a few political units that were more populous and economically and militarily more powerful. These were the voivodates, the result of the political integration of several knezates into a "country." The assembly of knezi chose the voivode from among their number and invested him with substantial political,

military, judicial, administrative, and fiscal powers. The voivode, like many medieval monarchs, had a tendency to transform his elective office into a hereditary one. The voivode Ahtum of the Banat, for example, succeeded Glad because of kinship ties.

The Eleventh and Twelfth Centuries

The indigenous Transylvanian civilization of the eleventh and
twelfth centuries in some respects can be seen simply as a continuing development of the culture of the preceding two centuries.
Agriculture expanded as more forests were cleared and new
grounds broken. Contributing to these advances were improved
agricultural implements. Plows equipped with multiple blades
of better-quality iron were introduced, and improved strains of
domestic animals. The number of wind and water mills rose
appreciably, which provides further evidence of the growth of
cereal production. There was progress in the cultivation of wine
and textile plants, and in mining, particularly of salt, but also of
iron, silver, and gold. Household crafts diversified, as did crafts
connected with mining; the overall number of crafts and trades
increased.

On the other hand, social distinctions became more sharply
defined, as the feudal type of social order began to take hold.
New "nobles," who ruled "domains" and "courts," were added
to the ranks of the older nobility who had risen from the upper
class of the communes. Since the new forms were only in their
infancy, the communes continued as the dominant type of social
and economic organization for some time, even after the equivalent of feudal lords were in their midst. In the new circumstances, the evolution of the knezates and voivodates kept pace
with social and economic transformations. The Romanian political units consolidated territorially, militarily, and politically.
At the end of the tenth century and the beginning of the eleventh, the voivodate of the Banat was led by the voivode Ahtum,
who was, according to the *P. magister Gesta Hungarorum* and
the *Legenda Maior Sancti Gerhardi,* a descendant of the voivode
Glad, who had ruled at the beginning of the tenth century. This
fact indicates that the rank had become or was becoming hereditary, which was characteristic of feudal institutions. Furthermore, the voivodate of the Banat had grown to include certain

territories north of the Mureș, which had been part of the voivodate of Crișana under Menumorut. The center of the newly expanded voivodate was established at a settlement on the Mureș; this was described as a "town" (*urbs Morisena*), which suggests a more developed settlement, and also a "fortress" (*castrum Morisena*), meaning that it was fortified as well. There were schools attended by many scholars, as, for example, that of Morisena, near the monastery of Saint George.

The Transylvanian voivodate was also more extensive than it had been under Gelu at the beginning of the tenth century. The eleventh-century voivodate took in a large part of present-day Transylvania, as far as the middle Mureș, and was very wealthy in grain, metals, and salt. Its voivode was Gyla, whose name perhaps derives from a Hungarian word meaning an army commander and high judge, or from the name of a Petcheneg tribe living in southeastern Transylvania. The center of Gyla's expanded voivodate was at Bălgrad, near Alba Iulia, a fortress town built of earth, wood, and stone. There were other fortified settlements—political and military centers—at Cluj-Mănăștur, Alba Iulia and nearby Teligrad, Dăbîca, Șirioara-Chiraleș, Moldovenști, Morești, and elsewhere. Both Transylvania and the Banat maintained active relations with the Byzantine Empire, from which they imported ceramics and jewelry, and from which, most likely, the Transylvanian voivode Gyla brought back a bishop, the monk Hierateas.

Such were the circumstances at the beginning of the eleventh century, when the Hungarian King Stephen I and the aristocrats of his court began to look toward neighboring lands, the home of Romanian farmers and herdsmen, miners and craftsmen. The changes that had occurred in Magyar society were the most important reason for the expansionist policy. Starting in the second half of the tenth century, the Magyar tribes were feudalized at a quicker pace, partly for internal reasons and partly because of external influences. Links to the German empire and the western church sped the process, and a feudal state was able to take hold at the start of the second millenium. The result was direct warfare between the armies of the voivodates and Stephen's army, a conflict Stephen eventually won, aided by the defection of some of the Romanian forces.

Magyar rule in Transylvania and the Banat remained uncertain for quite some time, however. The Petchenegs, for example, undertook several campaigns against the Hungarian state, some of which succeeded in reaching Pannonia. The power of the Magyar feudal state was weakened by struggles for the throne after the death of Stephen I; the German emperors took the opportunity to meddle in the internal affairs of Hungary in the hope of installing a ruler who would support their interests. Thus for some fifty years, the Magyar state was not only not in a position to enlarge its holdings, but indeed was forced to give up certain lands it had held.

The boundary of Magyar feudal rule was at the Meseş Gates, on the far side of the Bihor Mountains. There, at "the border of the land" in Crişana, a "great barrier of trees" was planted, as we learn from the Magyar chronicles of the twelfth to fourteenth centuries. The Magyars, unsuccessful until the end of the eleventh century in their attempts to reenter Transylvania, called the area Ultrasilva, Ultrasilvana, Transilvana, Erdeełu, and Erdeleu—which mean, both geographically and politically, the land "beyond the forest," "beyond the woods."

After this prolonged stay outside Transylvania, the Hungarian king and his aristocrats once again took action to conquer it. Their efforts were favored by the success of the feudal system and the Catholicism which supported it, as well as by the defeat of the tribal elements and non-Christians in the interior, and by the collapse of Petcheneg power in Transylvania. In the first quarter of the twelfth century, the Magyar feudal state had advanced as far as the Someş, Mureş, and Tîrnava Mică valleys. Nevertheless, Magyar control of Transylvania was made difficult by local resistance. The Magyar kings therefore sought to win over the leading groups among the indigenous population, and in certain regions they also established colonies, first of Magyars and later of Szeklers, Saxons, and lastly Teutonic knights.

The Szeklers are an ethnically mixed population, the result of the blending of a number of Turkic peoples. Their name derives from the Turkic word *sikil*, "well-born." According to the narrative sources, the Szeklers lived in the northwestern part of Transylvania before the Hungarians settled in Pannonia; when the Magyars passed through the western part of their lands, the Szeklers welcomed them, conquered Pannonia with them, lived with them for some time, and, as is the custom of nomadic peoples who attach themselves to another group, fought in the vanguard of their army. Eventually the Szeklers settled at the limits of the Magyar feudal state, with the mission of defending the frontiers. When Magyar rule reached Bihor, we find the Szeklers there too, living alongside the Romanians. (According to the chronicler Simon of Kéza, the Szeklers learned to write from them.) When it expanded to Transylvania proper in the twelfth century, however, either the Szeklers fled to avoid feudalization, or, more likely, were resettled by the Magyar kings on the Mureş and the Tîrnave. Finally, when Magyar authority took in the southeastern corner of Transylvania at the beginning of the thirteenth century, the Szeklers were settled there, alongside the indigenous population. There they remain today.

Because of the privileges accorded to them, the Szeklers were able to preserve traces of their old tribal way of life into the fourteenth and fifteenth centuries. Land was considered the common property of the whole tribe; the Szeklers did not recognize private property in their settlements. Administratively and politically, they were organized into "seats" around the middle of the fourteenth century; these seats were a type of administrative unit deriving from an earlier, less fixed territorial entity known as a "land" (terra) or "district" (districtus).

The Magyar kings also brought German settlers to Transylvania, and for the same reasons: they needed to consolidate the rule of the House of Arpad and to guard their southern border, and they also wished to exploit the colonized territories. The Germans arrived in several successive migrations. The first groups, who came in the mid-twelfth century, were apparently brought from Flanders; other, larger groups came from Luxembourg and the Moselle valley. Later the ranks of the colonists were further swelled by immigrants from the right bank of the Rhine—Saxony, at the time—which is probably the source of the generic name "Saxon" for all the German colonists. These groups were willing to emigrate because the mass of German peasants had become serfs and were impoverished by heavy taxes owed to the state, the church, and the feudal lords. The peasants—who were followed by craftsmen and merchants—who were established in Transylvania were granted hereditary title to their land in return for agreeing to assume some minor financial obligations. The head of a village of colonists—called a "count"—enjoyed certain privileges, such as a larger plot of land which was exempt from state taxes, and the right to a portion of fines and taxes paid by the peasants. The Transylvanian territories colonized by this first large German population were in the Sibiu basin and in the Olt and Hîrtibaciu valleys. Later they settled around Bistriţa, in Ţara Bîrsei, and in the Tîrnava Mare valley.

In 1211, King Andreas II brought Teutonic knights from Palestine to settle in Ţara Bîrsei, partly in order to defend the southern border against the threat of the Cumans, and partly in order to expand feudalism and Catholicism in Transylvania. As with the territories settled by Szeklers and Saxons, so with the lands granted to the Teutonic knights: they were already inhabited by an indigenous Romanian population, as is shown by place names and the remains of a few fortified settlements mentioned in contemporary documents. The king rewarded the knights handsomely, granting them significant economic, political, and religious privileges. However, the consequence was that they were able to rule independently of the Magyar state, and they soon came into conflict with the king. As a result, they were expelled from Ţara Bîrsei in 1225, the indigenous population remaining behind.

Social Changes in the Twelfth and Thirteenth Centuries

The establishment of Magyar rule over Transylvania in the twelfth and thirteenth centuries was followed by attempts to provide the territories with a new social, political, and economic organization. What happened in Transylvania was similar to what happened in England after the Norman Conquest: feudalization, which had already begun, progressed more rapidly. To combat the resistance of the local population, the Magyar kings settled Transylvania with groups of outsiders to prop up their rule, and they granted their most devoted supporters, the nobility and the church, extensive lands usurped from the village communes. For all that, however, the old institutions could not be abolished, and as a result we observe two aspects of feudalism in Transylvania. One developed from the Romanian voivodates, while the other was introduced by the conquerors and superimposed on the local forms.

The indigenous aspects of feudalism were maintained throughout the country in the Middle Ages, although most strongly in the peripheral areas. The *ţări* so often mentioned in the sources of the time—Ţara Bîrsei, Ţara Făgăraşului, Ţara Haţegului, Ţara Severinului, Ţara Oaşului, and Ţara Maramureşului, which completely surround Transylvania—are in fact the old autonomous Romanian political units, alliances of communes. Certain customs and institutions survived for some time in these areas. The village communes continued to distribute land by lot; they were led by

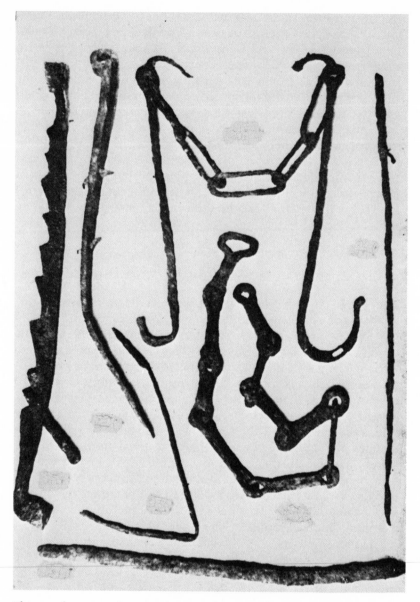

Thirteenth-century iron implements from southern Transylvania.

the judges, knezi, and wise old men; judgments at law were based on ancient custom, traditional land rights, or Romanian law (*jus valachicum*), which the authorities were compelled to recognize; and courts were composed of jurors, knezi, priests, and common people. The petty nobility mentioned as existing in Făgăraş, Chioar, and Maramureş were the successors to the dominant class of the communes. The Romanian "districts" retained traces of the old autonomous Romanian political structures in their internal judicial, military, and administrative organization, and they often acted together or affirmed their solidarity against the official authority.

Those institutions introduced by the Magyar feudal state in some cases superseded Romanian ones; in other cases they coexisted. For the most part, the conquered territories and the lands usurped from the communes became the property of the king. His holdings were composed of fortress domains and other properties spread out over all of Transylvania. Royal ownership also extended to salt mines and gold, silver, and iron mines. At the center of a royal holding was the fortress (*castrum regale*) or court (*curia, curtis regalis*). Since these royal fortresses played both an economic and a military role, their inhabitants included certain economically or legally privileged social groups. Among these were the "natural serfs" or "serfs of the holy king" (*iobagiones naturales, iobagiones sancti regis*), freemen by birth, who had certain privileges granted by the first Magyar kings; some of this group later became part of the petty or middle nobility, while others were reduced to peasant status. Another group living in the royal fortresses were "fortress serfs" (*iobagiones castri*), who had military obligations and were essentially freemen, although they were not free to leave the fortress when they wished. Some of them became servants of the king or of powerful feudal lords, but most fell all the way to the ranks of the peasantry. The construction and maintenance of the fortresses was the duty of still another group of fortress residents, the *castrenses* or *civiles*. In addition to all these groups, there were several different grades of dependent peasants: serfs (*iobagiones*), jerleri, or landless peasants (*inquilini*), court servants (*conditionarii*), freemen (*libertini*), and slaves (*servi*). They were the farmers, grape growers, and craftsmen, who made the land productive through their unpaid labor; they were obliged to tithe in grain, in wine, and in animals, contributing to the state's coffers with the taxes they paid either per head or per household.

Once a royal property had been established, the formation of other church or secular domains nearby quickly followed, either through royal grants or through the appropriation of commune lands. The beneficiaries of the earliest grant documents pertaining to Transylvania were churches and monasteries, followed soon afterwards by the high nobility. The lands granted were substantial tracts seized from the peasants, who lost their liberty along with their land and became dependents of the church or of the secular feudal lords. As serfs, jeleri, servants, or even slaves, the peasants were obliged to work or to pay taxes in produce and in money. They were compelled to perform such tasks as plowing, tending vines, haymaking, carting, cutting wood in the forests, mining salt, caring for animals, and making tools and clothes; they tithed in pigs, cattle, honey, grain, hay, hides, salt, and manufactured items, and paid taxes in money.

In the eleventh and twelfth centuries, the Roman Catholic bishops in Cenad, Oradea, and Alba Iulia organized to support the consolidation of royal power and the expansion of their Catholicism among Orthodox populations, to establish church and secular feudal properties, and to force the granting of some privileges. All of this made possible the establishment of a relatively rich secular and clerical aristocracy, which, because of its economic power and the political situation, was able to oppose the central authority when it wished to do so.

In spite of the inroads made by the feudalizing upper classes, a strong, free peasantry, composed principally of indigenous peasants in their old village communes, and of the larger or smaller "guest" colonies—neo-Latin (latini), German, Czech, and Ruthenian—managed to maintain itself down to the middle of the thirteenth century. Contemporary documents mention powerful communes from one end of Transylvania to the other. One source, for example, refers to some ten villages around Arad where peasants lived in free communes in the early years of the thirteenth century. Another source mentions about thirty such communes in the 1230s in the neighboring region of Zarand and in the Banat. In Țara Hațegului in southern Transylvania, the village communes also flourished: as late as the fourteenth century, five districts still retained the old rights of choosing judges and knezi and of governing themselves according to Romanian law. In the communes in Făgăraș, also in southern Transylvania, the free peasants were organized into the so-called Country of the Romanians (Terra

Blachorum; mentioned in 1222) and controlled the "forests of the Romanians and the Petchenegs" (mentioned in 1224). This Făgăraş peasantry played a significant role in the social and political life of Transylvania throughout the thirteenth century. Not far from Ţara Făgăraşului was Ţara Amlaşului, west of Sibiu, where Romanian communes also were to persist for some time. The most powerful Romanian communes, however, were those in Ţara Maramureşului in northern Transylvania, which managed, by steadfast struggle, to resist the coming of feudalism until the middle of the fourteenth century.

Peasant communes also existed in other parts of Transylvania (Alba in the central part, Dăbîca in the northeast, and Bihor in the northwest), but these were endangered, earlier and more seriously, by the onslaught of royal, noble, and clerical feudal power. This is not to say that these peasants lightly surrendered their land and their freedom; indeed, they resisted with every means at their disposal. The 389 cases tried by the ordeal of hot irons before the religious court of Oradea between 1208 and 1235 offer conclusive proof of the valiant struggle waged against feudalism by the village communes. The communes of Szekler peasants were also able to preserve their old freedoms.

The peasants, whether free or dependent, were the direct producers of the material goods needed by the whole society—clothing, shelter, agricultural implements, jewelry, and arms, as well as agricultural products. Crafts and trades were at first simply an adjunct to agriculture, and closely linked to peasant society. Craftsmen worked exclusively for the communities in which they lived. But as early as the second half of the thirteenth century, crafts began to become independent of agriculture. More and more craftsmen left the restricted environment of the feudal estates to settle in the fortresses, whose walls and whose rulers assured them their livelihood, and whose people bought their wares. Thus the foundations were laid for the further development of townlike settlements. In the same way, a few free villages in favorable economic and geographic circumstances were also transformed into towns.

Some medieval Transylvanian towns evolved from the fortified settlements that were the residences of the voivodes: tenth- and early eleventh-century Biharea, Satu Mare, Orşova, Dăbîca, Alba Iulia, and some others. The establishment of Catholic bishoprics at Cenad, Oradea, and Alba Iulia also contributed to the growth of these towns. Yet other towns appeared following the colonization by various groups in the twelfth and thirteenth centuries at the royal fortresses at Cluj, Satu Mare, and Timişoara, through the development of the economically well-situated villages of Braşov, Sibiu, Bistriţa, Sighişoara, Mediaş, Sebeş, and Orăştie, and at some mining sites such as Baia Mare, Rodna, Dej, Turda, Abrud, and Zlatna. At the beginning, however, all of these settlements retained a pronounced agrarian character and were inhabited by a very mixed population of soldiers, courtiers, officials, craftsmen, and farmers.

The Tartar Invasion

The foundations of town life were severely shaken by a Tartar invasion in 1241, and everything had to be rebuilt more or less from the start in the second half of the thirteenth century. At the beginning of that century, Genghis Khan managed to unite the Mongol tribes and raise them to a level of power they had never before known. After conquering Asia, the Tartars invaded Europe under the leadership of Batu Khan. One by one the peoples and states in their path were conquered, and the Romanian territory did not escape their destructive onslaught. In the middle of March 1241, a part of the Tartar army, which had just laid waste northern Moldavia, entered Transylvania through the Rodna Pass under the leadership of Kadan. Villages and towns along the way—Rodna, Bistriţa, Dej, Cluj, and Oradea—were devastated and a great part of the population killed or carried off. Another Tartar horde, after cutting across Moldavia from north to south and stopping briefly in the southern part, entered Transylvania from the southeast, via the Oituz Pass; they crushed the resistance of the Romanians and the Szeklers of the Transylvanian voivodate. The southern part of Transylvania met the same fate, from Ţara Bîrsei to the Banat. Appeals to the pope and the German emperor for help met with no response, and the army of the Hungarian king Béla IV was totally destroyed on the River Sajó on 11 April 1241. For more than a year afterwards, the Tartars were the tyrants of Transylvania, subjecting the masses to severe hardship and constant terror. But the struggles of the local population, the difficulties of organizing and controlling such a vast area, and the battle of the Russian people against the Mongols in the Russian knezates forced Batu to withdraw his

Mongol chieftain, 1241. Painting on silk.

armies from the territories west of the Carpathians in the summer of 1242.

The Tartar-Mongol invasion and conquest left vast material damage and destruction in Transylvania, and resulted in the death or abduction of many of its inhabitants. In order to reorganize the region, Béla IV put out a call for new colonists, offering substantial privileges to those who accepted his offer. In addition, numbers of noblemen whose properties on the Hungarian plain provided insufficient protection against future invasion resettled in the fertile river valleys in the hilly wooded areas of Transylvania. They either were granted new domains or simply seized the land and property of weaker groups; as a result, feudal ownership had a new period of growth at the expense of the peasant communes. The anarchy reigning in Hungary in the second half of the thirteenth century enabled the nobility to take over royal fortresses or build their own; these lords went about like royalty and resisted central authority in any way they could.

The masses, of course, were left to the whims of the landlord, and the rural communes were victimized by the dominant class to an unprecedented extent. Serfdom was widely extended, so much so that laws written at the end of the thirteenth century equate the terms for peasants or people in general with those for serfs (*populi seu iobagiones, rusticus seu iobagio*). The number of serfs was also swelled by the addition of slaves given as offering to the church (*dusnici*) and freed slaves (*libertini*). Under these circumstances, the condition of the peasantry and especially of the serfs worsened, while their obligations to the state, the church, and the landlord increased. Taxes were raised, especially those paid in agricultural produce and animals, but also those paid in money. To assure that the rulers would have as many subjects as possible—and thus all the more income—the serfs' freedom of movement was severely restricted. Those who wished to leave the lord's domain were required to obtain his permission and to pay a special tax (*terragium*).

Faced with these circumstances, the peasants did not simply submit. They rose up against their oppressors, refused to pay taxes, left estates and banded together as brigands, revolted in larger groups, or settled in other areas, even south and east of the Carpathians, where they lived with other Romanians, their own people.

5

The Transylvanian Voivodate

IN ITS EFFORTS to introduce its own institutions in Transylvania, the Magyar feudal state encountered active resistance from the Romanian population. In many cases, the deeply rooted indigenous institutions emerged victorious, and the knezates, voivodates, districts, and seats, led by knezi, voivodes, and judges, were able to survive as viable entities throughout the Middle Ages. From these indigenous institutions arose that special form of political organization, the Transylvanian voivodate. It represented the further development, for the whole region, of the old voivodates of the tenth and eleventh centuries, but it was unique to Transylvania within the entire Magyar kingdom.

The first political leader of Transylvania—a certain Mercurius—is mentioned in documents in 1111 and 1113, where he is referred to as "prince" (*princeps*). However, we have no evidence that he ever effectively ruled; indeed, that would have been difficult, since at the time Transylvania had only been partially conquered, and the natives were putting up stiff resistance to foreign institutions. This presumably explains why there is no further reference to political rulers in Transylvania for a considerable time. Not until 1176 do we find mention of Eustatius, and it is noteworthy that his title is "voivode" (*Leustachius waivoda Transilvaniae*) and not "prince." This appearance of the Transylvanian voivodate in the last third of the twelfth century proves two facts: first, that Transylvania was not conquered by the Magyar kings until that time; second, that the central authority was obliged to recognize the durability of the indigenous institutions. It was thus the realities of the economic, social, political, and geographic situation that forced the Magyar kings to respect the uniqueness of Transylvania and to recognize its character and its distinctive organization within the Hungarian kingdom. The line of the Transylvanian voivodes continued uninterrupted until the middle of the sixteenth century.

Transylvania experienced a separate development from the rest of the Magyar feudal kingdom during the whole time it was a part of it. This explains the fact, emphasized by the Hungarian historian Sándor Szilágyi, that Transylvania never entirely lost its identity: Transylvania and the Kingdom of Hungary remained two separate countries. As another Hungarian historian, László Kőváry, points out, Hungary was oriented politically more towards the west, while Transylvania naturally began to look east to the other two Romanian countries. Indeed, in the second half of the thirteenth century and the first half of the fourteenth, Transylvania was only formally a part of the Kingdom of Hungary; in reality it formed a separate country (regnum). In 1257, Béla IV of Hungary acceded to the insistent demands of his son Stephen and granted Transylvania to him; for thirteen years, Stephen assumed the privileges of a sovereign in his role as duke of Transylvania, and he governed it like an independent country. When Béla attempted to end these rights, Stephen, with the support of the local nobility, retained them by force. On several occasions he defeated armies sent against him, compelling the king to accept a peace under the same conditions as between two sovereigns and two separate countries.

Although the Magyar kings repeatedly tried to quell Transylvanian independence, it continued to be strongly felt. In the period of anarchy during the time of the Magyar king Ladislaus IV (r. 1272–90), Transylvania was again considered a separate country, and the voivode Roland Borsa exercised essentially sovereign rights, conferring privileges, appointing counts and councils, deciding disputes between nobles, and so on. Roland's successor, Ladislaus, assumed even greater autonomy for Transylvania. In his fortress at Deva, Ladislaus established a true court, with judges, squires, and notaries; he was the uncontested ruler of fortresses, towns, royal domains, and mines. He appointed and dismissed bishops, granted and revoked privileges, and became involved in arbitrating the succession to the Hungarian throne, confiscating the royal crown and defying papal orders. In return for recognizing Charles Robert of Anjou as king of Hungary, he imposed conditions like a sovereign, and when these conditions were violated at the beginning of the fourteenth century, he did not hesitate to turn against the king, forming pacts with other important feudal lords and even with foreign sovereigns, such as

King Stephen II of Serbia. These actions culminated in the establishment of a general assembly of the Transylvanian nobility, convened and presided over by the voivode or his representative in the same way as the king convened and presided over the Hungarian diet. The first mention of this Transylvanian institution is in 1288; in 1291 and 1355, Romanian representatives also participated. The assembly, a continuing reminder of Transylvania's autonomous position in the Hungarian kingdom, survived until 1541, when Transylvanian was officially tranformed into an independent principality.

The autonomy of the Transylvanian voivodate and its orientation toward Moldavia and Ţara Românească can be explained further by the fact that all three regions were ethnically homogeneous. Most of the people in Moldavia and Ţara Românească were Romanian, as were a majority of those in Transylvania. Of the approximately 550,000 inhabitants of Transylvania on the eve of the great Tartar-Mongol invasion of 1241, roughly 65 percent were Romanian and 35 percent Hungarian, Saxon, Szekler, or of other groups. The huge drop in population caused by the invasion was recovered by the end of the thirteenth century, partly through natural population growth and partly through new colonization. Thus, by 1300 the population of Transylvania presumably had returned to the level of sixty years earlier. This population, however, may have been even more heavily Romanian, since fewer Romanian lives were lost during the invasion and the number of Romanians grew more rapidly afterwards.

Demographic evidence for the first half of the fourteenth century is more abundant. From a church registry of tithes for 1334, for example, we know quite exactly the population of the settlements in the seat of Orăştie in southeastern Transylvania. In these nine settlements—eight villages and a market town—there were almost 5,200 inhabitants. Such a population was large for the time, since the average for Transylvanian villages was more like 200. It is true that there were substantial population differences among these settlements: there were over 1,300 persons in the market town of Orăştie, but barely 150 in the smallest village. In the mid-fourteenth century, the population of Transylvania as a whole was perhaps 900,000, or 9 inhabitants per square kilometer.

On the basis of records of papal tithes for the years 1332–37, we can determine for Transylvania as a whole the approximate ratio of the Catholic population (Hungarian, Saxon, and Szekler) to the Orthodox (Romanian), since only the former were subject to papal tithes. The records show 950 Catholic parishes, and since at this time there were approximately 3,000 settlements in Transylvania (more than 2,550 are specifically mentioned in documents up to 1350), roughly 2,000 contained no Catholic parish. This in turn means that either those settlements had no Catholic inhabitants or too few to constitute a parish, and it therefore follows that 2,000 settlements were entirely or very largely only Orthodox. In other words, more than 65 percent of the inhabitants of Transylvania were Romanian or, rarely, Ruthenian—and less than 35 percent were Catholic Hungarian, Szekler, or Saxon.

The steadily rising population was cut back in the middle of the fourteenth century by the Black Death, the great epidemic that raged throughout most of Europe. Though the effects of this frightful scourge were not as disastrous in Transylvania as in the countries of western and central Europe, where the population was reduced by 20 to 25 percent (rising to more than 50 percent in some towns), they were nevertheless not negligible. But the effects of medieval epidemics were directly proportional to the density of the population. Transylvanians were spread out in small villages, many of which were located in hilly and wooded regions, and they were therefore relatively well protected. The population of England, for example, was 3.7 million at the outbreak of the epidemic, but barely 2 million thirty years later. The population of Sweden dropped 42 percent, and that of Norway 26 percent. Transylvania's population returned to its former level in only slightly more than half a century, whereas the western European countries needed a full century. In Sicily, for example, the population did not regain preplague levels until the end of the fifteenth century.

The population of Transylvania in 1400 can be estimated to be about the same as in 1348–49—that is, about 850,000 to 900,000; the proportion of Romanians to other coinhabiting peoples also remained at roughly 65 percent to 35 percent. A century later, around 1500, it can be estimated at about 1,400,000 and another half-century after that at about 1,600,000; the same ethnic proportions were maintained.

The great majority of the Transylvanian population lived in what we may call villages. The typical settlement is referred to in contemporary sources as a village (*villa*), manor (*possessio*), or settlement (*praedium*). The head of a Romanian village was known as a judge (*judex*), mayor (*villicus*), or knez (*kenez*); he was called a burgrave (*gereb* or *gräf*) or count (*comes*) in Saxon villages, and judge (*biró*) or mayor (*villicus*) among the Hungarians and Szeklers. The judge was chosen by the community if the village were free, imposed from above if it were subject to a lord. The judge had a significant role in community life. He presided over all the village court of justice (*forum pedaneum*), which adjudicated all disputes between inhabitants of the village; he collected the taxes owed to the state and to the feudal ruler as well as the lord's income from mills and taverns. He was responsible for overseeing the involuntary labor (*robota*) that the inhabitants were obliged to perform for the lord; he distributed family lots from the village lands and was in charge of the rotation of fields and crops. In carrying out these functions, the judge was assisted by village leaders known as jurors (*jurati* or *Geschworenen*) in the Saxon villages, and the wise old men in the Romanian villages. The judge and his councillors held court weekly, on Sunday or some other day, outside when the season permitted, or in the "judgment house," the village hall, when the weather was inclement.

The character of any given village depended on its physical and environmental conditions and the occupations of the inhabitants. In higher, more mountainous regions, where the main activities were herding and stockbreeding, villages were dispersed: houses were widely separated and set in the middle of family plots of land (usually pastureland, less often cultivated fields). In gentle hilly regions, where stockbreeding and agriculture were found in roughly equal proportions, villages were predominantly detached, with the houses less far apart than in the dispered villages and strung out along long winding roads. In regions where the hills met the plains, the predominant type was the valley village, with a road or path along a watercourse, and the houses spread out on one or both sides of the road. Finally, in the plains, the villages were concentrated, crossed by a network of several streets and with houses set more closely together. The plains inhabitants engaged primarily in agriculture, with stockbreeding as an adjunct. The plains also had another type of village, the geometric village, which was usually square, with the houses set next to each other on both sides of the roads. These were usually the villages of colonists, who, because they settled as a group, were able to plan and organize. In these villages, too, the primary occupations were agriculture and its adjuncts.

Certain rural settlements, such as those at major crossroads, political and administrative centers, and fortresses where craftsmen and merchants had settled, underwent further development and became market towns (*oppida*) or cities (*civitates*). Those settlements that had begun to urbanize in the eleventh and twelfth centuries were seriously affected by the Tartar-Mongol invasion, since they contained greater wealth and naturally attracted the invaders, and they had to be rebuilt from ruins. Nevertheless, as time went on, more and more Transylvanian settlements came to be characterized as cities or market towns. They enjoyed judicial, administrative, and ecclesiastical autonomy; they had certain economic, political, and fiscal privileges, including the right to a weekly market and an annual fair; they fulfilled a significant economic, military, and cultural function; and they were important centers for merchants and artisans. The birth of towns was in fact a consequence of several forces: the increasing social division of labor; the separation of crafts and commerce from agriculture; the creation of new economic relations involving money in place of barter; more extensive trade; and the formation of permanent marketplaces. But the most important characteristic of these urbanized settlements was that the inhabitants were legally free. The proverb "Town air makes one free" ("Stadtluft macht frei") expressed the fact that a person who lived a certain length of time in a town—usually a year and a day—was freed of his feudal dependence.

Towns were governed by a "magistrate"—that is, by a council headed by one or two judges. The judges were assisted by a panel of jurors, who, like the judges, were elected by the citizens for a one-year term. Beginning in the second half of the fourteenth century, we see the appearance in some places of the burgomaster (*magister civium, Bürgermeister*) and even of the town manager (*villicus, Hann*), who was responsible for the town's economic affairs. Around the middle of the fifteenth century, certain towns began to elect larger councils of one hundred men, which were responsible for apportioning financial obligations among the inhabitants.

Several late thirteenth-century settlements are referred to as cities in contemporary sources, or mention is made of their judges and jurors or their inhabitants (*cives*). These are Rodna, a mining center in northeastern Transylvania; Sibiu, a manufacturing and commercial center in southern Transylvania; Alba

Iulia, the bishopric in central Transylvania; Bistriţa, a manufacturing and commercial center in northeastern Transylvania; and Turda, a salt-mining center in central Transylvania. By the first half of the fourteenth century, another twenty towns from all over Transylvania had been added to this list. Of all of these, the most populous and the most important were Braşov, Sibiu, Cluj, Bistriţa, Sighişoara, Oradea, Arad, and Timişoara. The Transylvanian towns had medium-sized populations. Cluj had about 6,000 inhabitants in the mid-fifteenth century and 9,000 in the mid-sixteenth—about the size of Heidelberg, Dresden, or Basel. By the last third of the fifteenth century, Sibiu had 7,000 or 8,000 inhabitants; Braşov had around 9,000 or 10,000; Bistriţa had around 3,500 to 3,700; and Sighişoara had 3,000 to 3,300.

In their layout and organization, the Transylvanian towns were very similar to those of central Europe. The largest were built on a radiating concentric plan, with a central square or plaza, from which streets led out to the periphery like the spokes of a wheel, and with the main streets connected by other smaller ones. The streets were well-worn dirt tracks, in some cases surfaced with boards. At first houses were made of wood, but later increasingly of stone and brick. The larger towns were usually encircled by mighty walls—in some cases by both an inner and an outer wall—made of stone and brick. At intervals along the walls were towers and bastions, either square or polygonal, which were constructed, maintained, and manned by a civil guard made up of members of the town's guilds. Arms and armaments were stored in these towers; from them a lookout could be maintained, the town defended from danger, and distant happenings observed. Access to and from the town was only through the gates, which were well watched by the toll collectors and guardsmen.

In addition to these fortress towns, there were fortifications in some rural villages and in certain other suitable locations that were not connected with any particular settlement. Some villages also had the court (*curia*) or castle (*castellum*) of the feudal ruler. In many cases—especially in southern Transylvania, but also in the center and even further north—churches were also surrounded by strong walls, thus becoming fortress churches. These fortified churches served as refuges for the population in time of danger. The same role was played by peasant fortresses built by village communities. These were made of massive stone blocks and generally were located high on a promontory. This type of fortification was more common in the south, since the south was more often exposed to danger.

Finally, the kings and feudal lords, both clerical and secular, also built mighty fortresses, with massive crenellated stone walls, towers, and bastions, surrounded by water-filled moats. Many such fortresses were built in all parts of Transylvania; the royal fortresses were especially common in the south, where the Ottoman threat was greater, while those of lesser feudal rulers were built throughout the voivodates. The fortresses served both defensive and offensive purposes, as they were used by major feudal rulers to maintain their resistance against the central authority and to launch attacks against other nobles.

The total number of fortified sites in Transylvania was about three hundred, which means one fortified settlement per 340 square kilometers. This figure becomes meaningful when we find it is comparable to the situation in the rest of medieval Europe. In this respect as well then, Transylvania clearly has its place on the landscape of European civilization.

6

The Late Middle Ages

THE FOURTEENTH TO SIXTEENTH CENTURIES saw the emergence of Transylvania as a politically, socially, economically, and culturally distinct region. It became an increasingly autonomous element in the Hungarian kingdom, through the consolidation of its own political and administrative institutions and because of its role in blocking the expansion of the Ottoman Empire. Moreover, it underwent significant economic development—significant, at any rate, in the light of internal and external historical factors. This economic development, especially a noticeable increase in the activities of merchants and artisans, was considerably influenced by Transylvania's trading relations with Țara Românească and Moldavia. Furthermore, the economic development helped to fix the social structure and stabilized the relations between the various social classes and groups.

Autonomy

Transylvanian autonomy was manifested primarily in the consolidation of the voivodate. The twenty-year rule of the voivode Toma Széchenyi stamped the voivodate with its own special character. With King Charles Robert's approval, the voivode extended his jurisdiction to include all the inhabitants of Transylvania; he convened and presided over the assembly of the nobility and imposed his will on their deliberations, making and revoking grants like a sovereign. His activities made possible such significant phenomena as the establishment of true dynasties of voivodes, like the Lackfis, who governed from 1344 to 1376, or the Csáks, who ruled from 1401 to 1437. Another aspect of Transylvanian autonomy was manifested after 1382, when Louis I of Anjou died and the Transylvanian

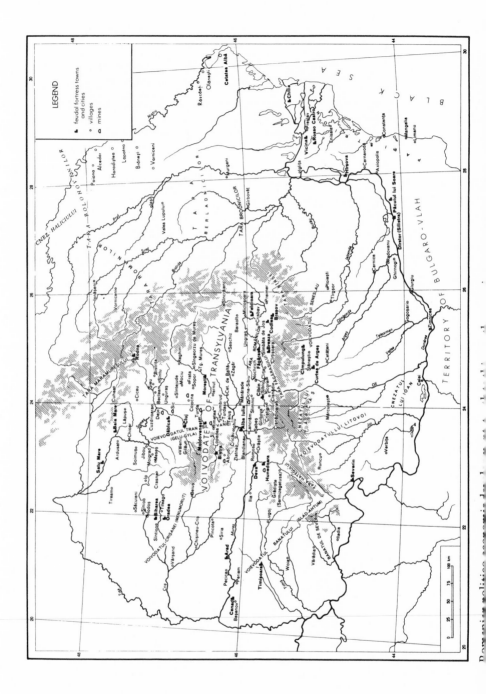

voivode Ladislaus of Losoncz joined a Balkan coalition against Hungary. Again, when Ladislaus the Posthumous and Vladislav Jagello fought for the Hungarian throne in 1440, a rebellion against Vladislav broke out in Transylvania.

In 1442, when Iancu of Hunedoara, the son of a family of Romanian knezi from southern Transylvania, ascended to the position of voivode, the country was in a unique position. It constituted a kind of center of gravity for Ţara Românească and Moldavia in their efforts to create a powerful anti-Ottoman bloc. This bloc, under Iancu's strong influence and for a time under his direct leadership, did in fact achieve exceptional results. The Turkish army that attacked Transylvania in the spring of 1442 was defeated with the help of the masses, whom Iancu had called into action. With the support of an army made up of members of the lower classes and with the army of Vlad Ţepes, called Vlad Dracul ("Vlad the Devil"), the lord of Ţara Românească, the Turks were defeated again, near Ialomiţa. These victories were the starting point of the gloriously successful "long campaign" of the Balkans, which the Transylvanian voivode undertook in the fall and winter of 1443. The success of this campaign—the result of cooperation among the peoples of southeastern Europe—seems all the more important when we remember that a crusade that included knights and nobles from a number of different countries was defeated at Varna in 1444. The year after the loss, Iancu's alliance turned defeat into a fine victory, again with support by Ţara Românească. It is therefore not surprising that this great military leader overcame the opposition of the Hungarian nobility and was chosen governor of Hungary, establishing himself as the true ruler of the Hungarian kingdom.

Under Iancu's leadership, a much closer unity was forged among the three Romanian countries, since he in fact controlled them. In 1447, in addition to his usual titles, Iancu of Hunedoara was also called "voivode of Ţara Românească" and "captain of Wallachia." Bogdan II, prince of Moldavia, considered him a "father," and pledged the fealty of his "squadrons" and "all his armies" to Iancu, since Transylvania and Moldavia "were one." This important political achievement was necessary in order to consolidate an anti-Ottoman front, since the Turkish threat was becoming ever more serious following Sultan Mahomed II's conquest of Constantinople in 1453. Concern about the Turks was also behind Iancu's efforts to assure that Vlad Ţepeş would have the throne of Ţara Românească, since he saw in him not only a faithful follower but also a real ally in the coming great struggle against the Turks. With Vlad Ţepeş in control of Ţara Românească, the defense of Transylvania was guaranteed. In 1456, Iancu's army, which included a great proportion of common people, scored important political and military successes, thanks to the support of the great masses of peasants, Romanian knezi, burghers, and petty nobles and to the fact that the clear object of the struggle was to defend and strengthen the cooperation among the peoples of southeastern Europe and the interrelations of the three Romanian lands.

The years following Iancu's death, however, were marked by struggles for hegemony among the various Romanian princes. A large-scale rebellion broke out in 1467 against King Matthias Corvinus, Iancu's son. This revolt was set in motion by the voivodes of Transylvania, in alliance with the Saxon and Szekler counts, who hoped to separate Transylvania from Hungary and transform it into an independent sovereign state, which would be ruled with the voivode János Szentgyörgyi as king. In the second half of the fifteenth century, Transylvania continued to play an important role in the struggle against the Ottomans and to express its aspirations for independence. In 1479, the Transylvanian armies, led by the voivode Istvan Báthory and by Pavel Chinezul (Paul the Knez), count of Timişoara and a descendant of Romanian knezi, won a great victory at Cîmpul Piîuii. By the end of the century, independence had gone so far that Báthory used to say that he was king and voivode of Transylvania, and that anyone who would dare complain to the king of Hungary about him would have to have two heads, so that when he lost one he would still have the other.

The glorious reign of Stephen the Great, prince of Moldavia, witnessed a shift in the relations among the three Romanian lands. The Szeklers fought bravely against the Turks at Vaslui under Stephen's banner. The Saxons likewise put their hopes in Stephen in the face of the Turkish threat, considering that he had been "sent by God to rule and protect Transylvania," and calling on him "with great love and longing" to have the "kindness to take over this country in order to defend it from the unspeakably cruel Turks." Vlad Ţepeş realistically described the contemporary situation when he wrote in 1476 to the people of Braşov that "by God's will we [Transylvania and Ţara Ro-

 allodium
serfs' tenures

Landholdings in a medieval Transylvanian village.

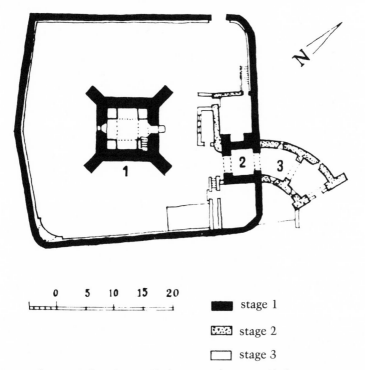

0 5 10 15 20

stage 1
stage 2
stage 3

Peasant fortress of Gîrbova: 1) the central tower; 2) the gate tower; 3) external addition.

mânească] are now a single country." Indeed, for a considerable time the Muntenians and Moldavians ruled extensive areas in Transylvania: the former held Amlaș, Făgăraș, Vînt, Vurpăr, Geoagiu, and for a certain time even the fortress of Bologa near Cluj; the Moldavians ruled Ciceu, the fortress of Balta, Unguraș, Bistrița, and Rodna.

Economic Development

Circumstances favorable for economic development followed the consolidation of the voivodate. Agricultural agreage was further extended by clearing forests, thus permitting agricultural development even in more mountainous regions, and the introduction of crop rotation made it possible for land to be productive at all times. At first this was done on a single lot, in order to extend its period of fertility, but then a system involving two and later three fields was developed: one part would be sown with winter grains, one with spring grains, and one left as pasture. This certainly meant an increase in grain production.

Urban development, meanwhile, and the opportunity thereby created to obtain higher prices for animals and agricultural products, provided a further incentive for landowners to increase their holdings. Feudal organization was extended into more mountainous regions—the Bihor Mountains, Zarand, Maramureș, Bereg—and the hilly areas of the counties of Hunedoara, Caraș, Bihor, and Sălaj, as well as to the Szekler seats, where rural communes had so far managed to preserve their freedom.

In addition to cereal grains, grapes and other fruit crops were widely grown, not just on feudal estates and church properties, but also on peasant lots and around towns. The existence of taxes in money alongside taxes in produce proves that part of the peasants' crops could be sold at market for cash. Transylvania's broad forests and rich pasturelands provided opportunities for large herds of animals, which could be sold as well as providing the peasants with food and clothing. Tithes in calves, pigs, and sheep were among the serfs' more burdensome obligations and constituted one of the major sources of income for the state, the church, and the feudal lords. Starting in the first half of the fifteenth century, then, agriculture began to be transformed into a commodity-producing sector of the economy.

Top: Iancu of Hunedoara, voivode of Transylvania (1441–1445). Bottom: A battle with the Turks.

Another proof of economic development may be found in the increase in the number of grain mills and felting and tanning shops. In the entire thirteenth century, only about 30 mills in twenty-four villages are mentioned in the surviving records, while in the fourteenth century over 150 are documented, including some with two or even three wheels. Presumably the actual number of mills would have been even greater.

There was also large-scale fishing in Transylvania, as is shown by the numerous ponds which the nobility maintained along watercourses on their properties and by the tithes in fish serfs owed to their lords. However, the fish taken in Transylvania were insufficient to meet domestic demand, and large amounts had to be imported from Țara Românească.

Like agriculture and stockbreeding, mining underwent a considerable development. Miners were brought in and settled beside the natives in order to increase the production of salt, iron, silver, and gold. Laws made in 1327–28 provided that landowners whose property contained precious metals were entitled to one-third of the entire yield, with the king taking two-thirds. Moreover, Abrud, Roșia, Zlatna, and Baia de Arieș, in the Bihor Mountains, and Rodna, Baia Mare, Baia Sprie, and other mining centers in northern Transylvania were granted the rights of towns. Moreover, new methods of mining required more substantial investments of capital. For example, gold and silver were mined in deep galleries, hydraulic power was increasingly used for the machines that crushed the ore, and the metal was purified in furnaces in special worshops. Rich local merchants, such as the judges of Sibiu, Brașov, and Bistrița, and foreign bankers like the Fuggers made major investments in the gold, silver, and salt mines of Transylvania in the first half of the sixteenth century. The development of certain trades, of military technology, and of commerce also gave an impetus to iron mining. There was some use of hired labor in the iron mines, but not to the extent seen in gold mining.

A number of large salt mines also were developed around this time, presumably because salt could be sold for money. There were mines at Turda, Ocna Dejului, Cojocna, Sic, and Ocna Sibiului, and in Maramureș at Rona and Șugatag. Five "chambers" directed by chamberlains and vice-chamberlains were responsible for the extraction and transportation of the salt to storehouses. Much of the work in the mines themselves was done by human labor, but there were also a few machines (*gepel*) for which the power was provided by horses or men. The workers were mostly local people, either freemen or serfs, though some were imported from Germany and Slovakia. Since the foreign workers had more experience, they were used for the more demanding tasks.

In the villages, the number of artisans grew steadily, in an increasing variety of trades. In most villages, all everyday needs were met by local tradesmen, although sometimes craftsmen such as smiths, potters, and furriers would produce goods for neighboring settlements as well. The distance between producer and consumer was still insignificant; most village craftsmen were still primarily peasants and engaged in their trade only as a supplementary occupation. As crafts developed, however, some spent less and less time in agricultural work, especially craftsmen living in market towns.

In the larger cities, the population gradually abandoned farming as a way of life and became artisans and merchants. This meant that the urban population depended on rural food production by the end of the fourteenth century, and the economic base of the cities was provided by the artisans. The number of trades increased until, for example, by the second half of the fourteenth century there were at least twenty-five in Sibiu, Sighișoara, Sebeș, and Orăștie. In the mid-fifteenth century, in Cluj, Brașov, Sibiu, and Bistrița, the number exceeded thirty, and in the first half of the sixteenth century there were between forty and sixty. This growth was due both to increasing specialization within old professions and to the appearance of entirely new trades, such as watchmaking, glassmaking, and paper manufacturing.

The development of trades led to the organization of guilds, legally recognized professional corporations or associations. A contemporary document might refer to a guild as a *societas, communitas, consortium, collegia, fraternitas, breaslă cehe,* or *Zunft,* but all of these terms mean an organization composed of the master craftsmen in a particular trade or group of related trades, with identical economic interests. A guild was formed when the number of local craftsmen in the same trade had grown large enough that they wanted to band together in order to control competition, both in their own town and in relation to craftsmen in other settlements. The guild was responsible for

The Gothic Black Church of Braşov (fourteenth century).

all aspects of a trade, from procuring raw materials to selling the finished product; it monitored prices and quality, and took an interest in the professional and family affairs of its members.

To become a guild member, one had to spend several years as an apprentice and several more as a journeyman, the length of time depending on the difficulty of mastering the trade. (To protect their own interests, journeymen also formed associations, beginning in the last quarter of the fifteenth century.) At the end of his period as a journeyman, a young artisan took an examination, consisting of practical work, to become a master. The guild was directed by deans of guild (*magistri fraternitatis, magistri cehae, cehmesterek, Zechmeistern*), usually two of them, who had financial, legal, administrative, and other powers. In discharging these responsibilities the deans of guild were assisted by other elected officers; together they formed a council.

As more abundant supplies and rising demand led to an increasing volume of trade, craftsmen could no longer personally manage the sale of their goods, particularly when it took place at distant markets. Thus a new class arose to serve as intermediaries between producer and consumer—the merchants. They, like the craftsmen, formed guilds to consolidate their economic power. One such was the so-called Great Society (*prima societas magna*) which wealthy merchants (*magni* or *grandi*) of Braşov formed in 1530.

In the later Middle Ages, Transylvania had commercial links with Hungary, with the Germans in the west, and with the Czechs and Poles in the north. But the strongest and most substantial links continued to be with Moldavia and Ţara Românească, a fact that explains the particular economic development of towns in the south and east, such as Sibiu, Braşov, and Bistriţa, and of many Muntenian and Moldavian towns, such as Cîmpulung, Tîrgovişte, Baia, Suceava, and Siret. Many contemporary documents attest to the uninterrupted and everstronger commercial links between the territories on either side of the Carpathians.

On the basis of numerous commercial privileges granted to Transylvanian merchants by the princes of Ţara Românească, beginning in 1368, and by Moldavia's rulers in the early fifteenth century, modern historians know what sorts of goods were exchanged. Exports from Transylvania to the other two Romanian territories included wool, linen, and hemp fabrics (both foreign and domestic), all kinds of weapons, including cannon, furs, and sheepskin coats, rope, clothing, wagons, agricultural tools, jewelry, unprocessed ores, and several types of small manufactured items. Master bowmakers, silversmiths, masons, and other craftsmen also went from Transylvania to Moldavia and Țara Românească, while journeymen traveled from those countries to perfect their trades in Transylvania. Transylvania, meanwhile, imported large quantities of livestock, fish, wax, cheese, skins, and wool, and merchants from the other Romanian territories were increasingly to be seen in Transylvanian cities and towns. In some cases there were such close links that merchants passed without hindrance from one country to another—"as if you were traveling in your own country," Vlad Țepeș wrote to the merchants of Brașov. The treaty between Matthias Corvinus, king of Hungary, and Stephen the Great of Moldavia assured the same rights of free entry and unrestricted travel to Moldavian and Muntenian merchants in Transylvania.

Fifteenth- and sixteenth-century customs registries from Sibiu, Brașov, and Bistrița provide us with information about the volume of trade among the three countries. On the average this was 150,000 to 200,000 gold florins per year. At the beginning of the sixteenth century, over 1,000 people from 120 different localities made roughly 3,000 trips a year in the commerce among the three Romanian countries. By the mid-sixteenth century, these figures had tripled. Brașov began to play the role of central marketplace for the three—it became their *emporium*, to use the word of writers of the time.

Social Stratification

The growth of feudalism in Transylvania led to profound social changes, and social divisions became more and more fixed and obvious. The Romanian and Hungarian peasants in general became serfs; only in peripheral regions could they preserve a certain nominal freedom. There was still a free Romanian peasantry as late as the fifteenth century, in Țara Făgărașului, Țara Hațegului, Țara Maramureșului, and the Banat, owning a part of their land in common and living according to the "tradition of the land" or the "old Romanian law." At least two things explain the survival of these autonomous Romanian communities: first, the authorities' desire to involve the local population in defending

The Braşov town hall (fifteenth century; restored in the eighteenth century).

the frontiers against Turkish assaults; and second, the close relations between the Transylvanian Romanians and the Romanians on the Muntenian and Moldavian slopes of the Carpathians.

The Saxon colonies for the most part were able to avoid serfdom because of their old privileges, which were repeatedly renewed. Nevertheless, the territories where they lived were transformed into feudal domains, and socioeconomic and political distinctions also arose within the Saxon population. The counts or landgraves and the urban elite used every means possible to impose a variety of obligations on the peasantry and the urban poor. Some of the Saxon counts who succeeded in joining the ranks of the nobility were granted property outside the Saxon seats, and Saxon peasants who settled there lived in the same circumstances as the Romanian and Hungarian peasants.

The Szeklers, meanwhile, had been able to preserve their freedom and continued to live in rural communes. But little by little even their communes fell apart. A few individuals became rich, thanks to their occupations or the spoils of war, while most, because of population growth and the resulting repeated division of plots of land, became poorer. In order to live, the poor had to work on the lands of the rich; the latter, in turn, occupied the positions of leadership in the seat for generation after generation, and thus tended to treat the poor as subordinates or inferiors. As a result, by the beginning of the fifteenth century Szekler society also had become differentiated in an essentially feudal way. In the following century the differences became even more pronounced, with society divided into the elite (*seniores, primores*), the knights (*primipili*), and the common people (*pixidarii*). The *primores* and the knights increasingly monopolized the positions of authority, and the common people were even excluded from the seat of justice. Like certain Romanian knezi, the Szekler elite even succeeded, with the help of the royal power with which they cooperated, in attaining titles of nobility, usurping larger and larger tracts of communal land and transforming some members of the commune into serfs.

As the ancient communal lands increasingly became feudal domains, the free peasants became serfs. A few voivodes, knezi, and judges managed to raise their status within the communes to that of ruler or proprietor; their collaboration with the higher authority was recognized by charters granting them title to part of the land usurped from the communes, and they thereby became feudal lords themselves. At first they were considered to be ennobled voivodes and knezi, but later some of them embraced Catholicism and married into noble Hungarian families, becoming part of the petty, middle, or even high nobility. However, most of the knezi and judges and even the voivodes remained as ordinary knezi or fell to the social and legal status of village mayor and eventually joined the ranks of the serfs.

Along with the subjugation of the peasantry, there was a continuous process of intermingling and changing status among the peasants who had become feudal dependents—serfs, jeleri, and servants. A small group of peasants attained a somewhat improved material situation, but the majority became ever poorer. The most obvious evidence of this is the breaking up of hereditary peasant holdings (sessiones). Some peasants had an entire sessio, many animals, and a large stock of agricultural equipment, while others would have only a section of a sessio, or no land at all, and still others did not even have animals or tools.

The noble classes were divided into the high nobility (magnates, magistri, comites); the middle nobility and the knights (nobiles, milites); the petty nobility, who owned a single property (nobiles unius sessionis); and different categories of vassals (servientes and familiares). The nobles of these last groups served the high nobility, performing certain duties in return for bequests of properties or other goods. The lines between these various classes were neither official nor especially sharp; the strata intermingled, so that a member of a higher group might drop in status to the next lower group, while those from a lower group might rise.

The town-dwellers also gravitated toward one of the two fundamental classes of society. The rich artisans and merchants—the urban elite—took control of guilds and towns, depriving the ordinary artisans, smaller merchants, and common townsfolk of their rights.

Peasants and poor burghers were burdened with severe obligations. The state needed men for the army and financial backing for it. By developing internal markets, the nobles and rich townsmen were able to sell agricultural products, animals, and manufactured goods. As a consequence, the serfs' obligations to the landlord, the church, and the state grew continually. Serfs paid tribute to their landlords in produce, labor, and money. The tax in produce—the tithe—consisted of both agricultural products and small animals. Until the mid-fifteenth century, the tithe remained at one-tenth of the whole crop, but from then on

Interior of the Gothic church Biserica din Deal, Sighișoara.

it was fixed at one-ninth for grain and wine. Increasingly, too, feudal obligations included payments three times a year in fowl, eggs, and bread. The landowners, in their desire to have more and more products available for sale, also began to set aside a part of their estates to remain under their direct control. These so-called seigneurial reserves were cultivated by *robota*, the involuntary labor of the serfs. As the seigneurial reserves grew, this obligation grew as well. In 1437 it was fixed at one day of work per year at harvest time. By 1514, serfs were obliged to work the lord's land one day a week, using their own animals, tools, and food. Furthermore, they were required to donate their labor for maintaining mills and ponds, perform various tasks in the landlord's court, and bring in wine, wood, grain, and hay for his use. Most of this work had to be done during the spring and summer, which made *robota* even more onerous.

As trade grew, the nobles needed money to satisfy their tastes for luxury and to procure arms and other things not produced on their own estates. As a result, taxes in money underwent a growth similar to that of the other forms of tribute. In 1437, in an accord reached between the peasants and the nobility, they were fixed at 10 dinars; in a second accord they were set between 12 and 100 dinars (1 florin), depending on the serf's material situation. After an unsuccessful rebellion in 1514–15, they would be raised to 100 dinars, regardless of economic status.

The Catholic church, in its turn, required tithes from Catholic peasants. In the fifteenth century, it was also able to impose the tithe on "schismatics" (that is, those of Orthodox faith) as well, a category which included Romanians, Ruthenians, and Serbs.

The peasants, town-dwellers, and mine workers were also obliged to provide revenue for the state. In the fourteenth century the state's tax had been set at 18 dinars per "door," or household. In the first half of the fifteenth century, this tax was raised to thirty dinars for a "large door" and fifteen for a "small door." Furthermore, the *subsidium*, a tax originally exacted to support the army under special circumstances, came to be routinely imposed.

Antifeudal Uprisings

In the face of heavy and increasing obligations, there were manifestations of discontent among the serfs and free peasants. They fled their homes and even the country, lived as outlaws (hai-duks), and otherwise fought the abuses by the privileged classes and resisted attempts to strip them of their land and liberty. Joined by other oppressed groups, such as miners, poor artisans, the urban lower classes, and a few petty nobles, the peasantry united in a great popular revolt in 1437–38. This rebellion first broke out in the spring of 1437 in the area of the Someş in northeastern Transylvania. From there is spread and intensified, taking in peasants from other towns and villages, workers from the salt mines of the region, and poor townsmen and petty nobles. The rebels, numbering between four and five thousand, set up camp on Bobîlna Hill, in the village of Olpret near Dej, modeling their organization on that of the Czech Hussites. They elected their own captains from among their ranks: Anton the Great of Buda, Mihail the Romanian from Vireag, and Pavel of Voivodeni, "the standard-bearer for the Hungarians and Roma-nians of Transylvania." This first phase of the revolt ended in victory for the peasants, when a truce favorable to the rebels was signed at Bobîlna at the end of June 1437.

The rebellion entered its second phase in the autumn of 1437, which ended with another battle in northeastern Transylvania, this time at Apatiu, and another truce, signed on the battlefield on 6 October. This new phase was marked by the regrouping of the antipopular forces. The nobles brought the Saxons and Szek-lers into their camp with an agreement known as the *unio trium nationum*, signed 16 September at Căpîlna.

The last phase of the revolt took place in the fall and winter of 1437–38. It reached its peak in November and December, when the rebels succeeded in taking over the towns of Aiud, Dej, Turda, and Cluj. But the high point of the revolt carried the seeds of its end. The peasant masses tended to localize their action, thus splintering the rebellion and dissipating their forces, while the nobles and their allies organized and armed them-selves more efficiently and obtained royal support. The final battle took place at the city walls of Cluj, where the rebels were defeated and their leaders killed. Once the rebellion had been put down, bloody reprisals against the peasantry followed.

The Bobîlna rebellion had great significance, not just at the time it took place, but also in the perspective of the develop-ment of society. The revolt involved a very large area, and it lasted an unusually long time. The rebels' social and political program surpassed the demands of previous peasant movements.

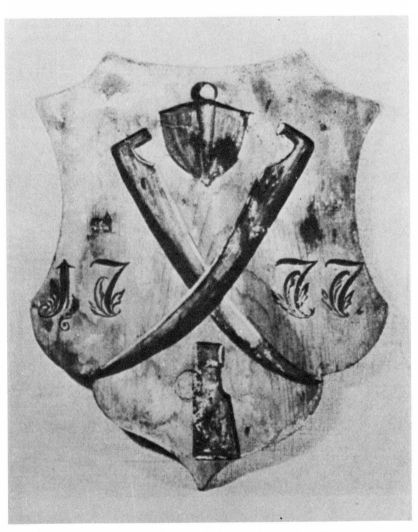

Fifteenth-century emblem of the blacksmiths' guild in Sighişoara.

In fact, the most progressive of the rebel leaders were concerned with fighting feudal organization itself. They wanted the entire country, including the nobility, to be subject to "popular power," exhorting the peasants to "shake off and throw down their insupportable burdens" and calling for the "removal of the unbearable yoke of serfdom." In a word, they demanded a radical modification of feudal organization and social relations, and the establishment of a new social and political order in which the peasants would be free. To ensure that their demands would be carried out, the peasants proposed bold measures: they wanted their own assembly, like that of the nobility, to which they would elect their own representatives. Thus they called for an annual assembly on Bobîlna Hill, to be attended by two "wise and trustworthy" men from each village, town, and manor, to investigate whether the nobles were respecting the peasants' liberty. The rebels repudiated royal authority, proclaiming their captains the leaders of the new popular power. In its program and its goals, and because of the numbers involved, the revolt of 1437–38 was comparable to other great medieval popular revolts: the French Jacquerie uprising in France in 1358, Wat Tyler's rebellion in England in 1381, or the Hussite War in Bohemia in 1434–36.

Despite its bloody end, the Transylvanian uprising was nevertheless an example and an encouragement for the masses. When oppression again had become intolerable, the peasantry once more rebelled, and with the same goals—the modification of social relations to improve their lot, either through reduction of taxes and other obligations or, more radically, by the abolition of serfdom. Such a program was put forth by the insurgents of 1514–15. When Bishop Toma Bakocz of Esztergom called for a crusade against the Turks in spring, 1514, peasants from Hungary, Slovakia, Transylvania, and Slovenia, led by their village judges, gathered in camps near Buda, along with poor townsmen and artisans and some of the petty nobility—"more because they could no longer bear the life they led than out of any love of Christendom," in the words of the Italian chronicler Paolo Giovio. Gheorghe Doja, a Szekler peasant who had been granted a title of nobility for bravery during the anti-Ottoman wars, was appointed military leader of the crusade. In a short time there were about forty thousand peasants and poor town-dwellers camped near Buda. Multitudes of peasants, farmers, herdsmen, poor townspeople, outlaws, and miners gathered in other places.

The nobility, horrified at the large number of serfs who had left their fields during spring planting time, attempted to prevent others from joining their fellows and to force those who had already left to return home. Whole families were humiliated, tortured, and yoked to carts and wagons. As a result, the peasants began to abandon any thought of a crusade and refused the order to set out against the Turks. In the beginning of May 1514, the crusade was transformed into a great popular rebellion. Marked as it was by a radical program, a large number of rebels from a vast area, and at least some degree of organization within the peasant army, the movement must be considered more than an ordinary rebellion. It was a peasant war.

The revolt quickly spread, and was particularly active toward the southeast, east, and in the northeast. The rebels won a great victory at Cenad in the Banat. One by one, early in June, they took the cities and towns along the Mureș. By this time the revolt involved large numbers of Romanian and Hungarian peasants from all over Transylvania, and the nobility, the high clergy, and the urban elite, greatly concerned, united around the Transylvanian voivode, János Zápolya. Desperate appeals for help, accompanied by threats, were sent out everywhere, calling for men, arms, food, clothing, and money. The ruling class was all the more worried by the fact that the peasant war took in great numbers of Romanians, Hungarians, and Szeklers. The poor people of Cluj, Turda, Dej, Bistrița, Sighișoara, and other Transylvanian towns allied themselves with the rebels and opened the city gates to them. Miners from Turda, Cojocna, Ocna Dejului, Rimetea, Rodna, and other mining centers also joined the revolt.

Once again, however, the peasantry could not consolidate their gains. Unified action was necessary, but the efforts of the more progressive elements to achieve it were thwarted by the inability of the mass of peasants to understand the need to subordinate their local actions to a more general plan. As a consequence, the rebel forces were splintered at a time when they needed to be concentrated, and the army of the nobility, gathering its forces in the Banat, decided the outcome of the war. The noble troops were centered in the well-fortified town of Timișoara, which was under siege by the rebels. However, the besiegers were themselves surrounded by the nobility and rich burghers of Buda, and by the noble army led by Zápolya. After a fierce battle, the peasant army suffered a severe defeat

Tower of Cisnădie, Sibiu.

on 15 July. Its leaders fell into the hands of the nobility and were subjected to terrible torture. On 20 July, Gheorghe Doja was burned at the stake, and the other rebel captains were put to death in barbarous ways.

However, the peasant war was not yet completely over. Bands of rebels in Transylvania continued the fight. Under the leadership of Lörincz Mészáros, who had escaped from the battle of Timişoara, a few groups were involved in skirmishes around Cluj. But the nobles' army was able to defeat such isolated groups of rebels in various parts of Transylvania. Bloody massacres were unleashed all over the country, and tens of thousands of peasants, miners, and poor townspeople fell victim to the reprisals.

As a result of this "general peasant war," the masses suffered redoubled oppression. The nobility met in a diet at Buda, and their decisions were codified into law by their legislative assembly. This law, known as the Tripartitum, was said to have been "written in the blood of serfs." *Robota* was fixed at one day a week; the tithe was set at one-ninth of all crops and animals; domestic fowl were not to be exempt from the tithe; the tax money was set at a minimum of 100 dinars; all peasant property was to be subject to church taxes; and the obligation to the royal treasury was doubled, from one gold florin per household to two. The peasantry was condemned to complete and perpetual hereditary serfdom (*mera et perpetua rusticitate* or *servitute*), in order, as the nobles put it, to "remind you what a crime it is to rise up against your master." The peasants were forever bound to the land (*glebae adstricti*), and the nobility remained in control of all property.

Another important consequence of the bloody suppression of the 1514 rebellion was the rout of the Hungarian army of Mohács in August 1526. Lacking the support of the people—whom the nobles were afraid to call to arms—the Magyar feudal kingdom succumbed to the onslaught of the Turkish cavalry and janissaries. This event had serious consequences for the history of southeastern Europe. Not only was part of Hungary occupied and transformed into a Turkish pashalic, but the fall of the Magyar kingdom weakened resistance to Turkish power, which now posed a greater threat to central and western Europe. For more than a century, the middle Danube was an outpost of the Ottoman Empire.

7

Turkish Suzerainty

THE DISASTROUS DEFEAT of the Hungarian army at Mohács led to the breaking up of the Hungarian kingdom and more intense struggles between rival feudal factions. There were two pretenders to the now vacant Hungarian throne: János Zápolya, the voivode of Transylvania who had the support of the petty and middle nobility, and Ferdinand of Habsburg, whom the high nobility supported. Each also sought the support of more powerful protectors. Zápolya at first asked for help from the king of Poland, but he was engaged at the time with the invasion of Russia, Byelorussia, and the Ukraine, and did not respond; subsequently Zápolya went to Sultan Suleiman himself, concluding a treaty with him in 1528. With Turkish help, Zápolya took the Hungarian throne in the autumn of 1529, and held it, in spite of Ferdinand's military and diplomatic efforts, until his death in 1540.

The action during the struggle for the throne took place principally in Transylvania, which the Habsburgs coveted both for its wealth and for its strategic importance. They actually succeeded in pressuring most of the Transylvanian cities and part of the nobility to join their side, but Zápolya kept the support of another group of nobles and of the Szeklers. Since neither side, therefore, had been able to gain control of Transylvania, each sought the support of the Moldavian prince Petru Rareş. Rareş knew how to take advantage of the situation to further his own ends, which were to increase his holdings—and hence his influence—in Transylvania. Siding with Zápolya after the defeat of Ferdinand's army at Feldioara in southern Transylvania on 22 June 1529, Rareş was successful: he acquired the fortress of Balta, Ciceu with its sixty Romanian villages, Unguraş with more than thirty villages, and Bistriţa and the Rodna valley, with twenty-three villages and gold and silver mines. He thus became the arbiter of the situation in Transylvania.

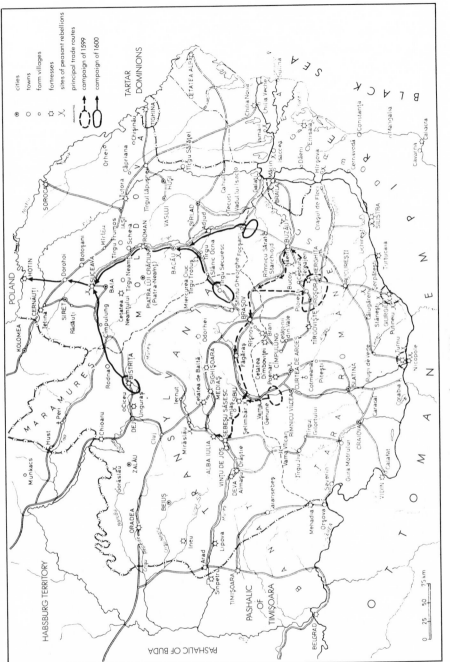

Romanian territories in the era of Mihai Viteazul, ca. 1600.

Meanwhile the Turks, who were trying to take over Transylvania, Moldavia, and Ţara Românească, also attempted to find some advantage. Rareş therefore joined the anti-Ottoman forces of Ferdinand of Habsburg. But Ferdinand had already seen the impossibility of realizing his goals by force, and on 24 February 1538, he signed a peace treaty with Zápolya at Oradea. By the terms of the treaty, Zápolya agreed that at his death, Transylvania and the part of Hungary he controlled would pass to the Habsburgs.

Sultan Suleiman could not stand by passively in the face of an agreement against Ottoman interests, and he decided to intervene with a powerful armed force. Petru Rareş was attacked first, in the summer of 1538, since he was considered most dangerous. Caught between a large Turkish army in the south and a Polish force in the north, Rareş was defeated and lost his throne. Zápolya hastened to placate Suleiman, paying him a large sum of money and promising an annual tribute. But Zápoyla and his governor, Gheorghe Martinuzzi, the bishop of Oradea, set up a rapacious regime which caused dissatisfaction among the Transylvanians. The Transylvanian voivodes Ştefan Mailath and Imre Balassa tried but failed to capitalize on this popular discontent, attempting to depose the Zápolya-Martinuzzi forces, seize power, and transform Transylvania into an autonomous principality.

Zápolya's death, however, left vacant the Hungarian throne, which, according to the treaty of Oradea, was to go to Ferdinand. But when Ferdinand tried to claim his inheritance, he aroused the ire of the Turks, who could not permit Hungary to be taken over by their enemy. On 29 August 1541, Suleiman's army occupied Buda, and for the next 150 years the part of Hungary that had been ruled by Zápolya was a Turkish pashalic. An area of Hungary on the other side of the Danube remained in Habsburg hands, while all of the counties, districts, and Saxon and Szekler seats in Transylvania proper, the Banat (until 1552, when it was gradually taken over by the Turks and turned into a pashalic), and the counties of the so-called Partium (Satu Mare, Crasna, Middle and Outer Solnoc, Bihor, Zarand, Arad, and Maramureş) became an autonomous principality.

The economic life of the new principality felt the effects of Ottoman suzerainty in the form of tributes and other obligations to Constantinople; at the same time, however, because of its economic importance, its geographic and strategic position, and its tradition of resistance to Turkish expansionism, Transylvania managed to obtain a more favored situation than that of other vassal states. During the time of the principality, therefore, Transylvania was able to preserve its autonomous institutions, and, within the framework of the conditions of the period, to maintain economic and political ties with Moldavia and Ţara Românească. Transylvania was also sufficiently independent to play an important role in various European coalitions, including a number directed against both the Turks and the Habsburgs.

The head of the principality was a prince chosen by the Transylvanian diet. The diet exercised this right in electing János Sigismund prince, and in 1566, Suleiman issued a decree confirming what he had already acknowledged from the beginning—that usually, after the diet had made a choice, Constantinople was to be notified, and the new prince would be confirmed or rejected according to the sultan's desire. In some cases, however, the sultan would name a prince directly, before the diet had a change to have its say, or would simply impose his favored candidate against the diet's wishes.

The prince of Transylvania, like the princes of Moldavia and Ţara Românească, theoretically possessed substantial powers: he guided foreign policy, waged war and made peace, appointed or approved the appointments of emissaries to other countries, and received emissaries to Transylvania. In practice, however, the Turks were heavily involved in foreign policy affairs, and the authority of the prince of Transylvania and of the Romanian princes was significantly circumscribed. There was less interference in the internal politics of the three Romanian countries; the sultan respected their autonomy so long as his own interests were not threatened—as, for example, by continued nonpayment of tribute or failure to fulfill various other obligations. However, the prince of Transylvania was free to choose his advisors among the high feudal lords, who then constituted his council. The number of council members varied during the sixteenth century, and was finally fixed at twelve, four from each of the three medieval Transylvanian "nations"—the nobility, the Saxon elite, and the Szekler upper class.

In principle, important domestic and foreign matters were debated and decided by the diet, which had fiscal, judicial, elective, and political powers. It set the taxes paid by the peasantry to the state and the feudal lord, adjudicated disputes between members of the privileged classes, and decided matters of foreign policy, as well as electing the prince. It represented the development of

A late sixteenth-century Renaissance door from Cluj.

the assembly of nobles from the period of the voivodate and of the conventions of the three nations that had taken place after the Bobîlna uprising. The diet included the representatives of the nations, of the four official religions (Catholic, Lutheran, Calvinist, and Unitarian), and of certain cities and towns, together with personal representatives of the prince (the so-called regalists). Representatives were elected by the nobility of the counties of Transylvania proper and of the Partium (the count and two representatives from each county), the leaders of the Szekler seats (two representatives per seat), the counts and leading citizens of the Saxon seats (two representatives per seat), and by the wealthy burghers of nine cities and fourteen market towns. In addition, the assembly included the captains of ten royal fortresses and a few other important officials, plus the regalists, who were chosen from among the prince's advisors and the high nobility. Altogether it had more than 150 members, who met when summoned by the prince—at first twice a year, but later only once—and in emergencies.

Like the assemblies and conventions of the preceding period and like later diets, the diet of this period represented the interests of the privileged classes and the high clergy. It excluded the common people, the Orthodox religion, and the most numerous group, the Romanians. Since the Romanian peasants were not one of the three constituent nations of the country, they were excluded from political life, and after 1437 they were doubly oppressed—socially and as an ethnic group—by the privileged nations. The Szekler and Saxon seats continued to possess some of their old powers, and their local assemblies decided certain administrative and judicial matters. But like the diet, these assemblies included only the Szekler leaders and the Saxon elite. The peasantry was not represented and did not benefit from their acts.

Relations between Transylvania and the Ottoman Empire were those of vassal to suzerain. The empire owed Transylvania protection and support, in return for which the principality was obliged to pay tribute and taxes, and to provide military and other forms of aid. The tribute was set at 10,000 florins per year, and remained at that level until 1575, when it was raised to 15,000. Taxes to the sultan and other high officials roughly followed the level of the tribute: about 10,000 florins at first and 15,000 later. Tribute in kind included grain and animals. Diplomatic relations between Transylvania and Constantinople were maintained by a permanent ambassador, or *kapukehai*, who was elected by the diet and confirmed by the prince, and by occasional ambassadors extraordinary, who were appointed by the prince and approved by the diet.

During the rule of Prince János Sigismund and his mother Isabella, Transylvania became involved in the war between the Ottoman Empire and the Habsburgs. Governor Gheorghe Martinuzzi, who was the real political leader of Transylvania, played the game of the nobility and added fuel to the Turkish-German rivalry—at great cost to his country. A number of Transylvanian politicians had the idea of making a pact with Petru Rareş, who had returned to power in Moldavia; they offered him his old domains in Ciceu, the fortress of Balta, Unguraş, and Bistriţa in return for defending Transylvania. However, in 1551 Germany temporarily managed to impose its rule, while the Turks had to be satisfied for the time being with the occupation of a few relatively unimportant towns and fortresses in the Banat.

Habsburg rule encountered grave difficulties because of popular dissatisfaction with German administrative and fiscal policies. Dissatisfaction grew even greater when, beginning in 1552, a large part of the Banat was gradually occupied by the Turks and transformed into a pashalic. Taking advantage of the unrest, the exiled prince János Sigismund and his mother were able to return from Poland under the protection of the Moldavian and Muntenian armies, but the Habsburgs continued to cause him a variety of troubles, and he sought protection from Sultan Suleiman. The sultan issued another decree ratifying Sigismund's election as prince, but Sigismund was nevertheless unable to consolidate his rule. In 1570, with the Treaty of Speyer, he renounced his claims, again leaving the door open for Habsburg rule in Transylvania.

On Sigismund's death, however, the Turks installed Istvan Báthory at the head of the principality. With Turkish help, Báthory was able to frustrate the German plans, especially after his victory over Gaspar Békes, the Habsburg pretender, at Sînpaul in 1575. With this victory, Báthory increased the prestige and authority of the Transylvanian principality, and he was able to persuade the Polish parliament to elect him king of Poland on 14 December 1575. In this way he personally achieved an alliance between Transylvania and Poland which lasted from 1575 to 1586. Báthory's reign, since it was not independent of the Turks, brought no special economic or social benefits to

Silver tumblers from the workshops of sixteenth-century Transylvanian craftsmen.

Fragment of a sixteenth-century tombstone.

103

Transylvania, but it did strengthen the country's international prestige and to some extent the authority of its central power.

The alliance between Transylvania and Poland ended with Báthory's death in 1586. His successor, Zsigmond Báthory, who was a member of a Christian league started by the German emperor, made plans for closer ties between Transylvania and Ţara Românească based on their common interests. These first steps could not be followed up, however, because of internal troubles and the Turkish-German rivalry. Faced with problems, the indecisive prince Báthory preferred to renounce his throne, now in favor of one, now in favor of the other.

Michael the Brave

The projected alliance between Transylvania and Ţara Românească that Zsigmond Báthory left unfinished was extended to include Moldavia and brought to fruition by Michael the Brave, prince of Ţara Românească. Uninterrupted cultural and economic links among the three Romanian countries; the beginning of a common marketplace at Braşov, which was also the center of Romanian printing and book distribution; ancient political ties, which had been strengthened in the face of the Turkish threat; and a common language, customs, and traditions meant that Romanians on both sides of the Carpathians were actively aware of their ethnic identity. It was this ethnic awareness that paved the way for Michael the Brave's attempt in 1599–1600 to unite Moldavia, Transylvania, and his own country under a single ruler. Michael had had such a plan in mind ever since he ascended the throne, and it was in keeping with the goals of the anti-Turkish forces at work in the midst of the Ottoman Empire. At his urging, the three Romanian countries achieved some measure of cooperation in 1594, and in the autumn of that year began to take action against their enemy, the Ottomans. They joined forces in the common cause in 1595, when Ţara Românească regained its independence through the victories Michael won, with Transylvanian help, at Călugăreni and on the Danube.

Romanian independence could be assured only by superior military and political power, which in turn could be achieved only through the union of the three countries under a single leader. This was brought about in the fall of 1599. The initiative came from Ţara Românească, but the way had been prepared some time earlier by Michael's envoys in Transylvania. The idea of Michael's rule caused the Romanian peasants to hope that the yoke of ethnic and social oppression would be lifted from their shoulders by a ruler who was one of their own. As a result, they supported Michael's actions by rebelling. His forces were also joined by the Szeklers, who were similarly discontented with their treatment by the nobility and the authorities. Thus, on 28 October 1599, the noble's troops were defeated in the battle of Şelimbăr-Sibiu in southern Transylvania. The Saxons surrendered to the conqueror, as did the nobles who had escaped from the battle, and Michael marched victorious into Alba Iulia, the capital of Transylvania, on 1 November 1599.

Michael's goals, however, were not yet fully realized, for the German emperor, Rudolf II, still sought to wrest his new domain away from him, and Zsigmond Báthory, the former prince of Transylvania, was in Moldavia with the Moldavian lord Eremia Movilă, awaiting an opportunity to retake his throne. To avert this danger and increase his own power, Michael crossed the Carpathians into Moldavia at the beginning of May 1600. In less than twenty days, Moldavia too was under Michael's rule, and he then referred to himself as "By the grace of God, I, Michael, voivode and lord of all Ţara Românească and Ardeal [Transylvania] and all of the country of Moldavia."

The turmoil created by the Turkish and the German threats and by internal dissension allowed Michael some time to institute measures designed to consolidate his achievement. In addition to Transylvanian nobles, boyars from Ţara Românească were added to the prince's council, in such high positions as marshal, treasurer, and chancellor; moreover, those holding these positions exercised authority over both Transylvania and Ţara Românească. Muntenian captains were installed in the most important fortresses; a regency was set up in Moldavia, but Michael retained the actual power. The new prince also claimed the fortresses of the Partium in order to create a western defensive line for the Romanian lands. Romanian was used in official acts in addition to Latin and Hungarian. Michael's seal was a combination of the coats of arms of the three countries. Customs barriers were eased and trade facilitated. Finally, the Orthodox metropolitan of Transylvania was subordinated to that of Ţara Românească, which meant that the countries were linked religiously as well as politically.

Title page of Ioan Sylvester's *Grammatica Hungarolatina* of 1539.

All these measures provoked even greater discontent among Michael's enemies—which encompassed the Viennese court, the Turks, and the Transylvanian nobility. When the Saxon nobles and burghers staged a revolt against him, they found support from the imperial general Giorgio Basta. The rebels and the imperial army united to defeat Michael at Mirăslău, near Aiud, on 18 September 1600. The accord that the German empire had made with Michael in the face of the nobles' rebellion was proved neither sincere nor durable, for after the nobility's defeat at Guráslău, near Zalău in northwestern Transylvania, on 13 August 1601, the same General Basta treacherously arranged for Michael's assassination, which occurred on the morning of 19 August 1601, near Cîmpia Turzii in central Transylvania.

The union of the three Romanian countries under a single leadership was an achievement of enormous importance in the history of the Romanian people, since it marked the first time that the territories inhabited by Romanians formed a political and administrative unit. The importance of this event was clear even at the time it took place, but with the death of its principal architect, the political union came apart. The boyars of Țara Românească undermined it, because they feared the growth of central power; the Transylvanian nobility had directly attacked it, both because they distrusted Michael's policies and because they were unfriendly towards Michael himself. The social classes who had an interest in centralized power—the town-dwellers and the peasants—had been neglected. The destruction of Michael's creation was also hastened by the hostility of the great powers to Romanian political unity, which struck at the interests of Poland and of the Habsburgs, who hoped to establish their own political and military dominance there, and at those of the Ottoman Empire, which was desperate to restore its rule. The Polish nobility supported the efforts against Michael, and the Turks renewed their own attacks.

Successors to Michael the Brave

For about ten years after the destruction of the political unity forged by Michael the Brave, Transylvania went through a period of uninterrupted warfare, with the imperial forces on one side, seeking to preserve and consolidate their rule, and the Transylvanian nobility on the other, who followed a number of princes in their efforts to avoid Habsburg domination. Not until Gabriel Bethlen was appointed and later elected prince, in 1613, was there an end to the turmoil. Bethlen was an excellent leader, and he understood the political currents in a complex situation. In particular, he understood the political and economic importance to Transylvania of the other Romanian countries. One of his first political acts after his appointment as prince, therefore, was to make a sworn agreement to be "brothers to the death" with Radu Mihnea, lord of Țara Românească, and Ștefan Tomșa, lord of Moldavia. He continued this policy, making a "friendly peace" and a promise of mutual aid against external enemies with Gavril Movilă, Mihnea's successor, in 1619. By checking feudal anarchy and strengthening central power, Bethlen consolidated his rule and was able to resist the pressures of both Germans and Turks. In 1618, at the outbreak of the Thirty Years' War, he fought against the Habsburgs; in 1620, the German Empire recognized both Transylvania's independence and its annexation of seven counties in Upper Hungary in the Peace of Mikulov. Bethlen was then drawn into the coalition of Protestant countries, with the idea of assuring Transylvania's independence and increasing its territory.

Failing in his plans to become king of Bohemia and then of Hungary by extending his rule over the Habsburg part of Hungary, Bethlen turned his attention to uniting the Romanian countries in a single state. He had witnessed the events of 1599–1600 which had led to the union under Michael the Brave, and he recognized the strength inherent in such a union. He was also a realistic politician, aware of the importance of economic and political links. Thus he developed the idea of creating a Protestant Kingdom of Dacia incorporating Transylvania, Moldavia, and Țara Românească. Bethlen sought support for his plan from Cyril Lukaris, the patriarch of Constantinople, whom he asked for help in converting the Romanians to Protestantism. Significantly, the patriarch in his reply reminded the prince that he would have to remember, in his proselytizing efforts, that there were "ties of blood and feeling which, though hidden, yet all the more strongly unite the Romanians of Transylvania with the inhabitants of Țara Românească and Moldavia."

Gabriel Bethlen stands out among his predecessors and even his successors. He believed in the absolutism and centralized authority that had made its appearance in western Europe, and he

Michael the Brave's triumphant entrance into Alba Iulia, 1 November 1599.

sought to put an end to feudal anarchy by restricting the power of the high nobility and by displaying a certain compassion for the plight of the lower classes. His economic reforms were aimed at reducing anarchy in the marketplace by introducing "limitations," or maximum prices. In his religious and educational policies as well, Bethlen showed a greater understanding of the people than other princes. He believed that a Protestant education for the masses would provide support for the absolutist state in its struggle with the feudal lords, and he therefore decreed that peasants' children should be able to attend schools—elementary schools, to be sure—in order that they might become priests, teachers, and scribes. For the children of the nobility and the rich burghers, he founded a Protestant academy in Alba Iulia.

After Bethlen's death, the high nobility, whose power had been restricted to some extent, took advantage of the weakness of the central authority to try to rescind all the economic and political measures that obstructed their power, and attempted to take control of the principality. The Habsburgs likewise hastened to take advantage of the situation, and tried to annex at least the seven counties in northwestern Transylvania that they had ceded to Bethlen. But the haiduks revolted against these attempts, and György Rákóczi, capitalizing on the haiduk movement, was elected prince by a part of the Transylvanian nobility at the end of 1630.

Prince György Rákóczi I took up his predecessor's policies, especially after he defeated the imperial and Turkish armies sent against him in 1636. In the consolidation of his power, a significant role was played by Matei Basarab of Ţara Românească. The alliance between the two princes, made in 1635, assured peace on Transylvania's southern border. Moreover, it was through Matei's good offices that the sultan confirmed Rákóczi as prince of Transylvania; this was acknowledged by the Transylvanian envoy, who told Matei, "your friendship served us well in a difficult situation." Because of Rákóczi's aspirations for suzerainty over the other Romanian lands, however, and because Vasile Lupu, the prince of Moldavia, planned to undertake military action against Transylvania, a treaty of alliance signed in 1638 between the Transylvanian prince and the Moldavian lord lasted only briefly. Nevertheless, the support he derived from the alliance, however temporary, was extremely valuable to Rákóczi, since it permitted him to reestablish the power of his central authority. This meant not only new curbs on the power of the high nobility, but also the possibility of entering the Thirty Years' War against the Habsburgs.

After long negotiations with Sweden and France, Rákóczi joined the continental war early in 1644, and with the support of peasants oppressed by the Habsburgs, he succeeded in 1645 in imposing on the empire the Treaty of Linz, which granted him the seven counties of northwestern Transylvania. On the basis of these victories, Transylvania was recognized as a sovereign state by the other European powers, and it participated in the Peace of Westphalia in 1648, which put an end to the Thirty Years' War. Through its role in the war and in the making of peace, Transylvania gained a significant place in the struggle against the Habsburgs and the Catholics.

György Rákóczi II, the son and successor of György Rákóczi I, continued his father's policies of strengthening central authority and of forging closer political links to the other Romanian countries. The opportunity to put these plans into effect arose in 1655, when, at the request of the boyars of Țara Românească, he intervened to help put down a rebellion. After the rebels' defeat in the battle of Șoplea in June 1655, György Rákóczi II of Transylvania, Constantin Șerban of Țara Românească, and Gheorghe Ștefan of Moldavia agreed at Gherghița to strengthen their existing alliance, which was essentially anti-Ottoman. To make the agreement more durable, in 1656 the three Romanian countries and the Ukraine signed a peace treaty, and a treaty of alliance was made between Moldavia and Russia, followed by a commercial treaty. In 1657, on the basis of these ties, Rákóczi, with the help of Șerban and Ștefan, embarked on an expedition against Poland. At the same time, Rákóczi was negotiating with Bogdan Khmelnitsky of the Ukraine over undertaking a joint military operation against feudal Catholic Poland. Their goal was to strengthen the anti-Ottoman front and free the Romanian countries from Turkish suzerainty. However, the expedition was a failure, and all three Romanian leaders were dethroned by the Turks. Rákóczi continued the anti-Ottoman fight until 1660, when he died leading his troops near Florești in central Transylvania.

The new prince of Țara Românească, Mihnea III, was meanwhile putting together a bold plan to bring back the time of Michael the Brave. The first sign of his intentions was given when he changed his name from Mihnea to Mihai (Michael) as soon as he took power. Other signs followed: his execution of pro-Turkish boyars and the fact that his rule was supported by merchants, petty nobles, and peasants, some of whom were even appointed to office. The revolt set in motion by Mihnea-Michael thus had a broad popular base within Țara Românească itself, and it was supported from outside by the army of György Rákóczi II and by assistance requested from Venice and the Vatican. Mihnea's army, with Transylvanian help and supported by the Moldavian army as well, was successful against the Turks. Once more, the Romanian countries, led by Țara Românească, dared to hope that they might shake off the Turkish yoke.

This hope was not realized. On the contrary, after 1659 Ottoman rule was strengthened. In Transylvania, the Turks crushed the resistance of the masses, who lacked the help of the central authority. In 1659 they extended their rule to the cities of Lugoj and Caransebeş and their environs, previously unoccupied territories in the Banat. In 1660, following the Peace of Oradea, they expanded to the north as well, controlling Zarand and Bihor.

The last period in the history of the autonomous Transylvanian principality under Turkish suzerainty was the reign of Mihály Apafi. It was a time of economic and political decadence. Under the leadership of the ambitious Miklós Teleki, "the scourge of God for Transylvania," as he was characterized by the chronicler Mihály Cserei, the nobility went unchecked by the feeble Apafi, whom the same chronicler described as "a better priest than prince." The high nobility increased their domains and monopolized state revenues, and, because they held the powerful offices, they were able to control state policies. As a result, the country was disoriented, weakened, and easy prey. Lacking independent policies, Transylvania went along with the Turks in joining a new anti-Habsburg coalition.

The Turks' object was the conquest of Vienna, which was the most significant obstacle to their penetration into the heart of Europe. In 1683, under the leadership of the vizier Kara Mustafa, they subjected Vienna to a long and difficult siege. It was only thanks to the intervention of the Polish king, Jan Sobieski, and his army that the city was saved. After the siege was lifted, the gradual process of driving the Turks out of Europe began.

The new circumstances posed problems for Transylvania. Both the emperor of Austria and the king of Poland coveted her riches. Ultimately it was the former, with the aid of diplomacy—and of his army—who succeeded in establishing his rule in Transylvania and, later, in wresting control from the Turks in the Banat. Thus both regions came under the "protection" of the Viennese court.

The Renaissance and Reformation in Transylvania

Despite the contradictions inherent in Transylvanian society and the turbulence of the times, Transylvanian cultural life from the late fifteenth through the early seventeenth centuries displayed the creative energy that marked European civilization as a whole. Transylvanian folk culture reflected the people's aspirations for progress and well-being, and common social themes transcended linguistic differences among Romanians, Hungarians, Szeklers, and Saxons. Folk epics composed in their own languages dealt with the fight against the Turks, and with the bold deeds of such military leaders as Iancu of Hunedoara, Pavel Chinezul, and Stephen the Great. While Latin continued to be the primary written language for most purposes, the Transylvanian vernaculars—Romanian, Hungarian, and German—now also began to be written as well as spoken. It is the growth and dissemination of formal education and the arts, however, that most clearly demonstrates Transylvania's place in the great intellectual movements of the Renaissance and the Reformation.

Village schools, where teaching was in Latin, Slavonic, and the mother tongues, provided at least a minimal education to the sons of peasant families. These increased in number throughout the late fifteenth and sixteenth centuries. Schools also were founded at major monasteries: Peri in Maramureş, Vad in the northeast, Scorei in Ţara Făgăraşului, and Prislop in Ţara Haţegului. Peasant children attending these schools were taught reading, writing, and ecclesiastical chant—all, of course, in Latin. The very best of the Romanian schools of the time was that in Şcheii Braşovului; founded in the fourteenth century, in the fifteenth it reorganized its curriculum along the lines of most contemporary European schools into a *trivium* (grammar, rhetoric, and dialectic) and a *quadrivium* (arithmetic, geometry, astronomy, and music). Other Latin schools were founded in towns, as, for instance, in Alba Iulia, Tîrgu Mureş, Oradea, and Sibiu. Learning no longer was the exclusive province of the clergy; there were educational opportunities for the sons of artisans, merchants, and even peasants. For higher studies, a number of young Hungarian, Saxon, and Romanian Transylvanians journeyed to the unversities of Prague, Vienna, Kraków, and even beyond.

Thus Transylvanian culture increasingly was swept into the intellectual and ideological currents of humanism, becoming part of the general European renaissance. Humanism, flowering in the fifteenth century in western Europe, spread east, until its growth was evident over most of Europe in the sixteenth century. Though humanism took on particular features in response to differing conditions in various countries, it nevertheless had a number of general characteristics. The civilization of ancient Greece and Rome was much admired and imitated. The economic, social, and spiritual emancipation of society and of mankind was a major tenent; culture was to be taken out of the hands of the clergy and spread to the masses, while scholasticism, mysticism, and obscurantism were to be replaced by reason. People were to be judged on their intelligence and personal worth, not by their birth or social station. Science was based on experiment and the observation of natural and social phenomena, and the vernaculars were used in addition to Latin to make knowledge as widely accessible as possible.

These ideas, as advanced by such giants of humanism as Leonardo da Vinci, Erasmus of Rotterdam, and Rabelais, are to be found in the humanistic culture of the sixteenth and seventeenth centuries in Romanian territory in general and in Transylvania in particular. We see them in the works of the Hungarian humanist Gáspár Heltai, the German humanist Johannes Honterus, and Romanian humanists such as Filip Moldoveanul and Deacon Coresi. The great humanistic scholar of Romanian origin, Nicolaus Olahus, was particularly active in spreading humanistic knowledge in history, philology, geography, and poetry. Olahus was a patron and friend of men of letters throughout Europe, including "the prince of humanism" himself, Erasmus. Such men, and others who were concerned with the dissemination of knowledge, were the founders and promoters of printing. Thanks to their efforts, presses opened in Sibiu, Braşov, and Cluj, where many of their own works and those of others were printed. The Transylvanian humanists also played a significant role in founding libraries in Sibiu, Braşov, Cluj, Alba Iulia, Oradea, and Orăştie. They recognized the importance of formal education, and one of their principal concerns and most important achievements was the founding of colleges in Braşov, Sibiu,

Cluj, Alba Iulia, and Oradea. Scholars such as Honterus, Olahus, and Johannes Sommer themselves became professors in the new institutions.

Teachers, scholars, and promoters of presses, libraries, and schools, the Transylvanian humanists were fully a part of European humanist culture. Moreover, they also had close links to humanistic thought in Moldavia and Țara Românească. Both Philip the Moldavian, who printed the first books in Romanian in Sibiu, and Johannes Sommer, who founded a Latin school and humanistic library in Cotnari, came to Transylvania from Moldavia. The son of Michael the Brave studied at the university of Cluj. Another Muntenian nobleman, Neagoe Basarab, wrote a political and philosophical treatise which some have compared to *The Prince* of Machiavelli. Basarab's activity influenced humanistic culture in Transylvania and was in turn influenced by events there; for example, his political philosophy reflects his thinking about the great popular rebellion of 1514. Another scholar from Țara Românească was Deacon Coresi, who, after working in Tîrgoviște, came to Brașov and printed numerous books. Transylvanian scholars, meanwhile, influenced those in Moldavia and Țara Românească. The work of the Transylvanian chronicler Laurentius Toppeltinus was adapted by the learned Moldavian chronicler Miron Costin in his own work. The mid-seventeenth-century Greek and Latin school founded by the Muntenian Udriște Năsturel and the Academia Vasiliană in Iași were both modeled to some extent after humanist education in Transylvania.

Humanist thought, progressive by comparison with scholasticism and ingrown church dogma, led to unorthodox ideas and movements within the church itself. Jan Hus, whose activities in Bohemia constituted a spiritual protest against Catholic teachings and a material one against papal tithes, found supporters in Transylvania and Moldavia as well. So numerous were his followers that the pope sent special legations, and the kings of Poland and Hungary intervened to combat them. Transylvanian Hussites had to take refuge in Moldavia, where they printed the first Hungarian version of the Bible.

The Transylvanian population was more strongly affected by the teaching propounded by Martin Luther in the early sixteenth and by John Calvin in the mid-sixteenth century. Lutheran ideas were spread in Transylvania by young men studying at Wittenberg and by merchants with commercial contacts in German towns. Brașov became a center of Lutheranism, and Johannes Honterus a principal spokesman for it. In 1543 Honterus published a book supporting the new faith, *Reformatio ecclesiae Coronensis*. In fact, Lutheranism spread so considerably that the Transylvania diet recognized it as an offical religion in the middle of the sixteenth century. On the other hand, while a number of Hungarians, especially those of higher social status, leaned toward Lutheranism, the majority of the Hungarian population was influenced by Calvinism and embraced Calvin's Geneva confession. This was recognized as the third official religion in 1564, after the Catholic and Lutheran (Evangelical) churches. The principal proponent of Calvinism was Gaspar Hoffneger-Heltai, a Saxon who had converted to the new faith.

The moderation of the new Lutheran and Calvinist doctrines did not satisfy the masses, who leaned toward another, socially more radical, new faith called Unitarianism. Unitarian ideas were preached in Transylvania by Ferenc David of Cluj, and Unitarianism became the fourth officially recognized religion in 1579. From this point on, the conflict between Catholicism and Protestantism made itself felt in Transylvania, as each creed tried to win adherents through schools and books. Schools in towns such as Brașov, Sibiu, Bistrița, Cluj, and Oradea were reorganized in order better to promote these goals, and new schools were founded for the purpose in other towns and villages. The Orthodox Romanian population was not for the most part receptive to the new religions. Calvinists managed to gain a small number of converts, especially among the townspeople in the Banat and Hunedoara, but the masses continued to resist, even in the face of political pressure. Indeed, the Romanian schools also were reorganized, but in order to fight Protestant propaganda. In addition to the school at Șcheii Brașovului, already flourishing by the second half of the sixteenth century, others were founded at Caransebeș, Lugoj, and Hațeg, all in southern Transylvania.

Clearly the time was ripe for founding a school of higher learning. Such a university was established in Cluj in 1581, headed by Antonio Possevino, a noted scholar. Run by Jesuits as a Counter-Reformation measure, it was nevertheless imbued with the spirit of humanism, and in the professors and the subjects taught in its four faculties—philosophy, theology, letters, and law—one could see the effects of the new cultural currents. The institution in Cluj was similar to contemporary universities in Italy,

France, Spain, and Germany, and its graduates—*doctores* and *magistri*—had rights similar to those of their colleagues from the western schools.

A mixed humanistic-religious character is also seen in published works from Braşov, Sibiu, Alba Iulia, Sebeş, Orăştie, Cluj, Abrud, and Oradea. Honterus wrote several books in defense of the Lutheran faith, Heltai wrote his *Dialogus* in order to spread Calvinism, and Ferenc David wrote numerous tracts and treatises in support of Unitarianism. The most active scholar of the time, however, was Deacon Coresi, who in the years from 1557 to 1581 published some thirty-five books in Romanian and Slavonic to disseminate the Orthodox creed.

Since much of the religious propaganda was printed in the vernacular languages, books of this sort were important to the spread of learning among the less privileged classes, and in this they were nicely complemented by various lay works in a number of different fields. Somewhere between history and literature were historical poems like the *Carmen historicum de oppido Thalmus*, composed by the Saxon Johannes Lebel. Johannes Sommer also cultivated this genre during his stay in Transylvania. His fifteen elegies titled *De clade Moldavica* were concerned with the events in that country in the second half of the sixteenth century. The humanistic spirit is also seen in Christian Schesseus's political and historical work *Ruinae Pannonicae*, which was written in twelve books and obviously was influenced by Virgil. Alongside this humanism modeled on classical forebears, there were also works inspired by Italian humanistic writers; for example, György Enyedi's story "Gismuda and Gisquardus" was indebted to Boccaccio.

From poetry inspired by history and by Italian humanism it is but a short step to philology. Grammars of Greek and Latin were published by Johannes Honterus and Valentin Wagner, Grigor Molnar, János Sylvester, and others. But it appears that the richest of the humanist genres, both quantitatively and qualitatively, was historical writing. The earliest example is a chronicle known as *Chronicon Dubnicense*, after Dubnic in Czechoslovakia, where it was found; it was written toward the end of the fifteenth century, probably by a Romanian, and it recounts events of the time in Transylvania and Moldavia. Another widely read historical work is the *Tractatus de ritu, moribus, condicionibus, et nequitia Turcorum*, written in prison by one "Captivus Septemcastrensis," a young Transylvanian who had been carried off by the Turks. The humanist spirit is also evident in the *Epistola de perdicione regni Hungarorum*, the work of György Szerémi, who came from Sirmium in Yugoslavia and became a courtier of the Transylvanian voivode. A similar approach—somewhat sympathetic to the people and somewhat critical of the nobility—characterizes the historical poem *Stauromachia* (*Stieröchsel*) by Taurinus.

These early humanistic works led to the fruition of Transylvanian humanist culture in the second half of the sixteenth century, in the work of Olahus, Honterus, and Heltai. Olahus distinguished himself as a poet and as a historian, ethnographer, and geographer with his *Hungaria* and *Chronicon*. Honterus was a geographer (*Chorgraphia Transilvaniae* and *Rudimenta Cosmographica*), historian (he wrote a "Description of the World," first in prose and later in verse), philologist (grammars of Greek and Latin), poet (*Odes*), and jurist (an edition of Justinian's *Pandectes* and a *Compendium juris civilis*, a collection of the civil laws of the town of Transylvania). Heltai was the author of fables and of a *Magyar Krónika* [Chronicle of the Hungarians], an abridgment of a chronicle by Antonio Bonfini. The line of humanistically tinged histories and chronicles continues uninterrupted to the end of the sixteenth century, when István Szamosközi completed his important *Libri, Pentades*, and *Hebdomades*. These have a pronounced humanistic structure and style, and many parts clearly are modeled on Livy's works.

Like literature, the fine arts were characterized by a higher conception of the world and society; it was interest in mankind, in mankind's uplifting and advancement, that formed the basis of the creative efforts of the Renaissance artists in Transylvania.

It is a great step from the Romanesque stone churches of the twelfth to the fourteenth centuries in Țara Hațegului to the Gothic churches of the fourteenth and fifteenth centuries in the cities of Transylvania. The churches of Cluj, Brașov, Sibiu, Sebeș, and Sighișoara are monuments of Gothic architecture, comparable to their counterparts in Austria, Germany, France, England, and Italy. Other Gothic constructions of the same period are various civil and military buildings in Sibiu, Brașov, Sebeș, Cluj, Sighișoara, Mediaș, Bistrița, and other towns. The Gothic style and spirit are seen even more clearly in the castles, most notably and spectacularly in the castle of Bran near Brașov and in that of Hunedoara, the work of the voivode Iancu of

Hunedoara. The former dates from the second half of the fourteenth century; it was modified and expanded in the fifteenth. The latter is fifteenth-century, and has since been modified and embellished several times. To these two castles we may add those of Făgăraş (fifteenth to sixteenth centuries), Vînţu de Jos, in central Transylvania (mid-tenth century), and Criş, which has a Renaissance watchtower.

In both the Gothic churches and the castle of Hunedoara, elements of the Renaissance of the first half of the sixteenth century appeared in the course of modifications and embellishments: portals, window and door frames, and altars. The Renaissance in architecture is even to be seen in the general style of town halls, schools, guild halls, and the houses of the wealthy burghers in such towns as Cluj, Sibiu, and Braşov. The new style is more evident in the decorative sculpture that adorns the facades of churches and other buildings, certain interior sections of churches (such as the choir), and the tombstones of nobles and wealthier town-dwellers, which are richly ornamented with floral and geometric motifs. Good examples are to be found in the cathedrals of Oradea, Alba Iulia, Cluj, and Sibiu.

A similar evolution occurred in painting. The Gothic style predominant in the fourteenth and fifteenth centuries gradually gave way, first to painting with some Renaissance elements in a Gothic whole, and finally to works of an entirely Renaissance character. Thus the murals in the church at Sighişoara are essentially Gothic, though with Renaissance features, while the altar of the church at Sebeş, dating from the early sixteenth century, is entirely Renaissance. Italian, German, Austrian, and Polish elements had some influence on this development; the school of the German-Polish Vit Stoss family in particular gave Transylvanian painting a substantial push toward the Renaissance.

Under the influence of the Reformation, the late-flowering humanism in Transylvania acquired a broader social base. Increasingly, Latin was abandoned in favor of the vernaculars, since a growing number of readers wanted works of literature and science in their mother tongues. One result was scientific works such as Peter Melius Juhász's herbarium and György Lencsés's work on medicine. The use of the vernaculars, in addition to Latin, in historical works such as chronicles in the second half of the sixteenth century also must be attributed to the influence of the Reformation. Alongside the Latin chronicles of István Szamosközi, Michael Siegler, and Eustatius Gyulaffi were the vernacular writings of István Székely, Sebestyén Borsos, Hieronymus Ostermayer, and others.

Transylvanian culture in the seventeenth century represents a transitional phrase between a late humanism and an early Enlightenment. Its representatives were desk-bound schoolroom humanists, no longer at the forefront of cultural change. Albert Szenczi Molnár, for example, though a learned linguist and notable poet, was not a fighter, but a scholar detached from the social disarray; János Rimay, also a talented poet, provides another instance of how militant poetry was transformed by these twilight humanists into an artificial, contemplative, and pessimistic literary game. Historians such as Gáspár Veress Bojtinus, János and Wolfgang Bethlen, and Laurentius Toppeltinus, who continued the humanist tradition, also persisted in writing in Latin. Education continued to be based on the reformist and humanistic principles established in the previous century, although there were certain attempts to modernize it by bringing foreign scholars to the college at Alba Iulia.

Progress in the culture of the day was represented by new currents of thought: puritanism, presbyterianism, and especially Cartesianism, a precursor of the Enlightenment. Puritanism came from the west and was an enemy of feudalism and absolutism. Adapting themselves to the social realities in Transylvania, its spokesmen began their activities in education, working to modernize instruction on the basis of the ideas set forth by the great Czech educator Jan Amos Comenius (Komensky); later they turned to the education of the masses and to church reform.

The desire for reform also is clearly seen in *Cărare pe scurt spre fapte bune îndreptătoare* [Short path toward good deeds], by Ioan Zoba, the Romanian archpriest of Vinț, and based on the work of several English authors. In 1648, the Romanian New Testament was published by the Orthodox metropolitan Simion Ștefan in Alba Iulia; in spite of Ștefan's ecclesiastical position, his preface expresses a concern about the need for a language understood by all Romanians that was progressive for his time, surpassing the narrow ideas of even the reformed religions. Even farther advanced in this direction is the work of János Apáczai Csere, who received his education in Holland, where he became acquainted with the new ideology, and who raised determined opposition to the feudal order. The fact that the Romanian scholar Mihail Halici from Caransebeş, a notable poet, owned a library of over five hundred volumes on diverse subjects shows his multifaceted interests.

The vernaculars, on the other hand, were well represented in historical writing. Works in Romanian included a chronicle of the Romanian church of Saint Nicholas in Scheii Braşovului, written by the priest Vasile between 1628 and 1633, and Gheorghe Brancovici's chronicle written in 1687; these works provided their readers not only with interesting facts of local history, but also with more general knowledge about Transylvania. Among historical works in Hungarian, memoirs were particularly common, including valuable books both by the nobility (János Kémeny and Miklos Bethlen) and by the burghers (Ferencz Nagy Szabo, Toma Borsos, and Miklos Kis Totfalusi). German historical works—by such authors as Georg Kraus, Johannes Tröster, and Mathias Miles—deal exclusively with the history of individual towns, though they sometimes contain scattered information about Transylvania as a whole or even about Moldavia and Ţara Românească.

The continuous contact among the three Romanian territories in the seventeenth century contributed to the spread of culture from one side of the Carpathians to the others. Ioan Caioni, in a rhymed chronicle, recorded the political events of the period of Matei Basarab, Vasile Lupu, and György Rákóczi II. Moldavian scholars were extremely active in Transylvania, and a few Transylvanian scholars worked in their country. Moreover, books printed in Moldavia—Vasile Lupu's *Pravila* (a compendium of laws), Varlaam's Romanian school book, and Dosoftei's psalter—were widely reproduced in Transylvania.

Finally, the progressive tradition is also seen in folk poetry, which reflects social antagonisms and the discontent of the masses. Ballads, in particular, vividly express these feelings. Like love songs and songs telling of struggles against the Turks or the Habsburgs, the ballads were spread not only orally, but also in manuscript form, copied down by village scribes and teachers. Some of them even have a common theme, like the Romanian ballad of Master Manole and the Hungarian ballad of Clement the Mason. Thus folk poetry played an important role in preserving and spreading the tradition of the people's struggle in Transylvania.

Social and Economic Developments

Social conditions in Transylvania in the sixteenth and seventeenth centuries did not favor economic development. The continued warfare between the Habsburgs and the Ottoman Empire brought with it the usual misfortunes of war. Cities and peasant homes alike were destroyed, and people were carried off into captivity. The preservation of feudal organization and obligations, and particularly the severe exploitation of the peasantry, was almost equally destructive.

The peasant farm continued to form the basis of agricultural production, since the seigneurial preserves which produced goods for market were as yet little developed. In Poland, Bohemia, and the northwestern states of Germany, peasant land was usurped and incorporated into such reserves as early as the sixteenth century, but this phenomenon was not to become general in Transylvania until the second half of the seventeenth. It was more profitable for the feudal nobles to increase their revenues by intensifying their exploitation of the peasants. Thus the goods in the marketplaces mostly came from tithes sold by the nobility, though to a lesser extent they were goods sold directly by the peasants.

It is true, however, that seventeenth-century village farmers began to make more rational use of the land, the crops they grew being dependent on the quality of the soil. Winter wheat took first place in agricultural production; spring wheat, which yielded less, was less commonly grown. After wheat came oats, and then rye, barley, millet, and buckwheat. A new crop, cultivated as early as the middle of the seventeenth century, was corn. At first it was used for fattening pigs and chickens, but gradually it came to occupy a more and more significant place in the peasant diet, replacing millet. In general, Transylvania's cereal production was consumed domestically, although occasionally trading took place if any of the three Romanian lands had suffered a bad harvest.

In addition to farming, herding and stockbreeding continued to be the major occupations. They were important to the serfs not only because of their obligations to their landlords, the church, and the state, but also because of greater opportunities to sell goods locally and abroad. The large number of animals also explains the increase in the old practice of transhumant herding; Transylvanian herdsmen crossed to the southern and eastern sides of the Carpathians in search of pastures in the Romanian plain and Danube valley, and on the Moldavian plateau and in the valleys of the Siret and the Prut.

Transylvania's mineral wealth, on the other hand, was unevenly exploited. During times of actual warfare or domestic unrest, the mines were relatively inactive, but interest always revived when conditions improved. Several measures were taken in the course of the seventeenth century to promote mining and thus to increase state revenues. Gabriel Bethlen, for example, in addition to granting individual concessions, had the diet decree in 1617 that anyone, local or foreign, could open a mine anywhere that ore was found. Thanks to such measures, mining did indeed develop; the state's need for iron was thus satisfied, and significant additional revenues were derived from gold and silver in the second half of the seventeenth century. Transylvania also continued to produce large quantities of salt, of which a significant proportion was exported to Hungary and to the Balkan Peninsula. These exports brought tens of thousands of florins each year to the state treasury. Mercury, which was mined especially at Zlatna and Abrud in the Bihor Mountains, also became important in the seventeenth century; it was exported to Poland and Venice, and, in the absence of coins, several princes used it to pay their taxes to the Turks.

The central authority also had an interest in encouraging individual artisans and manufacturing. With the growth of markets came an increase in both the quantity and the quality of artisans' products in the sixteenth and seventeenth centuries, and manufacturing began in the seventeenth century. Artisans' guilds produced a wide variety of items that were much sought after, not only in domestic markets but in foreign ones, especially in Ţara Românească and Moldavia. These included cloth of various types, leather, weapons, and silver articles. The number of trades and skills continued to grow. In Cluj, for example, there were thirty guilds and almost sixty specialities in the sixteenth century. As early as the mid-sixteenth century, there were a small number of paper mills in Braşov, Sibiu, and Cluj which could be regarded as incipient factories. However, not until the opposition of the guilds could be overcome—and then only incompletely and temporarily—could the central authority succeed in establishing actual factories. The glasswords at Porumbacul de Sus (Făgăraş) produced a large variety of glass items in significant quantities in the second half of the seventeenth century. In 1645–46, a cannon foundry at Alba Iulia employed 204 blacksmiths, 47 fitters, 84 carpenters, 80 wheelwrights, and about 1,300 auxiliary laborers.

Increased production and the general economic development of the country made possible somewhat more substantial domestic trade. The towns of central Transylvania, especially Cluj, played a significant role in this development; another strong influence was the army's demand for goods. Saxon merchants and predominantly Saxon towns had held a privileged position in Transylvanian commerce, but beginning about the middle of the sixteenth century, Romanian, Greek, and Armenian merchants offered growing competition. The large number of non-Saxon merchants and the importance of their commercial activity enabled them, in spite of opposition, to form commercial "companies" in the first half of the seventeenth century. These organizations or societies were known by the generic name "Greek company," although in fact they included many Romanians, as well as Armenians and Ragusans. They were founded in all of the more important Transylvanian towns—Sibiu, Brașov, Alba Iulia, and Cluj—as well as in a number of smaller ones inhabited largely by Romanians, such as Făgăraș, Hunedoara, and Orăștie.

After the complete separation of Transylvania from the Magyar feudal kingdom and its transformation into an autonomous principality, its commercial orientation toward the south and the east intensified. Transylvania's economic links with Vienna, Venice, and Poland were sporadic and generally of secondary importance; the best commercial outlets and best sources of raw materials for Transylvania continued to be Moldavia and Țara Românească. Overcoming both the backward economic policies of the feudal nobles and Turkish efforts to monopolize commerce, the Romanian countries maintained active trade relations. Brașov continued to hold its position as the commercial center for the three countries, and it also drew Turkish, Arab, Armenian, Greek, Italian, and Polish traders.

The political and economic changes that Transylvania was undergoing affected its social structure as well. The nobility grew in numbers and in economic and political importance. For one thing, noblemen who had fled from territories occupied by the Turks and the Habsburgs settled in Transylvania. These newcomers, taking advantage of the political struggles that were dividing the principality, soon acquired large estates and filled powerful offices. The princes, meanwhile, sought to create a more stable social and military base by strengthening the petty nobility; they granted titles to various free peasants and townspeople who had distinguished themselves in battle or through acts of faith. In the sixteenth and seventeenth centuries, a substantial number of Romanians, Szeklers, and Magyars became armigers (*armalisti*)—nobles entitled to a coat of arms—in this way. The same route to nobility was taken by the so-called riflemen (*puşcaşi*), serfs who performed military duty around fortresses, and by many Romanian knezi and voivodes from Haţeg and Maramureş, boyars from Ţara Făgăraşului, and haiduks from Bihor. But the economic and political power of these ordinary noblemen was rather restricted compared to that of the high nobility. Materially they were scarcely better off than the peasant serfs with whom they lived in the villages, the only difference being that they had no feudal obligations.

There were many causes for the impoverishment of the peasantry, but exploitation by the feudal lords must certainly be counted as the most important. In addition to the tithes in animals and farm products, the peasants were obliged to pay another tax, based not on the size of their crop but on the amount of land they used. There were also various taxes in kind. The "census," or tax in money, likewise increased, and on top of it there were various use taxes on pastureland, fishing grounds, slaughterhouses, mills, and taverns, as well as fines and so on. The sixteenth century saw further breakings-up of peasant holdings and an increase in the number of jeleri, peasants who had no land and therefore were also known as *pauperes*. The number of jeleri, together with the increase in cases where free peasants sold themselves into serfdom, shows the want in which the Transylvanian peasantry were living. Another confirmation is the drop in the number of animals on peasant farms. By the mid-seventeenth century, 56 percent of the peasants did not have enough draft animals to plow their fields and had to rely on the comradely help of others, while 26 percent had no animals at all, and survived only by the work of their own two hands.

The growth of domestic markets and the consequent increase in opportunities for the feudal lords to sell goods for money motivated them to increase the size of the fields cultivated for their own benefit. Larger seigneurial reserves implied the shrinking of peasant landholdings, which meant further impoverishment and, on a societywide scale, even more feudal dependence.

Moreover, the number of days of involuntary labor on the lord's land increased, from one day a week—the number fixed after the suppression of Doja's Rebellion—to two or even more. In winter, too, the women were required to do various domestic jobs at the manor, including spinning and weaving. One of the worst aspects of *robota* was long-distance carting, with the peasants being forced to provide their own food and draft animals. Another major hardship was abuse by the *slujbaşi* (petty nobles who were vassals of the high nobility), who demanded still further days of *robota* or even work on their own land.

Turkish rule in the Banat brought significant changes in the social and economic life of that region. In general, there was a noticeable economic decline. Extensive areas were left fallow; only on the properties of well-protected fortresses was there any substantial agricultural activity. Stockbreeding therefore became one of the inhabitants' principal occupations, since animals could be more easily protected in the woods and mountains. Social relations also were modified, as Turks took the places of the local nobility who had fled. Since all land ruled by the Turks was regarded as the sultan's property, hereditary feudal rights were abolished. Part of the conquered land was granted to religious institutions and a smaller part to important dignitaries, but most of it remained at the sultan's disposal. He granted a few fiefs to civilian and military officials, in return for which they owed military duty and, in times of war, had also to provide armed soldiers in proportion to the revenue from their fiefs. Such grants were temporary and contingent upon the character and duration of the grantee's service; land could not be inherited or disposed of in any way.

The Muslims of the pashalics—soldiers, officials, and priests— lived as parasites, supported by the peasants. The latter were bound to the land, and if they fled they could be hunted for fifteen years or, in the seventeenth century, for thirty. Serfs had obligations to the state in money, in labor, and in kind. The principal tax was known as the *harachi*, but there were also other regularly and specially levied taxes. Furthermore, the peasants owed rent in money, a tithe in all agricultural and animal products, either paid in kind or in money, and days of involuntary labor to Turkish landlords.

The binding of the peasants to the land in 1514, the frequent Turkish and German incursions, and the combined power of the privileged few had sapped the peasants' strength, and their ability to resist was substantially weakened. The struggle against exploitation did not cease, however; instead, great numbers of serfs fled their homes. Flight from one estate to another, or to towns and mines, became so common that in some villages more than 20 percent of the farms lay deserted. Those who fled were hunted down tirelessly by their masters and forcibly returned to the land they had left, and therefore some peasants left the country altogether. No safeguards, no threats were enough to stop this exodus; the authorities feared that all of the inhabitants would leave and no one would be left to pay the sultan's taxes.

Those peasants and poor town-dwellers who stayed at home continued to struggle in ways dictated by the circumstances. In 1556, the poor population of Sibiu revolted over increased taxation and other obligations. Prince János Sigismund sent an army, but it was forced to pull back in face of the determined rebels, and the city's leaders were compelled to hide. Only the dispatch of more troops put a bloody end to the Sibiu unprising.

The most significant and consequential of the uprisings of this period, however, took place in 1562. Burdened with heavy taxes to the prince's treasury and the feudal lords, and threatened with the abolition of their old privileges and mass serfdom, large numbers of Szekler peasants revolted in the spring of the year. They assembled at Odorhei in May, armed with agricultural tools and other weapons, demanding restoration of their lost freedoms and abolition of the feudal-style obligations that had been imposed on them. The prince sent representatives to try to calm the uprising by promising to restore their former rights, but these efforts failed, since the Szeklers had lost faith in the state and the feudal class. The rebels scored a few victories and even defeated the army sent against them near Odorhei. However, they did not have enough men, were poorly armed, and lacked organization and strong leadership, and they eventually lost to another feudal army in a battle near Miercurea Nirajului in southeastern Transylvania. The nobility was merciless: the captains of the revolts were impaled, while other rebels had their ears and noses cut off or were imprisoned.

To prevent another rebellion, the Szeklers were forced to build two fortresses, strongholds for the nobility; these were given the significant names "Szekler Attacks" and "Szekler Regrets." The consequences of the revolt indeed were severe for all the Szekler peasantry. The diet officially did away with their privileges, and

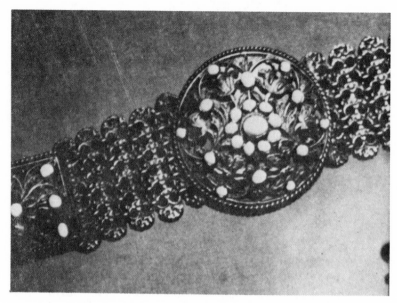

Prince Gabriel Bethlen's golden and jeweled belt.

Fortified wall in Cluj (fifteenth to seventeenth centuries).

the peasants were declared serfs, subject to state taxes and obliged to pay tithes and perform involuntary labor. The Szekler leaders (*primores*) were rewarded for their collaboration in putting down the rebellion, afterwards being considered part of the high nobility.

In some circumstances, the fight against feudalism even took on mystical forms. Thus in 1659, in northern Transylvania, a man named Gheorghe Crăciun appeared, presenting himself as "God's representative on earth." Crăciun made a deep impression on the masses. He was himself a peasant, from around Baia Mare in northwestern Transylvania. According to our sources, he was possessed of extraordinary physical and mental characteristics: the strength of Hercules, a black birthmark covering part of his body, remarkable craftiness, and a gift for oratory. The peasants flocked to him, calling him "the Black Man" and "divinely inspired," "a saint." The Black Man claimed to be able to work miracles—to multiply bread and wine—and his followers believed him. His rebellion against the Ottoman "infidels" and the "pagan" landlords broke out near Debrețin. At the news of this crusade, ten to fifteen thousand peasants, ignoring their lords' prohibitions, left the estates and headed for Debrețin. Gheorghe Crăciun told the assembled throng not to worry about anything, as God would take care of his chosen ones. His ill-prepared and disorganized forces did manage to destroy a few castles and rob and kill a few noblemen and priests who fell into their hands, but at their first encounter with the Turks they were, in the words of a contemporary chronicler, "slaughtered like lambs." The Black Man, together with a group of rebels who remained faithful to him, escaped the massacre and returned to Debrețin; there he fell victim to a conspiracy by the town's judges. The rebels were completely defeated and the revolt suppressed.

8

Transylvania under the Habsburgs

NOT LONG after the Turks were driven away from the walls of Vienna in 1683, the Austrians turned their attention to Transylvania, which they had long coveted for its wealth and strategic importance. In order to convince the Transylvanians to accept the emperor's "protection," they first sent an envoy, the Jesuit diplomat Antidius Dunod. But when the Transylvanian nobles tried to obtain as advantageous a compromise as possible, the Viennese court refused to accept their conditions. The imperial army was then sent to do what diplomacy had failed to accomplish—to convince the Transylvanians that "the emperor will afford you protection whether you want it or not" ("*nolentes volentes, proteget vos Sua Maiestas*"). The Treaty of Blaj, imposed by the army at the end of October 1687, forced the Transylvanians to accept Habsburg rule, to permit imperial troops to winter in twelve cities, and to pay 700,000 Rhenish florins in tribute. Any discussion of the conditions of the settlement was cut short by the arrival of General Antonio Caraffa; the general extracted from the diet the declaration of 9 May 1688, which stated that the Transylvanians, "of their own free will and motivated only by Christian zeal, renounce Ottoman protection . . . and do sincerely and in good faith accept the fatherly protection of His Majesty for themselves and their descendants." This declaration marked the end of Turkish suzerainty in Transylvania, and the beginning of the Austrian rule that lasted until 1867.

The imperial army proceeded immediately to occupy four fortresses named in the Treaty of Blaj. However, at Braşov it met with resistance on the part of the artisans and the town's poor, who had been organized by the goldsmith Gaspar Kreisch. General Veterani was forced to shell the city, and he inflicted bloody reprisals after the resistance was broken. The leaders of the movement were tried and executed and the town burned. Similar conflicts broke out at Bistriţa and Baia Mare. In the end, however, nothing—not the intervention of France, an ally of the Turks, not the fact that the Austrians were driven back from Ţara Românească by Constantin Brâncoveanu, not the Austrian defeat at Zărneşti and the appointment of Imre Thököly as prince of Transylvania by the Turks—could stop the Habsburg occupation of Transylvania. The Turks, who had suffered several defeats, recognized the new situation in Transylvania in the Peace of Carlowitz in 1699.

The general principles according to which Transylvania would be governed as a part of the Habsburg empire were established by the eighteen points of the Diploma Leopoldina of 4 December 1691. Continued recognition of the Catholic, Lutheran, Calvinist, and Unitarian religions was guaranteed. All privileges granted to the nobility under the principality were reconfirmed. The country's old laws were to remain in force, and the old administrative, judicial, and economic status quo was recognized. The Saxons and the Szeklers were to retain their old privileges. Only Transylvanians were to hold office; the political head of the country was to be elected from among the nobility and was to be a Catholic or a member of one of the other "received" religions. The commander-in-chief of the Transylvanian army, the chancellor, and the councillors and other officials were to be Transylvanian, while the commander of the Austrian army could only be Austrian. Transylvania's contribution to the Viennese court was fixed at 112,500 gold florins annually in time of peace, and 400,000 in time of war.

The Diploma Leopoldina, which was to serve as the constitutional foundation of the principality of Transylvania for more than a century and a half, was very skillfully written. In principle it recognized Transylvania's traditional autonomy and its separate status directly subject to the emperor, but it contained certain ambiguous phrases, which left open the possibility of Austrian interference in Transylvania's internal affairs. The Romanians, who represented the majority of the population, continued to be excluded from political life; only the three medieval nations and the four received religions constituted the state.

On the basis of the Diploma, the emperor was able to organize the principality in such a way that its autonomy was limited and the court's power increased. Transylvania was run by a Gubernium with administrative and judicial powers; the head of the Gubernium was a governor chosen by the diet and confirmed by the Austrian court. A Transylvanian "Aulic Chancellery" was set up to represent the Gubernium at the court, which also chose its members. This chancellery quickly became the most important political institution in Transylvania, as it served the interests of the Habsburg dynasty. Financial matters were the province of the treasury, which looked after taxes, customs, the salt monopoly, and the mines. Military affairs were in the hands of the Aulic Council of War, whose representative in Transylvania, the commander-in-chief, was the most important agent of the country's new rulers. The supreme judicial body was the King's Table, which continued to dispense feudal-style justice. The diet remained the country's legislature, composed of representatives of the three nations and the four received religions. The Habsburgs took control of the key positions—foreign policy, military power, financial administration, and internal government—and gradually transformed the political institutions into executive organs of the central authority.

Since the Habsburg empire was a conglomerate of different states and peoples, the Roman Catholic religion served to stengthen the other forces of cohesion—dynastic, absolutistic, bureaucratic, and military—and provided a political instrument for domination and unification. In addition to various measures designed to protect Catholicism, which at the time was very weak in Transylvania, the Austrians tried to strengthen the religion in other ways. An excellent opportunity lay in the fact that the Romanian people and their Orthodox religion were only tolerated. By winning over the Romanians, the Habsburgs would strengthen their position in Transylvania and be better able to send out feelers to Moldavia and Ţara Românească. In order to accomplish their goal, they used every means possible, from blandishments and persuasion to tricks and threats. As a temporary measure, a plan similar to the 1692 union with the Ruthenians was devised. The Uniates were to become "Greek Catholics" by retaining their Orthodox ritual but accepting the four doctrinal points established by the Council of Florence in 1439: the pope as the supreme head of the church; the existence of Purgatory; the recognition of the Son, Jesus Christ; and the use of unleavened bread in communion. The clergy had first to be won over with the material advantages of union, which would mean equality with the Catholic priesthood, including their income and their privileges. These were tempting promises, since the Romanian priests were almost serfs. The Romanian peasantry also would be recognized as one of the constituent nations. The beginnings of the union took place at a synod at Alba Iulia in 1697, but the final decision was made at another synod the following year, with thirty-eight protopopes in attendance. Union was accepted on the condition that the Orthodox ritual and customs could be retained. The Diploma Leopoldina of 16 February 1699 legalized the union, and raised the Uniate clergy to the same position as the Catholic.

Negative reaction, however, was not long in coming. The dominant classes were opposed to the union because it accorded fuller rights to the Romanians; the nobility would lose an important source of income. But the greatest opposition came from the Transylvanian Romanians themselves, especially those in the south. A new diploma, in March 1701, guaranteed the clergy and peasantry of the Uniate (Greek Catholic) church the same privileges as the Roman Catholic church, but also restricted the actions of the Romanian Greek Catholic bishop through the presence of a Roman Catholic theologian in his court. The provisions of the new diploma that offered the Romanian people the prospect of being one of the constituent nations, on the other hand, was never put into effect.

However, it should not be inferred that the union of part of the Romanians in Transylvania with the Roman Catholic church had nothing but negative consequences, for there were benefits as well. Through it the Romanians came into contact with Latin-based cultures in western Europe. In their schools and through other means, the Romanians became more aware of their Daco-Roman origins, of the Latinity of their language, of their uninterrupted ties to the land on which they lived, and of their historical rights. Thus began the national, political, and cultural renaissance of the Romanian people. In the schools in Blaj, the center of the new Greek Catholic faith, generations of young people from all over Transylvania were educated without regard to differences of religion, as were many from Țara Românească and Moldavia. For Romanian culture in the eighteenth and nineteenth centuries, Blaj became what was described at the time as "Little Rome."

Social and religious discontent imparted a new intensity to the anti-Habsburg struggles. There was constant turmoil and agitation, and huge numbers of peasants fled or became haiduks.

In this troubled atmosphere, in 1703, a rebellion broke out in the Tisza region under the leadership of the nobleman Ferencz Rákóczi II. Rákóczi called on nobles and commoners alike to join the struggle against Habsburg rule, promising exemption from taxes and *robota* to those who responded. With such promises he was able to assemble men of all ethnic groups and all classes, and his rebellion was further favored by the political situation in Europe. The war of succession in Spain and the Nordic war meant that many of the Austrian troops were occupied in the west. Furthermore, Rákóczi was able to obtain promises of support from Louis XIV of France and Peter the Great of Russia. In these circumstances the revolt spread quickly. Bands of rebel peasants, believing Rákóczi's promises, appeared all over Transylvania. The movement began to take on the appearance of a social rebellion, as serfs, the urban poor, the free peasantry, and the petty nobility joined it. The battles between the Lobonts, the Habsburg partisans, and the Curuts, Rákóczi's adherents (recalling the "crusaders" of 1514), ended in many cases in victory for the rebels. In July 1704, the diet, assembled at Alba Iulia, proclaimed Rákóczi prince, on the condition that he respect Transylvanian independence and not attempt to unite the country with Hungary.

Between 1705 and 1708, Transylvania passed from one rule to another—from the hands of the Curuts to those of the Habsburgs—depending on the fortunes of the battlefield. Then, in 1709, the rebellion began to decline. Louis XIV was ignoring the situation, Peter the Great was involved in a war with the Swedes, and the imperial army was returning from the western front. Internally, the situation was growing worse; the tax exemptions and easing of obligations which had drawn the peasantry into the rebellion were no longer possible, and the army could no longer be supplied. But the decline of the rebellion was principally due to the social contradictions within it. The peasants had risen up not only in opposition to foreign rule, but also in the hope of freeing themselves from serfdom. The nobility, on the other hand, was interested in strengthening its political position without any loss of its privileges. The enthusiasm and resolve of the peasants fell off, and at the crucial moment the nobility sought a truce with the imperial forces. Sándor Károlyi, the leader of the nobility and Rákóczi's second-in-command, was more concerned with saving his property than with the long-term goals of the battle, and he made peace with the Habsburgs at Satu Mare in 1711. The rebellion was defeated.

The year 1711 marked the beginning of the consolidation of Habsburg rule in Transylvania and of Phanariot rule in Moldavia; five years later Phanariot rule began in Ţara Românească as well. The Viennese imperial court, deliberately using any means to strengthen its dominance over Transylvania, gradually stripped the diet of its powers, and the emperor was assured his control by direct appointment of a number of deputies. The Gubernium's role was reduced to that of executive body for court decrees; the governor was named directly by the emperor and ignored the diet's votes. The treasury was subordinated to the Aulic Chancellery of Vienna. Together with the commander-in-chief of the imperial army, these Austrian-run institutions ruled the country.

The Banat, freed of Turkish rule in 1718, was declared crown property and governed directly by the court. Military commanders—none of them from the Banat—were appointed to act as governors for the province. The military government continued until 1751, when a civilian administration, consisting of an Austrian president and six councillors, was instituted.

The emperor also used Roman Catholicism as an instrument of domination, appointing Catholics to public office regardless of whether they met the conditions prescribed by law. Moreover, the Austrians repeatedly tried to extend the hold of the Uniate church on the Romanians; the union, which in any case had attracted only part of the clergy and the petty nobility, had been seriously shaken by the Curut rebellion. The Romanians, meanwhile, were attempting to use the Uniate church to help them obtain political rights. The person who put this tactic to best use was the Greek Catholic bishop, Inocenţiu Micu Klein. For sixteen years, tirelessly and fearlessly, he deluged the Gubernium, the diet, and the court with petitions and memoranda, presenting arguments in favor of his demands and offering harsh criticism of the social order and of those who had created and continued to defend it. Vladica Inochentie, as he was known to the people, went beyond religious differences and fought for the entire Romanian people, even if it meant abandoning the union. The demands he made in twenty-four memoranda to the court, in numerous others presented to the diet, and in speeches delivered on a variety of occasions, may be summarized as follows: the Romanians should no longer be merely tolerated, but should have equal rights with the other nations; they should be represented in the Gubernium, the diet, and in public office; the Romanian common people should be put on an equal footing with the common people of the constituent confessions. Furthermore, the property that the lords had usurped should be restored to the serfs; serfdom should be abolished in southern Transylvania, where the authorities forced *robota* on the peasants even though they were free; serfs should be allowed to move about at will, attend school, and learn a trade; involuntary labor should be reduced to two days a week, "for the serfs are wearing themselves out with uninterrupted toil." In order to support these demands, Micu invoked the Romanians' ancient origins and continuous presence in Dacia. He further argued that the Romanians had twice as many obligations as all the other nationalities put together, and, according to natural law, "he who bears the burden should share the rewards" ("qui sentit onus, sentiat et commodus"). "The Romanian nation," wrote Micu, "is inferior to no other in Transylvania, neither in its character, nor in its culture, nor in its aptitude for public affairs. Not only are the Romanians much the oldest inhabitants of the hills and valleys of Transylvania, but they are also the most numerous." Consequently, they should be represented in the Gubernium, the diet, the King's Table, and in all high offices.

Micu's demands were summarized in 1744 in the *Supplex libellus* and presented to Empress Maria Theresa. They treated the Romanian people as a whole, including the common people of the towns and villages and the peasantry. His program called for elevating the economic, social, political, and educational status of the Romanians, and for an end to all inequality. Inocenţiu Micu's campaign thus mixed progressive ideas with outdated ones. Such concerns as equality of rights between the Romanians and the coinhabiting peoples, serfs' rights to attend school and learn a trade, the restoration of usurped land, and the right of free movement, for example, were clearly progressive ideas. On the other hand, the preservation of the medieval nations and the reduction rather than abolition of *robota* were notions whose time had passed. But the mere fact that Micu raised issues that no one had raised before him, that he persevered in his campaign for almost twenty years, that he brought up certain irrefutable truths that no one previously had dared mention—these facts were enormously important to Transylvania in this time of profound social change.

The importance of Inocenţiu Micu (whose work was to serve as an ideological foundation for decades) was not lost on those at whom his effort was directed. The most eloquent proof was the declaration of the nobles' diet in May 1736. "These demands," declared the nobles, " . . . overturn the rights and liberties which the nations of our country have hitherto enjoyed . . . and in fact shake the foundation of the whole social system of the land, politically, economically, and in religious matters as well." By the time Micu realized that the route he had chosen was not the way to achieve reforms which would "shake the foundation of the whole social system," and that he would have to appeal to the masses and rouse them to battle, it was too late. He could not carry out threats made at the synod of Blaj in 1744, for the Habsburgs and their allies the nobility had taken steps to prevent an uprising and to destroy the courageous bishop.

The struggle of the Romanian people for social emancipation and political rights during the years when Micu was active gave birth to a clear awareness of the justice of their claims. As the Romanians of the city of Hunedoara wrote to the Magyar nobles in a memorandum in 1761, "We continue to be amazed and to wonder why . . . you oppress us so and impose on us the yoke of servitude, when we are and always have been more numerous than you, and more importantly, have been in this country longer then you, since we are the descendants of the ancient Dacians." This change in social and political awareness affected even foreigners who observed it while traveling or living among the Romanians. The Austrian geologist I. Haquet, who did research in Transylvania in 1763 and 1764, wrote:

> . . . the whole time I remained among them I found many things that demonstrated the goodness of the Romanian people. How moved they are when they are treated like equals! In the two years that I lived among them, I observed in many of them traits that would not be unworthy of the most civilized of men. How badly this nation, once so noble and great, has been broken by the hate and oppression of the monarchy! Whatever anyone might say, the Romanians have their merit, both in terms of numbers and in terms of their rightful ownership of the country.

The frequent uprisings and rebellions of the Transylvanian masses presented the Austrian rulers with the problem of finding more effective means of consolidating their control; the army, the financial officers, and the Jesuit priests obviously were not sufficient. Formation of a border militia seemed a possible way to meet this pressing need. Moreover, such a militia would be able to block the flight of Transylvanian peasants to Moldavia and Țara Românească. The militiamen would serve the centralizing efforts of the Habsburgs, could be used to help spread the religious union, and, finally, could be mustered against the nobility if they failed to support the state. Between 1762 and 1765, therefore, five border regiments were created. Two of these were Romanian—one in the Năsăud region and one in the south, from Hațeg to Țara Bîrsei—and three were Szekler, taking in the whole eastern region and providing a link between the two Romanian regiments. Two more were established in the Banat between 1764 and 1768, one Romanian-Illyrian and one Banat German. However, the officers were exclusively German, and they neither knew nor respected the language, customs, and aspirations of the Romanian and Szekler peasants. The liberty promised to those who enlisted left much to be desired, and efforts to convert soldiers to Catholicism continued unabated.

The consequences came quickly. Discontent spread through the regiments, manifesting itself in mutinies and rebellions. The first to revolt were the Romanians of the Second Regiment in Năsăud, who in May 1763 expressed their dissatisfaction by refusing to take the oath to the emperor and throwing their weapons on the ground. The ringleaders were condemned to death on the spot where the revolt broke out, at Salva in northeastern Transylvania. Some were broken on the rack (the fate of one Tănase Todoran, who was over one hundred years old), while others were hanged. The Szekler regiments were even more unhappy. A true rebellion broke out in 1763 in Siculeni (Madefalău); by the following year it had involved large numbers of peasants from almost all the Szekler seats. The revolt ended with the thunder of Austrian cannons. Over two hundred rebels died in the battle, while many drowned crossing the Olt River, and still others, gravely wounded, died later.

New regulations for the border regiments, put into effect in 1766, together with other Austrian measures, prevented a recurrence of such events. The Romanian border troops soon had a chance to prove their bravery on the battlefield, in the Russian-Austrian-Turkish warfare of 1768–74. Prove it they did, to the admiration of eyewitnesses. The Austrian Ignatius von Born, for example, wrote after the end of the war, "To the glory of this people, it must be said that its men were most valiant and brave.

Captain Duca, who is eighty years old, provided the most splendid service to our court in the last war with the Turks."

Habsburg Policies and the Transylvanian Economy

The basis of Habsburg economic policy in the eighteenth century was an Austrian variant of mercantilism, a doctrine with many adherents throughout contemporary Europe. It was a tenet of mercantilism that restrictions should be imposed on the export of raw materials and the import of goods that could be produced locally, in order to assure the consumption of domestic products. The application of this policy, however, invariably worked to the detriment of the economically less developed countries in the Austrian Empire—such as Transylvania—and to the advantage of the hereditary Habsburg provinces. The Viennese court saw Transylvania as a marketplace for Austrian manufactured goods and as a supplier of raw materials for industries in the crown countries.

Austrian attempts to stop the import of certain products that Transylvania needed and the export of products of which Transylvania had a surplus failed, however, because of the economic interdependence of Transylvania, Moldavia, and Țara Românească. The links among these three countries continued to be very strong; there was no break in the import of hides, wool, and livestock from the other side of the Carpathians, or in the export of iron and glass articles, linen, hemp, and woolen cloth, leather goods, rope, and so on. The value of exports from Transylvania to Țara Românească and Moldavia exceeded the value of imports, which meant a gradual improvement in the Transylvanian balance of trade. To encourage the exchange of goods, the Oriental Company was founded in 1719 and the Commercial Society in 1723. Their purpose was to sell domestic products abroad and expedite goods in transit. They did not achieve the expected results, however, because the eastern trade was for the most part controlled by Greek, Armenian, and Bulgarian merchants from the Ottoman Empire and from Țara Românească.

In the first half of the eighteenth century, the Habsburgs became particularly concerned with mining. Especially after the loss of Silesia in 1764, Transylvania had the richest metal resources of any imperial province, and mining operations therefore were expanded. Alongside the traditional peasant mines, there was an increasing use of modern methods and technologies. The Austrians established mining bureaus in the Banat, the Bihor Mountains, and elsewhere, whose mission was to maximize the state's mining revenues. Surface deposits worked by serf labor gradually gave way to underground mines which, to an increasing extent, used paid workers. Private capital became ever more involved in mining; companies were formed with both the Austrian and the local bourgeoisie as stockholders. Hired labor, capital investment, the introduction of superior technology, and the use of child labor signaled the emergence of capitalism in mining, a development carried even further as the feudal system declined in the second half of the eighteenth century.

The Habsburg state also intervened to establish a number of factories in Transylvania, although only for purposes which would not compete with Austrian products. Thus the earliest were set up to process ore in the crown territory of the Banat, at Reşiţa and Bocşa for iron ore, and at Dognecea and Ciclova for copper. Others made goods from local raw materials, such as cloth in Caransebeş and Timişoara, leather and tapestries in Timişoara, and glass in Călina. Paper mills were founded at Gheorgheni and Făgăraş, glassworks at Porumbacul de Jos, and ironworks at Hunedoara. Following the state's example, a number of noblemen established small factories on their estates in order to manufacture goods from local raw materials. In Timişoara, Sighişoara, and Gherla, local merchants also set up factories in the mid-eighteenth century, although these never became very large.

In factories run by the state and by the nobility, the work force was composed primarily of serfs, who provided what amounted to involuntary labor; they were paid only a small sum in money and in kind. In addition, there was a small class of hired workers, specialists who in most cases were brought in from other countries. All of the workers were paid in the merchant factories. It might be said, therefore, that the noble factories were somewhat feudal in character, the merchant factories primarily capitalistic; those run by the state represented a transitional form between feudalism and capitalism. The growth of capitalistic forms in manufacturing presaged the development of capitalism in the following century, and contributed greatly to the decline of feudalism.

The development of production and the general economic growth of the country made more extensive domestic trade possible, in which the towns of Transylvania, especially Cluj, played a more and more significant role. Romanian, Saxon, Greek, and Armenian merchants were all involved in this trade.

For a number of reasons, including the needs of domestic markets, the supplying of the Austrian army and official class, and the growth of the nonagricultural population, grain production also rose in the first half of the eighteenth century. This profited the nobility, who used every opportunity to increase the holdings that they controlled directly and worked with the *robota* of serfs. The increase in these lands was accomplished both by dispossessing the peasantry of their plots of land and by restricting rights of use in forests and pastures. This process was even seen in the so-called Fundus Regius, where small peasant properties predominated; there were numerous cases of Romanian peasants dispossessed and even banished by the officials of the towns or Saxon seats. In the Szekler seats, the same usurpations occurred, as the last remnants of communal organization were destroyed.

The territory of the Banat, declared a crown domain in 1718, was administered in accordance with the interests of the Viennese court. German, Italian, French, Spanish, and Bulgarian colonists were brought in to populate the region and given the most fertile land. This colonization served both to consolidate Habsburg rule in the region and to put the extensive tracts of uncultivated land into production. More rational land use was attempted, and cotton and rice crops were introduced. But even if agriculture was rationalized in certain regions of Transylvania, the continued existence of the *robota* system robbed the peasants of initiative and profit.

Social Change

Since the Austrian treasury had been depleted as a result of numerous wars with the Turks, the court sold property and titles of nobility to foreigners who settled in Transylvania and the Banat. Though the ranks of the aristocracy were thus swelled, the power of the old feudal lords was weakened by the competition of the newly ennobled, who collaborated with Vienna. Some of them received titles in return for their support, while others were put in charge of customs or other royal offices which afforded major sources of income. The peasants' situation, meanwhile, grew steadily worse, partly because of the sheer size of the privileged class. At the beginning of the eighteenth century, the Transylvanian nobility represented 4.4 percent of the total population, but thanks to the Habsburg policy, the proportion was 6.7 percent by 1767. This was the largest noble class of its time in Europe. However, the nobility still was not a homogeneous group. A small part was the high nobility, the magnates; then came the middle nobility, the landed gentry; these were followed by the petty nobility, who had little or no land. For the most part the first two groups were composed of Hungarian nobles, while the ranks of the petty nobility included many Romanians as well.

The free peasantry—including mine workers—amounted to only 20.5 percent of the population at the beginning of the eighteenth century. This class included Romanians, Magyars, Saxons, and, especially in the mines, other groups. The great majority of the peasants were serfs—73.23 percent of the total population. They were primarily Romanian, and then Magyar; in the eighteenth century the number of Szekler serfs grew, but there were still only a few Saxon serfs, concentrated in a few counties. The serf class was composed of the two older categories, namely, serfs in the strict sense of the word (those with their own property on the lord's domain), and jeleri (those who had no land of their own and worked on the nobleman's property). As the peasantry grew poorer, a new category known as *vagi* appeared in contemporary documents. These were peasants who moved from place to place in order to make a living.

Town-dwellers made up 2.8 percent of the population. They were tradesmen, merchants, and the urban poor who worked in factories.

The peasants' two masters—the nobility and the Austrian state—cooperated in oppressing their subjects. The imperial treasury burdened them with the usual taxes, plus military contributions and other special levies; at the same time they still owed work, money, and produce to the feudal lords. In 1714 the diet set the number of days of *robota* at four per week for serfs and three for jeleri. All members of the peasant family who were able to work were subject to this obligation, especially when there were pressing agricultural tasks. The Urbarial Law of 1769 (known as "Certain Points," *Certa puncta*), which governed relations between the serfs and the nobility, set the obligation at four days a week for hand work and three days for work with animals; the jeleri's obligation dropped to two days a week. But many nobles reinterpreted the law, and, when the demands of agricultural work were high, forced the serfs to spend four days a week with animals and three days working with their hands—in other words, every day of the week. Serfs continued to be obliged to give the landlord one-tenth of all agricultural products, with the only exceptions being the products of their own household gardens. One-tenth of the total production of animals also was required. The third major obligation in Transylvania was the "census," which could be required either in money or in kind. Peasants also had to give tribute in kind three times a year, of grain, fowl, butter, eggs, honey, fish, and lambs, or even of large animals. Furthermore, the peasantry paid use taxes on pasture-land, forests, taverns, slaughterhouses, and mills, as well as hunting, fishing, and acorn-gathering fees. In general, the lords monopolized anything that could increase their own incomes and sold it for money to the peasants.

The state of affairs was very worrisome to the imperial court, which feared that the peasants would no longer be able to pay their taxes to the state or would flee the country. Joseph II was full of indignation when he reported to the state council and to his mother, Empress Maria Theresa,

> Conscience compels me to emphasize that Transylvania is a fine and beautiful country, but in need of immediate help and radical reform. Mere improvements are not enough, as the nobles' mentality is totally corrupt. . . . They are all trying to defend their privileges, and they do whatever they want to their subjects. . . . The Magyar nobility is not afraid of anything in the world, except reductions to their income and curbs on their privileges. They increase their power as much as possible, in any way possible, so as to exploit their serfs more fully. The serfs are essentially slaves; they have no way to defend themselves, and must work as much as their master says, wherever and whenever he wants. No wonder whole villages are ready to move to Moldavia.

The court itself was concerned with finding ways to increase its own revenues. The Treasury demanded from the peasants a whole assortment of taxes on crops, animals, households, and income, as well as a head tax. What made the state obligations more burdensome was that increasingly they had to be paid in money, which the peasants generally lacked. In addition to taxes paid to the treasury, there were also military contributions, significant sums of money and large amounts of food and fodder. In

1714, for example—a war year, it is true—Transylvania's military tax was 600,000 Rhenish florins, of which 455,547 were to be paid in money, and the rest in tens of thousands of bushels of grain and bales of hay. The Austrians introduced yet another tax to support its public officials, which came to 50,000 florins, and additional obligations to individual communities and counties. The peasants justifiably complained that "the emperor's taxes on us are so great that we can no longer bear them." The taxes to the treasury averaged out to as much as five florins per year per taxpayer, which was the price of six bushels of wheat or a two-year-old bull. Finally, in villages where soldiers were quartered, the abuses by the army were disastrous.

In response to these conditions, antifeudal and anti-Habsburg activities on the part of the serfs ranged from complaints to the authorities all the way to outright rebellion. When repeated complaints brought no results, the peasantry began to lose faith in the procedure and even in the emperor, although they had once considered him "a good man" and "understanding" of their hardships—a belief that was ably promoted by imperial propaganda. Other forms of peasant resistance included refusing to perform *robota* and hiding or withholding animals from official enumerations. Massive numbers of peasants continued to flee or move to other estates. Moving was encouraged by lords who offered peasants easier conditions; after they had moved, however, conditions soon became harsh once again, sometimes even harsher than those the peasants had fled. Especially after the expulsion of the Turks, a significant number of peasants from more mountainous regions went looking for places to settle in the less populous plains of Hungary and the Banat. Fugitive peasants, despite the severe punishments with which they were threatened and the strict watch kept on the borders, went primarily to Moldavia and Țara Românească.

Uprisings also multiplied, for the peasantry was rebelling against the nobility as much as against Austrian rule. In the first decades of the eighteenth century, there were numerous local rebellions from the Banat to the Bihor Mountains. These uprisings broke out sporadically throughout the area and took the most varied forms. Religious movements against the union spread across southern Transylvania, from around Brașov to Făgăraș, from there to Sibiu, and thence to Țara Hațegului. Bold priests and peasants died in Austrian dungeons for the same "impermissible" deeds. Elsewhere the discontent emerged in rebellions which had social causes and took on religious forms; these occurred from one corner of Transylvania to another, and were led by both clerics and laymen. Romanians belonging to both the Orthodox and the Uniate churches were involved, which suggests that the real causes were feudal and Habsburg oppression, not religion.

In the Banat and around Arad, discontent was aroused when the militiamen lost the so-called Illyrian privileges that had been granted to them when the military borders were set up in 1699, and they thereby became subject to taxation. This unrest, together with the pressures for conversion to Roman Catholicism, resulted in 1735 in a revolt led by Pitr Seghedinaţ. The uprising quickly spread to southwestern Transylvania, involving both Romanians and Hungarians. The movement represented an effort to revive the time of the Curuts, in that it was directed against Catholicism but almost equally aimed at feudalism. When the rebel leaders were captured, they were broken on the rack, and some of their troops were hanged.

The harsh punishment of these rebels could not prevent the outbreak of similar revolts. In the Banat, the Romanian masses were aroused not only by the oppression of the Habsburg authorities and the feudal lords, but more specifically by the court's policy of importing colonists, who were primarily Catholic and German. The Habsburg goal, of course, was to Catholicize and Germanize the region, but the cost of transporting the settlers had to be borne by the local populace. Moreover, the natives were heartlessly driven out of the most productive lands and replaced by the new arrivals. The colonists enjoyed all sorts of immunities and privileges, while the burdens fell solely on the shoulders of the original inhabitants.

When a new war with the Turks broke out and the Habsburgs brought many troops to the Banat in 1737, the discontent grew into a major revolt, taking in a wide area and substantial numbers of peasants. Rebel bands attacked the Austrian army everywhere during the winter of 1737–38. In the spring of 1738, the revolt grew and was directed at the army, imperial institutions, and the colonists. There were full-scale battles between the rebels and the imperial army in Lugoj, Caransebeş, Slatina, Bănia, and elsewhere. New imperial troops were brought in and began a ruthlessly repressive campaign, making no distinction between those who had participated in the revolt and those who had not. Dozens of villages were burned to the ground, and women and children were given no quarter. The only positive result of the rebellion was that colonization was halted for forty years.

The peasantry's resistance to Catholicism, at first local and spontaneous, became a general movement in 1744. The Serbian monk Visarion Sarai found conditions in Transylvania favorable for a mass uprising. As a result, his simple sermons, though preached in Serbian, a language not understood by the people, nevertheless had the effect of channeling the discontent to such an extent that the whole country was soon in revolt. Visarion's arrest and imprisonment in a dungeon in the Tirol could not stem the popular tide. In the summer of 1759, therefore, Maria Theresa felt compelled to issue a decree of toleration which recognized the legal existence of the Orthodox religion in Transylvania. The intention, however, was simply to gain time in order to take more drastic measures.

In the fall of 1759, the revolt erupted again, under the leadership of the monk Sophronie (Stan Popovici), who was from Cioara in southern Transylvania. Beginning in the Hunedoara area, it soon spread to the neighboring county of Alba. Sophronie's capture in December 1759, far from demoralizing his followers, strengthened their resolution. They faced the army sent to put them down and freed the monk, whereupon the action spread to Zarand and all of southern Transylvania. The authorities reported to the Viennese court, "It is possible that this country could catch fire in an instant and be reduced to ashes." The center of the unrest moved to the Bihor Mountains, where the inhabitants generally were unhappy over their heavy obligations to the state and restrictions on their forest rights. In April 1760, Sophronie led a large crowd into Zlatna, and other troops led by captains chosen by the peasantry occupied Abrud and Cîmpeni. The peasants now considered themselves in control of the situation, declaring that "the time of the landlords' power has passed, and we are now the masters." Sophronie sent ultimatums to the imperial military commanders, threatening that "unless our requests and wishes are fulfilled, then because of the many trials and hardships we have endured, we will no longer follow a single order."

The course of events in Transylvania worried not only the local authorities, but also the Viennese court, where it was feared that "this spark, ignited by religious causes, [will] become a great conflagration." The situation for Austria was especially bad, because it was involved at the time in the Seven Years' War with Prussia.

The revolt had achieved great momentum when the people of the Bihor Mountains faced the troops at Zlatna, and the masses planned to extend the action to the other parts of the country. Sophronie, however, fearful of the extent to which the rebellion had grown, attempted to rein in the people's revolutionary zeal, advising them to keep the peace and trying to turn their attention from social problems to confessional ones. His negotiations with Austrian representatives meant the breakdown of the rebellion, and the capture and punishment of its leaders and participants brought it to an end in the spring of 1761.

In the first half of the eighteenth century, the struggle of the peasant masses was often intertwined with that of the miners and factory workers. This is entirely understandable, as these workers maintained their close links to the peasantry and continued to farm and raise animals. Once capitalist features began to appear in mining and manufacturing, however, the workers' struggle began to take on anticapitalist forms, such as resistance to the introduction of technological innovations that brought a lowering of average wages. One example of the fight against new machinery was that recorded in 1726, in Baia Sprie, when the workers refused to return to work until the ore crushers and furnaces that had been installed in the mine were abandoned. Elsewhere unrest was brought on "because of small earnings and low wages," as happened in the mines in the Banat in 1733. The leaders of that rebellion were sentenced to several months of chaingang labor on the fortifications. This sentence, meant as "an example to the other workers," did not have the intended effect; the workers continued their struggle even more boldly and killed the mine foremen, whom they regarded as tools of their oppressors. Severe punishment was meted out to the rebels, especially their leaders, who were tortured with hot irons before being quartered or broken on the rack. Yet not even these reprisals discouraged the mineworkers, who either alone or, as in 1784, in alliance with the peasants, continued their resistance.

Population

The economic and social changes in Transylvania were reflected in the demographic situation. The data presented in various contemporary reports, especially in the earliest conscription records assembled about this time, give us a more accurate picture of the demography of Transylvania in the first half of the eighteenth century than we have for earlier periods. There was some population growth, but not as much as might be expected. The explanation lies first of all in the devastation caused by the endless warfare of the late seventeenth and early eighteenth centuries, and second in the continued loss of population across the Carpathians. Nor should one ignore the high mortality rate— particularly infant mortality—due to inadequate sanitation.

Several official reports concerning the union of part of the Romanians with the Catholic church in 1700 put the number of those accepting the union at 200,000. It is known, however, that the Romanian population of the principality (that is, without the Banat, Crișana, and Maramureș) was much larger. This fact is confirmed by all the conscriptions in the first half of the eighteenth century. According to the conscription of 1733, there were 462,465 Romanians in the principality, while according to that of 1750 there were 578,382. These conscriptions were not censuses in the modern sense of the term, but only partial estimates of the Romanian population, and the figures thus should not be considered exact, a fact which also explains the large discrepancy between the different estimates. How many inhabitants of the other nationalities there were is not known with any accuracy. However, the approximate proportions of the cohabiting peoples in the Transylvanian population is known from the conscription of 1760–62, which reported that about 66 percent were Romanian, 21 percent Hungarian and Szekler, and 11 percent Saxon.

These figures correspond entirely to the statements of contemporary observers who were well acquainted with the demographic situation. The Jesuit priest Freiberger, in a report addressed to the Viennese court in 1701, wrote, "The Romanians are found all over Transylvania, even among the Szeklers and in the Saxon seats and territories. There is not a village, town, or suburb without Romanians." In 1766, the learned Hungarian polymath Jozsef Benkö likewise commented, "The Romanian population is so large that it not only equals but much surpasses that of all the other ethnic groups in Transylvania put together." This fact was also acknowledged in the highest circles in Vienna; in 1748, Maria Theresa, addressing the clergy, nobility, and Romanian inhabitants of every status and circumstance, referred to Transylvania as "our Romanian principality."

As for the Banat, we can rely on a conscription from 1743,

which recorded communities according to the ethnic background of their inhabitants. This record shows five times as many Romanian communities as Serbian ones, and suggests a proportion of about 72 percent Romanian villages, 22 percent Serbian villages, and 7 percent village inhabited by other groups. The Hungarian historian and geographer Mátyás Bél, who studied the Banat between 1720 and 1730, reported that even in Timişoara, the political, administrative, economic, and cultural center of the region, the Romanian language was widely spoken ("sermo valachus Temesvarini est vulgatius").

9

The Dawn of the Modern Era

The Enlightenment

THE EIGHTEENTH CENTURY has been characterized by Michelet as "the Great Century" (*le Grand Siècle*). While his phrase perhaps exaggerates the creative energy, it offers a fair assessment of the creative works. Prodigious developments in the exact sciences were crowned by achievements in the humanities. Mankind inquired, probed, learned, and became convinced that ignorance was disappearing. The Great Century represented the ideology of a new social group, a group which considered itself entitled by its economic position to political and cultural dominance. This was, of course, the bourgeoisie. The bourgeoisie associated itself with other deprived groups, the peasants and the workers, at least to the extent of bringing them into the fight against those who had until then been the recipients of most of society's benefits—the nobility and the clergy.

The bourgeoisie was rationalist, positivist, and utilitarian. Human reason should discover the natural laws governing society, and society should be organized for the happiness of mankind. It followed that men had the right to elect the form of government that guaranteed them their rights. Moreover, continued human progress depended on the spread of enlightenment. Education, the most important component of progress, was to be natural and practical, with studies in the language of the country, modern history, geography, natural history, mathematics, physics, and manual training. It should be accessible to all, for the principle of the French Encyclopedists was that "the truth is simple, and can always be put within everyone's reach."

Transylvanian culture in this period reflected the economic and political changes that were taking place throughout Europe. Prominent Transylvanians spoke out against the contemporary educational system, which the Austrian court tried to use as an instrument of domination and Catholicization (through legislation such as the *Ratio Educationis* of 1777 and the *Norma Regia* of 1781). Romanian, Hungarian, and even German teachers urged that Latin and German, the languages of instruction promoted by the Viennese court, be replaced by the Transylvanians' mother tongues—Romanian, Hungarian, and German.

After overcoming much opposition and resistance, the Romanians did succeed in founding many elementary schools. One of the distinguished figures in this effort was Gheorghe Şincai, the director of the Greek Catholic schools in Transylvania, who founded approximately three hundred schools in as many villages. Two other important founders were Dimitrie Eustatievici, director of the Orthodox Romanian schools, and Teodor Iancovici, director of the Romanian schools in the Banat. Numerous other schools were founded in Transylvania around this time, including Latin-language secondary schools (later transformed into Romanian, Hungarian, and German schools) in Oradea and Beiuş in northwestern Transylvania; a normal school in Arad in southwestern Transylvania; and an agronomy school in Sînnicolau Mare in the Banat. There were also various higher institutions: the Romanian seminary at Blaj, the Academy of Law in Oradea, and the Surgical Institute in Cluj.

The fight for educational reform was supported by excellent scholarly work. Progressive historians and linguists—men such as the Romanian Radu Tempea from Braşov, the Hungarian Péter Bod, and the Saxons Johannes Seiwert and Johannes Filstich—waged an ongoing battle against feudal ideas. The old order was effectively undermined by the many cultural innovations and achievements in the spirit of the Enlightenment: schools at all levels; textbooks, grammars, and dictionaries for both school and private use; original works, especially in history and philology; and translations, adaptations, and abridgments of the works of the boldest thinkers of the age. The collapsing feudal society was in the midst of a crisis from which it could not escape. The great popular rebellions, such as Horia's in Transylvania and Tudor Vladimirescu's in Ţara Românească, would make this abundantly clear. The new ideology undermined the old system's ideological foundations, the peasant revolt of 1784 its social foundations, and the *Supplex* national movement of 1790–91 its political ones. The leaders of the national movement were exponents of the national ideology,

Gate of the fortress at Alba Iulia (early eighteenth century).

learned historians and philologists such as Samuil Micu, Gheorghe Şincai, Petru Maior, Ioan Molnar-Piuariu, Ioan Budai-
Deleanu, Paul Iorgovici, and Gheorghe Lazăr.

The ideas introduced in the first half of the eighteenth century
by the tireless and courageous Bishop Inocenţiu Micu were
greatly strengthened in the works of the militant scholars of the
late eighteenth and early nineteenth centuries; Şincai, Maior,
Molnar-Piuariu, and Budai-Deneanu in Transylvania, and Gheorghe Lazăr (originally a Transylvanian), Dionisie Eclesiarhul,
Zilot Românul, Dinicu Golescu, Ioniţă Tăutu, and Eufrosin Poteca in Moldavia and Ţara Românească. For all these and others,
the pen was a political weapon. Their actions were dominated
by the idea of the social and ethnic emancipation of the Romanian people. Moreover, national consciousness no longer was restricted to a small group of scholars and intellectuals, but had
reached the masses, who were now pursuing the same goals.

The "Transylvanian School" developed the ideas of the great
seventeenth-century chroniclers from Moldavia and Ţara Românească, in particular those of Dimitrie Cantemir, a humanist and
pre-Enlightenment scholar and prince of Moldavia. The representatives of the school focused their ideas and their scholarly
and political work on the most important questions: the origin,
continuity, and unity of the Romanian people. Their zealous
defense of their cause occasionally led them to exaggerations—
for example, they asserted that the Romanian people were of
purely Roman origin, and the Romanian language purely Latin.
Some of their other ideas, however, were entirely correct, as
they sought to demonstrate the continuity of the Daco-Roman
people in Dacia, the ethnic unity of the Romanian people, and
the Romanian people's right to their own national life. The tireless activity of these scholars had as its final goal the complete
emancipation of the Romanian people. Samuil Micu, for example, took aim at anachronistic institutions and at those who
had created and defended them, both in his practical activities
and in such scholarly works as *Scurtă cunoştinţă a istoriei
românilor* [A brief account of the history of the Romanians] and
Istoria, lucrurile şi întîmplările românilor [History, works, and
deeds of the Romanians].

The fruit of all the scholarly work of the Transylvanian School
was the foundation for the Romanian national movement. The
Enlightenment ideology ignored artifical political boundaries,
both in the way it spread and in its concern for the Romanian

people. Micu, Șincai, Maior, Budai-Deleanu, and Lazăr fought to raise the people from their condition, urging them to unify and pointing the way back to the ancient glory of their Roman ancestors. Micu, Budai-Deleanu, and Maior emphasized the need for unification of the Romanian countries if the Romanians were to progress, again drawing on the Romanians' glorious past in urging them to fight for freedom. Convinced that Romanians had a right to a new place in economic, social, political, and cultural life, because of their numbers, because of their contribution to the material and military preservation of society, and because of their historic past, some proposed to achieve these goals through reforms instituted from above, while others advocated revolution. Two leading representatives of the Romanian Enlightenment, Paul Iorgovici and Gheorghe Șincai, were involved in the Jacobin movement, and both were severely punished.

In 1795, through the efforts of the same Iorgovici and of Molnar-Piuariu, the Philosophical Society of the Romanian People in the Grand Principality of Ardeal was founded; in its membership and its concerns, it went beyond the boundaries of Transylvania and took in the other two Romanian countries as well. Indeed, emancipation of all Romanians was equally important to the major Enlightenment scholars in Țara Românească and Moldavia. Șincai's *Hronica Românilor și a mai multor neamuri* [Chronicle of the Romanians and of several peoples] and Maior's *Istoria pentru începutul românilor din Dachia* [History of the beginnings of the Romanians in Dacia] were read avidly; these works had an inestimable effect on such well-known nineteenth-century Romanian scholars as Costache Negruzzi, Ioan Heliade Rădulescu, and Petrache Poenaru, as these writers testify. Equally influential were *Scurtă cunoștință a istoriei românilor* [Brief account of the history of the Romanians] and *Istoria, lucrurile și întîmplările românilor* [History, works and deeds of the Romanians], both by Samuil Micu, Ioan Budai-Deleanu's, *Țiganiada* [Gypsy saga] and his Latin works, *De originibus populorum Transilvaniae* and *Fundamenta grammaticae linguae romanicae*, and Petru Maior's *Disertație pentru începutul limbii române* [Dissertation on the origins of the Romanian language].

Just as important was the activity in Moldavia and Țara Românească of a significant number of Transylvanian intellectuals, led by Gheorghe Lazăr, the founder of national education in the latter country. Dionisie Eclesiarhul and Dinicu Golescu painted a devastating picture of the peasants' suffering under the boyars and of their country's suffering under foreign domination. Eufrosin Poteca, a student of Gheorghe Lazăr's analyzed the social situation and concluded that monarchs who strayed from the interests of the people should not be recognized. The ideas contained in the Proclamation of Padeş and in other documents of the 1821 revolution in Ţara Românească—which were to no small extent the work of Lazar himself, the mentor and adviser of Tudor Vladmirescu—appear again in the protest writings of Zilot Românul and even more strongly in those of Ioniţă Tăutu, who at the time was urging armed revolt as the way to social and political change.

As men of the Enlightenment, the leaders of the Transylvanian School knew that it was important to fight to extricate the masses from the ignorance and illiteracy in which they had been kept by the exploiting classes. The best means of achieving this goal, in addition to founding village schools for the children of the peasantry, was to prepare textbooks for those schools and for the already existing city schools. Gheorghe Şincai wrote primers and arithmetic books; Samuil Micu prepared texts on logic, ethics, and politics; Petru Maior was personally involved in teaching children. Works like Micu's philosophical texts or Şincai's *Istoria naturii sau a firii* [Natural history] and *Invătătură firească spre surparea superstiţiilor norodului* [Lessons in science to overcome folk superstitions] taught rationalist and materialist modes of thought. One must also mention Micu's contribution to the coining of Romanian philosophical terminology and Şincai's efforts to devise terms for scientific notations based mostly on native Romanian words. These concerns sprang from the scholars' need to make themselves understood by those for whom they were writing.

Another means by which the Enlightenment writers in Transylvania hoped to educate the masses was the publication of books on practical economic matters. The first such work printed in Transylvania was Ioan Molnar-Piuariu's *Economia stupilor* [Beehive economy] in 1785. Şincai published *Povăţuire cătră economia de cîmp* [Advice on farming] in 1806, and Grigore Obradovici, the director of the Romanian schools in the Banat, translated useful books on agriculture. In addition to offering practical economic advice, these works also dealt with more general matters, giving instructions on how to read and master their contents. Along these lines we may also mention Micu and Maior's *Calendarele* [Almanacs], which had historical supplements designed to spread the doctrines of the Transylvanian School to a larger circle of readers.

The term "Transylvanian School," however, should not be understood to apply only to its four leading members. Many other scholars in other towns, including Oradea, Braşov, and Sibiu, enriched the nation's cultural heritage with their work. They were guided by the same ideas and in some cases helped to develop them. The poetic works of Dimitrie Tichindeal, Vasile Aaron, and Ioan Barac, even though artistically undistinguished, nevertheless contributed to the cultivation of the language and the enlightenment of the people. Ioan Molnar-Piuariu's rich and varied works, which included a grammar, dictionary, rhetoric, and economic and historical writings, entitle him to a place among the most important representatives of the Transylvanian Enlightenment of the late eighteenth century.

The historical and philological concerns of the school were carried on by Damaschin Bojnică, Radu Tempea, Paul Iorgovici, and Constantin Diaconovici-Loga. Bojincă, who was from the Banat, translated some of Petru Maior's polemical works, and was himself the author of a similar reply in defense of the ideas of the Transylvanian School; later he wrote *Vestitele fapte şi perirea lui Mihai Viteazul* [The celebrated deeds and death of Michael the Brave] and a treatise on practical pedagogy, *Diregătorul bunei creşteri* [Guide to good upbringing]. Tempea, from Braşov, was primarily concerned with philological matters, as can be seen from his grammar of 1797, in which he attempted to Romanianize grammatical terminology. Iorgovici and Diaconovici-Loga, both from the Banat, were also philologists; the former's *Observaţii de I. R.* [Observations on the Romanian language] tends toward Latinist exaggeration, while the latter's *Gr. Românească pt. îndreptarea tinerilor* [Romanian grammar for the instruction of youth] is also concerned with Romanianizing grammatical terms.

Vasile Pop, from Braşov, wrote the first Romanian *Diplomatarium*, with documents pertaining to all three Romanian countries (1821–24). Another of Pop's works, *Disertaţie despre tipografiile româneşti* [Dissertation on Romanian publications], is a valuable investigation of old Romanian literature and contains excellent ideas about the importance of the language in the formation of the nation. "A nation," he wrote, "naturally cannot be divided by high mountains, broad rivers, or other political boundaries." Contemporary with Pop was Ioan Monorai, from Arad, who was the author of a history of Transylvania containing a lengthy, dramatic, and somewhat sympathetic description of Horia's revolt. Another writer of the time was the Hungarian György Bessenyei, whose rich and varied oeuvre, influenced by French materialism, rather inconsistently expressed materialist ideas on the world and society. He strongly criticized feudalism and Catholicism in one work, which was adapted into French as *Système de la nature.* Similar ideas were found in the works of other Transylvanian scholars of the late eighteenth and early nineteenth centuries. Paul Iorgovici, who was in Paris at the time of the Jacobin dictatorship, professed radical Enlightenment ideas in his *Observații de I. R.;* it contains hints of advanced social and political thought and even materialist elements, ideas for which he was imprisoned.

The most forward-looking social and political ideas of the time, however, are to be found in Ioan Budai-Deleanu's Gypsy saga, which indicts clericalism in any faith, feudalism, the bureaucratic mentality, and the monarchy. The work expresses, in the strongest terms, the ideas of Rousseau, Voltaire, Robespierre, and Saint-Just, the avant-garde of the day. It calls for social emancipation through the abolition of feudalism, and national liberation through the removal of Ottoman and Habsburg domination; these ends are to be reached by armed struggle on the part of the masses, and by the replacement of the army and of feudal justice with a popular militia and people's justice.

The struggle against feudalism and the exploitation of the masses is reflected even more vividly in Transylvanian folk poetry of the eighteenth and early nineteenth centuries. Satirical poetry attacks the ways of the Hungarian nobles and the Orthodox priests, contrasting them with the behavior of the common people. Love songs and domestic ballads shed light on the social inequalities in village life; exploitation by the nobility and wealthy burghers is clearly seen in songs about taxes and poverty. Laments and ballads of haiduks (as, for instance, Pintea the Brave) exhort their audience not to give up the battle against oppression. The eighteenth-century peasant revolts, which left profound traces on the life of the people, were immortalized in popular lyrics and historical songs. The bloody suppression of the Szekler rebellion of 1764 also is reflected in these songs, and the great popular uprising of 1784, led by Horea, Cloşca, and

Crişan, gave rise to a veritable wealth of popular literature in which the rebel leaders are presented as warriors for freedom and social justice. The folk poetry of the Romanians, Hungarians, and even the Saxons have many themes and traits in common, since the lives and socioeconomic situations of the masses of all three peoples were similar.

As the eighteenth century drew to a close, the intellectual ferment continued. Páriz Pápai compiled a Latin-Hungarian dictionary and Teodor Corbea a Latin-Romanian one; Eustatievici produced his *Gramatica Românească*, and Micu and Şincai their *Elementa linguae daco-romane sive valachicae*. The bourgeois intelligentsia fought to organize progressive cultural institutions in the most important cities. A society to develop the Hungarian language in Transylvania was founded in 1793, on the initiative of György Aranka; it dealt not only with linguistic matters, but with scholarship in general. The same goals were adopted by the Philosophical Society of the Romanian People, founded in 1795 by Ioan Molnar-Piuariu, and by the Saxon Society of Dedicated Historians of Transylvania, which developed from earlier reading societies. These educational advances were followed up by Sándor Bölöni Farkas, who worked tirelessly in many fields. The theater, which had its beginnings around the end of the century, was dedicated to educating the townspeople and spreading new ideas through dramatic works in Romanian, Hungarian, and German. A significant impact also was made by the great libraries founded around this time in Sibiu, Alba Iulia, Tîrgru Mureş, and other places.

The printing press further served to spread the new ideas, although the Austrian censors strictly watched over newspapers to make sure that no ideas appeared which might be dangerous to the dominant class and the Habsburg monarchy. Publications appeared in Romanian, Hungarian, and German, such as the *Siebenbürger Zeitung* (1784); *Siebenbürger Bote* (1792); *Erdélyi magyar hirvivö* [Transylvanian Hungarian, 1790]; *Erdélyi Múzeum* [Transylvanian museum; 1814]; *Biblioteca românească* [Romanian library; 1821]. A few issues of Molnar-Piuariu and Iorgovici's *Gazeta* for the peasants, and of *Vestirile filosefeşti şi moraliceşti* [Philosophical and moral information], published for the Romanians in Ţara Românească and Moldavia as well as in Transylvania, appeared in 1795. These publications contained a wide variety of articles on language, literature, science, art, eco-

Romanian peasants in Transylvania.

nomics, and politics. Zaharia Carcalechi's *Biblioteca româ-nească* also circulated in all these Romanian countries.

As a result of the social and economic changes during the century, a number of new scholarly disciplines developed whose findings could be used as weapons against the feudal order and for the country's economic progress. The Hungarian linguistic studies of Sámuel Gyarmathi and Sándor Csoma Körösi, for example, were particularly concerned with the origins of the Hungarian people and language, while Johannes Seiwert and others studied the Saxon dialects. Legal studies were often used in political battles and in antifeudal and anti-Habsburg ideology; a good example is the work of Károly Szász, which is filled with the progressive thought of the Enlightenment and even of certain Encyclopedists. Historiography passed from the phase of simply chronicling events to that of researching and critically selecting original sources. Gh. Pray assembled a vast collection of documentary sources; another collector was Daniel Cornides, one of the first historians to treat sources critically. Jozsef Benkö, in his *Transsilvania*, demonstrated his great knowledge of Transylvanian history of the eighteenth century and earlier. Among Saxon historians were Martin Felmer, who wrote the first textbook on Transylvanian history, and I. C. Eder, who was the founder of Saxon critical history.

The Demographic Revolution

In the second half of the eighteenth century and the first half of the nineteenth, there was an appreciable increase in population in Transylvania, as in Europe in general. The situation represented a normal evolution from the preceding periods, in that the proportions among the different Transylvanian peoples remained about the same, with an absolute majority of Romanians. This is true despite the fact that documents of the time record a steady Romanian emigration to Moldavia and Țara Românească, with no significant movement in the opposite direction. For example, the Prussian ambassador to the Ottoman Empire reported in 1767 that 24,000 families had moved from Transylvania to the other Romanian countries in that year. In 1782 the number of Transylvanian families who paid taxes to the state in those two principalities rose to 13,000. The memorandum sent to the Viennese court in 1773 by the Romanians in

Transylvania is particularly eloquent: it says that the large number of Transylvanians emigrating was arousing such concern that the inhabitants of Moldavia and Țara Românească were seized with panic and had been heard to exclaim, "All Transylvania is moving here" ("Tota Transilvania ad nos venit").

Nonetheless, the written sources record, not a drop, but an increase in the Transylvanian population in the second half of the eighteenth century. These sources include conscription records and the testimony of local and foreign observers who knew the area well; it should always be remembered, however, that such sources are not always accurate. In any case, according to the report submitted to the court in 1772–73 by General Preiss, commander of the imperial army in Transylvania, the principality of Transylvania was made up of about 63 percent Romanians, 24 percent Hungarians and Szeklers, and 12 percent Saxons.

In the Banat, where the Austrians continued the massive colonization of various peoples during the latter part of the eighteenth century, the situation around 1772–80 was as follows: of 310,000 inhabitants, 181,000 (60 percent) were Romanian; 78,000 (25 percent) were Serbian; 43,000 (14 percent) were German, Italian, French, or other.

From all the statistics for the first half of the nineteenth century, including those from Austrian and Hungarian sources, we arrive at the same proportions in Transylvania, the Banat, Crişana, and Maramureş: Romanians constituted over 60 percent of the population. This was also the situation in every administrative unit except for a few Szekler seats, where naturally enough there was a majority of Szeklers. According to Sollner's statistics in 1844, the Romanians equaled 60 percent of the population of Transylvania, the Hungarians and Szeklers together 29 percent, the Germans 9 percent, and others 2 percent. His figures are confirmed by official Austrian statistics from 1850.

Analyzing these data, we can see two things very clearly: 1) the uniform distribution throughout Transylvania, except for three Szekler seats, of villages inhabited by Romanians; and 2) the presence of Romanians, living together with other populations in almost every village, so that there were few villages in Transylvania without some Romanian population. This state of affairs, attested by official records, also was observed by contemporary writers. The early nineteenth-century Austrian statistician J. A. Demian concluded his investigations by writing:

Among the older "nations," the Romanians, by their numbers, undeniably occupy first place. Their number may be estimated at around four-sevenths of the entire population. Compared to the Szeklers, Hungarians, and Saxons, the Romanian population is so disproportionately large that wherever the Romanians live together with the other groups, they take the latter's place immediately. They are found throughout the country, both in separate villages, or villages where they form half the population, and outside Hungarian, Szekler, and Saxon settlements. Following the Romanians, in terms of numbers, are the Szeklers, then the Saxons—who in 1790 numbered 76,548 families in the 130-square-mile area where they live—and finally the Hungarians. All others form only a small part of the total.

Further confirmation of the demographic scene in Transylvania before the 1848 revolution can be found in the work of the Hungarian historian L. Kőváry. In the counties of Transylvania, he wrote, lived more than 1 million Romanians and only 213,000 Hungarians. One could travel for days in Transylvania without hearing a single word of Hungarian; one would think one was in Țara Românească.

Obstacles to Modernization

The changes in social and economic life in Transylvania in the second half of the eighteenth century can be seen everywhere. They are most evident in mining and manufacturing, though they are not entirely lacking in agriculture. Agricultural development was blocked by the policies of a Viennese court interested in maintaining its ready access to Transylvanian agricultural products and its marketplace for the industrial products of its own hereditary provinces. Only in the period of the Napoleonic wars and of the continental blockade, when agricultural products were increasingly in demand, did circumstances favor the marketing of Transylvanian grain. Meanwhile, the cultivation of new crops and improved strains of old ones had favorable consequences, reminiscent of the results of the much earlier introduction of crop rotation and certain machines. In some cases, paid workers were used on large estates to supplement serf labor.

The growth of internal markets resulting from the general increase in population—and particularly from the growth of the

Saxon town-dwellers in Transylvania.

urban population—created a new demand for grain in the first half of the nineteenth century. The Transylvanian nobility therefore concentrated on grain production as a source of money income, which led them to increase their holdings and concentrate scattered properties, primarily through dispossessing serfs of all or part of their lands, and through seizing forests, pastures, and fields that peasants had cleared. Increased impoverishment meant that their contributions to the Austrian state fell off, and as a result the court grew concerned with regulating the relations between landlords and serfs. Attempts were made to curb the seizures of peasant land and to limit the number of days of involuntary labor. The nobility of course opposed the controls, and eventually a compromise—unfavorable to the peasantry—was reached. The urbarial regulation of 1759, kept the number of days of work at three per week for serfs with animals, four for serfs working with their hands, and two for jeleri; it left to the discretion of the landlord the amount of land to be retained by the peasants. The same rules were established in the Banat by the regulation of 1780. Yet landlords still did not abandon their custom of making unlimited use of serfs when they needed them for agricultural work during the spring and summer.

In his travels in Transylvania, Emperor Joseph II discovered numerous cases where whole families of serfs were forced to work all summer on the lord's property. Such abuses were also personally observed and reported by Gheorghe Șincai, the principal representative of the Transylvanian Enlightenment; in his chronicle, he emphasized the nobles' practice of forcing their dependent peasants to perform involuntary labor every day of the week.

The Uprising of 1784

The events of the summer of 1784 in Transylvania confirmed the opinion of most realistic observers that when "the bow is bent too far, it will surely break." The bow had indeed been bent to the limit of its resistance. The peasantry's discontent had long been building, until it reached the point where it could no longer be contained. *Robota* had been increased; taxes had been raised and had been extended to apply to all peasant property. Abuse and coercion by the nobility had gone too far.

No one knew these things better than those who bore the burden. The oppression the serfs endured was expressed simply but powerfully by Gheorghe Crişan, one of the leaders of the peasant revolt of 1784, when he was asked what had aroused the peasantry. "The landlords have saddled us with ever-greater burdens; some have taken our wheat and other grain, not to mention the tithe on everything. The only thing we do not pay for is water." The complaint continues: "Moreover, each of us must perform four days of work per week. The lords force us to bring them wood even on our holy day of Christmas; what do they care about our holidays, they ask!" Women and children were forced to do other tasks at the manor house, including spinning, weaving, caring for animals, and much more. Whenever a serf with any property died, his widow was locked up until she confessed the details of the inheritance, which was then taken away from her. She and her children were sent away to earn their daily bread however and wherever they could. Moreover, to the material oppression by the nobility and the imperial treasury was added religious oppression by the Catholic church. In response, the peasants intensified their struggle in various ways. In the Bihor Mountains, villages joined in confederations and offered community resistance to the authorities. Petitions and delegations were sent to the local authorities, to the Gubernium, and to the court. Peasants hid their draft animals, fled to the forest, and joined bands of haiduks. There were local uprisings, skirmishes with the army, and even revolts.

The time was ripe, and bold leaders were at hand. Horea and Closca, serfs from the Bihor Mountains, had already given expression to communal discontent on different occasions. Horea had emerged as a respected leader following an uprising on 24 May 1782 at the market square in Cîmpeni, an outbreak brought on when Armenian leaseholders destroyed some of the peasants' wares. Now the peasants decided to confront injustice with open revolt. Twenty-three of them were captured, but their imprisonment, mistreatment, and sentencing had the opposite effect from that the authorities expected. The encouragement Joseph II offered to Horea and his comrades in an audience on 1 April 1784 was taken by the peasants to mean that the emperor was on their side, and that only the Hungarian nobility opposed the measures designed to correct the existing injustices. The peasants therefore began to make plans to win their rights by force.

On 31 January 1784, an imperial patent was issued concerning military conscription in the villages along the border. The peasants, however, interpreted it as referring to the whole country, and, spurred by the desire to escape from serfdom, they streamed by thousands into the towns to enlist. Once enlisted, they considered themselves free men. They refused to fulfill their feudal obligations, threatened their landlords, and thought of taking over noble lands. There were incidents and disturbances everywhere. Yet the nobility did not heed the lesson. The mistreatment of the peasantry increased, and castle cellars were transformed into dungeons for bold peasants. The army was sent to terrorize villages.

These events only increased the peasants' resolve to match their strength with their perennial oppressors. The occasion presented itself in the autumn of 1784, when Crişan addressed the inhabitants of Ţara Zărandului and the peasants who were gathered at the market in Brad. Speaking in Horea's name, Crişan called on them to send representatives to an assembly to be held in Mesteacăn on 31 October 1784, where recent events would be discussed. Over six hundred people assembled, representing numerous villages in Zarand and the Abrud Mountains, and were urged to revolt. Their decision was exceptionally important, since they were aware that such a step would entail enormous consequences. Force of arms would now decide the age-old struggle between oppressor and oppressed.

On the way to Alba Iulia, where they were to receive arms, the peasants were attacked, on the night of 1 November, by soldiers under the vice-count of Zarand. The revolt then erupted in full force, and Crişan urged the peasants to wipe out the entire noble class. In five days, all of Zarand was engulfed in the flames of rebellion. From there the revolt spread in every direction: to the county of Hunedoara in the south; to the Bihor Mountains and thence toward Turda, Cluj, and Baia Mare and on as far as Maramureş in the north; to the country of Arad and on into the Banat in the west; and toward Alba Iulia and Sibiu in the east.

The center of the revolt was established in the Abrud Mountains. On 4 November, in the commune of Blăjeni, large numbers of peasants swore an oath before Horea to annihilate the nobility. Although it started in a purely Romanian region, the revolt spread to areas where the population was mixed, and the Hungarian serfs rebelled as well. Romanian, Hungarian, and Saxon miners joined the fight. The movement thus became much more complex, much more deeply rooted. On 8 Novem-

Title page of Petru Maior's *Istoria pentru începutul românilor in Da-chia (1812).*

ber, Horea called for a new assembly at Bucium, in order to inform the rebels of plans for future action.

While the original goal was escape from social and ethnic oppression, the program and final objectives of the revolt were clarified as events unfolded. In the minds of most progressive leaders, the objective of the struggle more and more was seen as the liquidation of the nobility as a class and the abolition of serfdom and of the feudal order in general. This was the intent of the so-called Ultimatum of 11 November 1784, addressed in Horea's name to some nobles who had sought refuge in the fortress of Deva. "Let the nobility henceforth cease to exist; instead, let every person earn his living from a job he receives from the emperor. Let the noble landlords abandon their estates forever, and the lands be distributed to the peasants according to the emperor's orders. Let the nobles pay taxes like the poor." Similar demands were included in the negotiations between the rebels and the authorities a few days later: peasants should be freed of serfdom and allowed to enlist in the border regiments, and those imprisoned in earlier uprisings should be freed. Subsequently, the peasants' representatives declared that Hungarian nobles and county officers would no longer be permitted in the country. The latter's place was to be taken by others, whom Horea would appoint.

In addition to the emancipation of the peasantry, the revolt of 1784 sought national emancipation for the Romanians. Certain of the leaders, notably Horea, even thought of uniting Transylvania with Țara Românească and Moldavia. The authorities had good reason to fear the links between Transylvanian Romanians and the peasantry across the Carpathians; the large number of those who had emigrated were still closely bound to their old homes. The connections were further maintained, and even strengthened, by the almost three hundred young Romanians from Transylvania who were studying in the other two Romanian lands. They could not remain indifferent to the decisive battle being fought by those at home. Many of the peasants who had left thought of returning, accompanied by Moldavian and Muntenian peasants. A few even seem to have put these thoughts into action. One of those who did may be Petru Muntean, the rebel captain in the Mureș region; there were others as well. It was presumably such occurrences that caused Joseph II to propose an understanding with the sultan on joint measures to prevent relations between peasants on opposite sides of the mountains. This agreement was easily reached, since the sultan was equally interested in preventing the spread of the revolt to the Romanian principalities, which were only uncertainly calm. The agreement proved useful. Many villages of rebels did try to cross the Carpathians, and though some succeeded in reaching Țara Românească, others met bloody interference at the frontier.

The measures taken by the Habsburgs and the Turks are attested in written sources. The Hungarian newspaper in Bratislava expressed the reality of the situation when it reported that the Romanians in the Banat and the Arad region were thinking of calling on the Muntenian peasants for help. The Reform priest of Turda, meanwhile, wrote that at the beginning of 1785, "the rebels were in contact with the neighboring countries . . . and expect help from them." He added that at the beginning of that year about thirty thousand Romanians from Moldavia had sought to invade Transylvania via the Ghimeș pass, but had been stopped and then put to flight by the Szeklers and the Turks.

In all of this and more, we can see not only the bonds of ethnic solidarity among the Romanians, but also their active awareness of their national identity, an awareness noted by contemporary writers. In the midst of the revolt, on 14 November, the priest of Aiud, Jańos Nemegyei, informed the authorities in Tîrgu Mureș that the village clerics were preaching "ideas of national liberation"; they were telling the "indigenous" people of the country that "the time [has] come to throw off the yoke." Other peasants in the Alba, Hunedoara, and Mureș areas declared that they wanted to obtain help from other countries, and they advanced the idea of electing "a new emperor" to replace the one in Vienna.

These were manifestations of a national consciousness which lived even in the lowest stratum of the population. It was experienced emotionally by some, intellectually by others, and was propagated by the boldest and most enlightened. The efforts, even in this period, to found as many village schools as possible sprang from the desire of the masses to learn and of the more educated to teach them. Gheorghe Șincai, who directed the Romanian Greek Catholic schools from 1782 to 1794 (and thus during the time of the revolt), not only set up countless such schools, but was also, according to charges made by the vicecount of Lower Alba County, "involved in many disorders during the revolution."

The clear national consciousness is attested in numerous contemporary references to the rebels' intention of expelling the nobility from the country and replacing the foreign administration with a Romanian one. Even the serfs knew of the general desire for Transylvania to become a *țara românească*, a Romanian country. Others knew even more: the rebels planned to unite Transylvania with Țara Românească. This plan was even known to the authorities and to the foreign press. Thus the Hamburg *Politisches Journal* informed its readers that the Transylvanian Romanians meant to unite with their Muntenian brothers and thus bring back the old Roman Empire. Horea was known by the title *rex Daciae* on medallions and engravings. Similarly, he was reported to have said in the last moments of his life, "I die for my nation," which was recorded in engravings and a few newspapers.

The size of the rebellion and its radical character, the social groups involved, and its goals aroused great concern among the dominant class and the Habsburg authorities. If the revolt could not be put down by force of arms, then other ways would have to be found, and deception by false promises was considered an effective means. Representatives of the imperial army and of the Gubernium made three truces with the rebels, at Tibru on 12 November and in the Brad Valley and at Sălciua on 16 November. Unfortunately for the peasants, the drive and determination they had shown in the first two weeks were weakened by these agreements, and the antipeasant forces gained time to organize suppression of the revolt. Gallows were erected everywhere, and on them hundreds of peasants met their end. County prisons and castle dungeons overflowed. Massacres of peasants without trial were commonplace, and a price was put on the heads of the rebel leaders. The priesthood was sent in to urge peasants to keep the peace.

Once the deception was revealed, the revolt broke out again with greater force. However, conditions had become much more difficult for the rebels. They were forced into a defensive posture and surrounded in the mountains. Instead of facing a disorganized nobility, they were up against a large and well-organized army. In place of a kindly emperor sympathetic to the suffering of the masses, they found an emperor who sent in his army with orders to crush the revolt at any price. Nevertheless, faith in Horea and in the support of the masses throughout the country strengthened the rebels, who at first managed to resist the army's incursion into the mountains. With the arrival of reinforcements, however, the peasants were defeated on 7 December after a fierce battle at Mihăleni. Yet not even this defeat could

Horea, Cloşca, and Crişan, leaders of the peasant uprising of 1784.

Horea and Cloşca leading the peasants.

break their resolve. Horea, recognizing that the rebels were in a difficult position, on 14 December ordered them to stop the fight and return home, but, like his peasant followers in the mountains, he intended to revive the revolt once spring had come. Horea, Crișan, and Cloșca clung to such thoughts during nearly two months of imprisonment in Alba Iulia; so too did the thousands of peasants in other jails, and the millions more who had seen their original hopes shattered.

The peasants' enemies were aware of their plans, and took every step necessary to prevent another outbreak. Barbaric measures, even including mass executions, were prescribed, and the process that led to the martyrdom of the rebel leaders was speeded up. Backed by Emperor Joseph's decree of 10 January 1785, the investigating commission under Count Anton Jankovich pronounced sentence on Horea and Cloșca on 26 February; Crișan, no longer able to withstand the physical and spiritual mistreatment, had taken his own life on 13 January. Horea and Cloșca were broken on the rack on 28 February 1785, on the so-called Gallows Place outside Alba Iulia, in the presence of a mass of peasants who had been forced to attend and of a number of noblemen who had gathered for the "princely festival."

The revolt of 1784, taking place during the decline of feudalism, stands out from ordinary peasant revolts precisely because of the conditions under which it occurred. It roused the peasant masses and the other oppressed groups to an unprecedented extent; it developed a revolutionary consciousness among them; it forged the most progressive social and political program in Transylvania at the time. This important event was justly considered by Nicolae Bălcescu as the preparation for the Transylvanian revolution of 1848. He described Horea as the one who, through his actions, wrote the "rights of the Romanian nation and its political and social program for future revolutions." Avram Iancu, the leader of the Romanians in Transylvania in 1848, took as his model of how to defeat the tyranny of the nobility not "philosophical arguments," but the accomplishments of "Horea's spear."

Technological Advances and the Growth of Industry

Although the feudal social structure and Habsburg economic policies tended to retard the development of advanced methods in agriculture and industry, Transylvania participated in the pan-European progress toward the Industrial Revolution. It advanced from simple plows to farm machinery, from the water wheel to the steam engine, from the distaff to the spinning and weaving machine, and from village blacksmiths and master fitters to inventors and specialized manufacturers of machinery. To be sure, the fruits of this technological progress were still only sporadically distributed, and could not become general until the death of feudalism.

Certain technological innovations began to be seen both on the peasant farms and on the manors. The three-year system of crop rotation became general; new crops and new strains of various plants and animals could be found on many peasant farms. Yet worthwhile peasant initiatives met with resistance from many landlords who were interested in prolonging the feudal order.

So-called liberal landlords were more aware of the advantages of modernization. Cultivation of commercial fodder plants, such as clover, alfalfa, and rape, increased, and new types of wine grapes were grown. Improved agricultural tools and machines made their appearance alongside the plow. The same nobles also used raw materials from their own estates directly in their own factories. The number of such factories increased; potash, glass, sugar, brandy, iron products, paper, oil, and lumber were among the products manufactured. Nevertheless, these factories were still relatively undeveloped, both technically and in terms of the number and degree of specialization of the workers.

Manufacturing was better developed in the state and city factories, but even there progress was hampered by the court's protectionist policies, despite the fact that the artisans' guilds were no longer able to satisfy domestic needs. An enumeration in 1792 showed that only the following were then in operation: several sawmills, seven wax factories, six glassworks, two scythe factories, two paper mills, two potash plants, and one factory each for textiles, leather goods, candles, saltpeter, gunpowder, and mercury. A few years later, there was also a number of oil presses and sugar refineries.

In the factories of the nobility, the workers at first were paid partly in food and partly in manufactured goods; later they were paid in money. However, while the use of paid workers continued to spread, both old and transitional forms—serfs performing involuntary labor in industrial production and serfs working in factories but being paid in money—were preserved for some time. An example of the latter was the well-known china factory of Batiz in southern Transylvania, established in 1813, whose sixty paid workers had been recruited from among the factory owner's serfs.

In the first decades of the nineteenth century, the bourgeoisie, the guild masters, and the merchants established many manufacturing enterprises in the cities. For the most part these were typically capitalist factories. Paid labor was widely used; the workers, whose numbers included dispossessed peasants, journeymen from the guilds, and foreign specialists, were paid by the month or by the day.

Development of the forces of production is also seen in improved machines. In 1831, the sugar refinery at Gîrbou in central Transylvania imported from Vienna powerful iron presses and machines which could process a ton of beets per hour. The sugar refinery in Sibiu imported machinery from London, while Sibiu's textile mill obtained spinning machines from Brno, Moravia. The paper mill at Orlat in southern Transylvania operated with an imported rag-shredding machine. Businesses manufacturing iron tools and machinery, especially for agriculture, were set up in Arad in 1825, in Ruschiţa in 1834, in Cluj in 1840, and in Oradea in 1844 and 1847. The founder of the Cluj factory was Peter Rajka, a graduate of the Vienna Polytechnic. Struggling with lack of capital, low demand, and competition from the guilds, he invented and built a variety of implements that were more advanced than those made in other countries.

Around Braşov there was extremely diversified industry making use of agricultural raw materials. Women and children worked the machines that spun cotton and wool. The wool-washing plants of the area employed 1,500 to 2,000 seasonal workers and exported a million pounds of washed wool to Holland. Romanian and Saxon merchants and artisans operated factories that made blankets, leather, tallow, wax candles, alcohol, china, and paper, and employed 1,000 to 3,000 paid workers, both temporary and permanent. Around Sibiu the situation was similar. The paper mill at Orlat employed 180 workers, the one in Sibiu itself 32; the sugar beet refinery—a stock company—employed 105. Altogether in this industrial center there were over 500 factory workers, as well as those who worked at home. In 1838, for example, the textile mill in Cisnădie employed 1,400 women from the Făgăraş region, mostly as spinners.

Such early steps toward modernization did not transform Transylvania from an agricultural to an industrial country, nor did they radically change the basic social structure. In 1840, while the proportion of the population involved in industry and commerce in the Habsburg empire as a whole was one in twelve or one in fourteen, in Transylvania the ratio was one in thirty-two. The per capita value of industrial production in Lower Austria was seventy-seven florins, but in Transylvania barely seven.

The guilds, waging a desperate battle against the factories, used their power in city councils to obstruct new enterprises and the sale of manufactured goods; the Habsburg hereditary provinces, protected by tariffs, offered severe competition in both domestic and foreign markets. Transylvania's young industry had great difficulty in meeting these challenges. A movement called the Defense Union obliged its members to buy only domestically produced goods in order to protect the Transylvanian market from Austrian competition, but the Viennese government countered by prohibiting such associations.

On the other hand, Austrian interests favored the development of an almost exclusive state control in the mining industry. Transylvania's mineral riches were extensively exploited, especially gold and the iron needed for the industry of the hereditary provinces. These profitable undertakings attracted the interest of the Austrian state, certain members of the imperial court, and even a few local merchants. To maximize their return, they supported deep-pit mining and the granting of private concessions to certain mines. As a result, there were noticeable technological advances in mining and a much greater use of paid labor at Săcărîmb, Băiţa, and Baia Sprie. In the last of these places there were more than a thousand paid workers. Rudimentary tools were replaced by more sophisticated machines, including some built by local mineworkers with long experience and inventive minds. Bourgeois capital, both Austrian and local, was added to state investment, and stock companies were formed.

The new system prospered in part because adult workers were poorly paid and child labor was used extensively. At Săcărîmb, for example, 39 percent of the workers were children; at Baia Sprie there were 228 children between eight and fifteen years old at work in the mines. Production increased: for example, in 1830 ten times as much gold was traded as in 1710, which means that gold production itself had increased tenfold. Production of silver, copper, iron, and lead ore saw a similar growth. Large-capacity smelters were set up in the Banat and in Hunedoara, the most important being that in Reşiţa.

Innovations in mining technology followed. Machines were invented and built by local peasant miners; significant improvements were made to the ore crusher by three "folk artisans" (artifex naturalis), the Romanian miners Idu Crăciun, Munteanu Urs, and Constantin Palade. Their invention merited the description "miracle machine." Similar significant contributions were made to the modernization of mining by German and Hungarian inventors. Among these were Felix Franzenau and Márton Debreczéni, whose spiral blowpipes were introduced in smelters throughout western Europe. In the 1840s, water power began to be replaced by steam. The first steam engine was put into operation in the mine at Zlatna in 1838, and the second a short time later at Baia Mare. In 1845, three steam engines were installed at Reşiţa and a new rolling mill was completed. This mill included twenty-one furnaces and other advanced machinery. It also employed steam hammers for the first time in Transylvania.

Again production increased. Between 1825 and 1830, the annual production of gold, silver, copper, lead, and mercury had a value of 1,088,671 florins; in 1842, after the introduction of the steam engine, it had risen to 1,556,990 florins. L. Kőváry's statistics for 1847 put iron production at about 6,000 tons annually. In 1842, just nine mines produced an income of 412,770 gold florins. On the eve of the 1848 revolution, in other words, mining was one of Transylvania's most significant sources of wealth.

Such changes, however, did not mean an improvement in working conditions. Pay was low, occupational diseases were rampant, and there was an endless series of mine accidents. In the larger establishments in the Bihor Mountains and in Hunedoara, there were more and more cases of miners leaving their work, which finally led to major strikes. There were also frequent protests over arbitrary withholdings of wages, fines, the cost of food, the lack of medical care, and the system of paying workers according to the metal content of the ore mined. Similar unrest occurred among the salt cutters in several mines.

The End of Feudalism

In the second half of the eighteenth century, the type of government known as "enlightened despotism" began to take hold in the countries of central and eastern Europe. Represented in Prussia by Frederick II, in Russia by Catherine II, in Austria by Joseph II, and even, to a lesser extent, by certain Phanariot princes in the Romanian principalities, the absolutist theory was strongly opposed to revolution, holding that societies should adapt to new socioeconomic developments through reforms instituted at the top. Essentially, this policy served to prolong feudal rule in those countries where capitalism was little developed; the bourgeoisie was not in a position to overthrow feudalism by force, as happened in the countries of western Europe. Among the characteristics of absolutist regimes was centralization and a greatly developed bureaucracy. Constitutionally, Transylvania was independent, having been elevated to a grand principality in 1765; the Banat was annexed to Hungary in 1779, without, however, losing a certain autonomy. But the growing authority of the Austrian military commander, who was also, for most of this period, the country's governor, contributed to Transylvania's increasingly close bonds to the Austrian court.

When Joseph II ascended the Habsburg throne in 1780, he brought about a number of reforms, designed both to limit the power of the nobility, which was resisting centralization, and to forestall any revolutionary movements. These reforms affected Transylvania as well as the rest of the empire. They included the removal of censorship from clerical control and the creation of a commission to review books; abolition of a number of monastic orders; the institution of religious toleration, albeit with certain limits; the establishment of a new administrative division intended to do away with medieval autonomous territories; the separation of executive and judicial powers; the granting to everyone of the right to live in towns; the replacement of Latin by German as the official language of the state; and reform of education, including an attempt to introduce free mandatory elementary education. These reforms, though limited and adapted to the interests of the Austrian state, nevertheless curbed the power of the high nobility and the clergy, who therefore opposed and resisted them whenever possible. By contrast, the bourgeoisie welcomed them, especially those professional and intellectual groups who had been forced to accept political inferiority—doctors, engineers, professors, officials, and the like.

Horea's great popular rebellion—a premonition of the French Revolution, which erupted less than five years later—gave the Austrian court food for thought. Joseph II had helped bring about the defeat of the revolt and had decreed the execution of its leaders, yet he was spurred to improve the situation of the peasantry, since individual servitude represented a serious obstacle to social progress. Thus he took steps to lighten the peasants' obligations, and subsequently to abolish serfdom in his patent of 1785. Serfs were freed of their bondage to the land and were granted the right to move to other estates and to sell their own earned property, while the children of serfs gained the right to learn a trade.

However, because the nobility opposed it, the patent could not be put fully into effect. After Joseph's death in 1790, the nobles demanded "full restitution," the rescission of all Joseph's reforms and the restoration of all rights that they had previously enjoyed.

The diet that convened in Cluj on 21 December 1790 was heavily weighted in the nobles' favor. It was composed of 296 regalists and high officials and only 120 elected representatives, and its membership was 85 percent noble. It voted for the restoration of the old autonomy and feudal institutions and of the rights and privileges of the nobility; it also approved harsher social conditions for serfs, though it did not dare to restore serfdom for fear of rebuilding the revolt. The court approved the diet's decisions on the rights and privileges of the nobility, and intervened only to weaken the separatist tendencies.

This diet also debated the memorandum of the Romanian nation known as the *Supplex libellus.* Though based on ideas formulated half a century earlier by Inocențiu Micu Klein, the document nevertheless reflected the changes that had taken place since he wrote. For example, there had been an increase in the number of Romanian petty nobles who sought advancement through the creation of a Romanian nation; an intellectual class, which included respected scholars, had formed as the result of the opening of Romanian schools; in certain towns a Romanian merchant class had emerged; and a number of Romanians in the border regiments had succeeded in becoming officers. Romanians had become more aware that they had a right to a new place in the economic and political life of the country, and they voiced their concern in several memoranda. The *Supplex,* which was presented to Emperor Leopold II in 1791, formed a synthesis of these works. Written by Iosif Meheși, a high official at the Transylvanian Aulic Chancellery, in collaboration with the most learned Romanians of the time, it made several proposals for reforms: 1) that the Romanian nation should be restored to its rightful position next to the Hungarian, Szekler, and Saxon nations; 2) that there should be Romanian officials and Romanian seats in the diet in proportion to their numbers; 3) that administrative districts containing a majority of Romanians should have Romanian names, while others should have mixed names or be named after rivers or fortresses; 4) that all Transylvanians should enjoy the same rights, in accordance with their social status or condition, and should bear the same obligations, in accordance with their economic status; 5) that Romanians should have the right to meet in a national assembly and elect deputies who could represent them wherever the need arose. The petition was supported by the familiar historical, demographic, and economic arguments.

The *Supplex* was the first political manifesto of the Romanian people in Transylvania, a synthesis, expansion, and ideologically more solid grounding of Micu's ideas. Like his program, the memorandum combined older principles with more modern ones. It can be considered a progressive document in that it is based on the belief that those who bear the greatest burdens should enjoy corresponding rights, and that there should be equal rights for all nations and proportional representation in public life. On the other hand, it neglects the interests of the masses. Even the principles of the French Revolution—abolition of the nobility's privileges, abolition of serfdom, and granting of land to peasants—were given short shrift. The means suggested for attaining the proposed goals were, to say the least, moderate; matters were left in the hands of the imperial court. Compared to the political and ideological programs of the western bourgeoisies, then, the *Supplex* is undistinguished. In the light of the situation in Transylvania in the late eighteenth century, however, it was far ahead of its time.

The feudal diet assembled in Cluj was "indignant" and "disturbed." Turned over to a study commission, the *Supplex* was rejected on the grounds that recognition of a new nation would severely shake the principality's constitutional system. A new memorandum was then written, containing the same demands but with fuller documentation, and presented to the emperor by the two bishops, Orthodox and Uniate. The result was the same. Fearing the danger to their social and political regime, the Habsburgs and the feudal nobles joined forces to postpone the fall of an anachronistic social order.

The resistance of the empire and the feudal nobility was nevertheless rendered futile by irresistible social changes. The Transylvanian political progressive movement underwent a change of orientation after 1790, in part because of the reactionary policies of the nobility and the Viennese court, and in part because of the success of the French Revolution. Revolutionary societies were formed on the model of the French Jacobins. The Hunting Society of Diana, whose members were the most radical Transylvanian Jacobins, had branches in Sibiu, Cluj, Oradea, Satu Mare, Timişoara, and Tîrgu Mureş. The Liberty and Unity Society, which included Romanians, Hungarians, and other nationalities, was formed on its model, and was also active in several Transylvanian towns. One important center of Jacobinism was in the western region of the country; it was led by writer Ferenc Kazinczy, and included in its membership other fighters for democracy, such as Miklos Balugyánski ("the great Jacobin," a professor at the Academy of Law in Oradea), Moisin (the administrator of the district of Beiuş), and Gy. Szlávy. The Jacobin movement took on such dimensions that it "produced agitation and revolt among the common people, while *La Marseilleise* was widely sung in French, Latin, and Hungarian. A newspaper edited by I. Molnar-Piuariu and Paul Iorgovici spread "the French Revolution's dangerous ideas of freedom."

The court, backed by the nobility, succeeded in putting down the Jacobin movement, trying and imprisoning the leaders and active participants. Without the organized support of the masses—which in any case the Jacobins had not sought—the movement was doomed from the start. The masses, meanwhile, were acting more and more independently of the bourgeoisie. Numerous local rebellions and uprisings broke out in the 1790s and early 1800s. The revolution in Ţara Românească in 1821, which was led by Tudor Vladimirescu and in which the Transylvanian Gheorghe Lazăr played a role, together with the Polish rebellion of 1830 and the rebellion of 1831, showed that the revolutionary spirit was still alive among the peasantry.

Faced with these social and national movements, a segment of the nobility took up various reform ideas which were intended to slow the antifeudal and national struggle. This group recognized the need for modernization, and sought a political compromise which would give them a leading role in economic and political life. Only a few recognized the need for more thorough social reforms to improve the lot of the peasantry, and they could not lead the fight against feudalism; this task fell instead to the merchants and factory owners. Although the commercial and industrial bourgeoisie were joined by the bourgeois intellectuals, their ranks were not yet strong enough to overthrow feudalism. Some of their weakness was caused by internal ethnic splits, but it was also true that the bourgeoisie feared the peasants, the one ally who could have been decisive in the fight against Transylvanian feudalism.

10

National Consciousness and the Revolution of 1848

Prelude to Revolution

A NATION MAY BE DEFINED as a stable human community, with its own language and culture, territory and economic life, specific spiritual traits, and national consciousness. It is a historical entity founded on certain traits, traits which long exist unseen, gradually developing until they emerge and mature in the period when feudalism declines and the elements of modern capitalism appear. A nation may be considered a historical synthesis of the centuries-long evolution of the most significant aspects of the life of a human group.

In general, the nation-forming process is the same everywhere, but when the process actually is completed is related to specific historical circumstances. The formation of the English nation may be seen as completed in the fifteenth to sixteenth centuries, that of the French, Spanish, and Italian nations in the sixteenth to seventeenth centuries. The American nation may be considered to have been formed when it gained independence in the second half of the eighteenth century, about the same time the nations of central and eastern Europe also were established. The formation of the Romanian nation followed essentially the same course as that of other nations. The unifying traits of the Romanian nation were present—in embryonic form, but with potential for development—throughout the Middle Ages, being strengthened as feudalism developed and especially later, as it declined.

Linguistic unity is evident in the fact that Romanian has been a single language ever since it developed, in the seventh and eighth centuries, in the entire area inhabited by the Romanian people. It never had dialects in the strict sense of the word, but only slight local variations, unimportant peculiarities in one or another of the historical provinces. Inhabitants of two different regions, no matter how far apart, could understand each other with ease. When the standard literary language began to be formed the second half of the sixteenth century, it was based on the usage in northern Țara Românească and southern Transylvania. Naturally, it developed gradually, adding elements from local speech throughout the national territory of the Romanian people. The changes that the language underwent should not be understood as structural modifications, but rather as the result of a continual enrichment, necessitated by social change, to make the language capable of expressing new social, cultural, and political realities.

The importance of linguistic unity is also seen in the steadfastness with which the Romanian people fought to preserve their language in the face of attempts by the schools, the church, and the government to take it away from them. The fifteenth-century Italian humanist Antonio Bonfini wrote that the Romanians fought harder to save their language than their lives. Linguistic unity, based on ethnic unity, became a part of the national awareness, not just of educated Romanians, but also of the masses. This awareness is expressed with increasing clarity beginning in the fifteenth century; it is particularly marked in the sixteenth and seventeenth centuries, in both clerical and lay writings on history and law.

It is therefore only natural that the Romanian people should also exhibit *cultural unity*, which is seen in popular songs, poetry, and tales and in educated lay and clerical writings, all of which circulated without interruption on both sides of the Carpathians. The first printed texts, from the late sixteenth and early seventeenth centuries (the catechism of 1544 and the writings of Deacon Coresi), gave a substantial new strength to this unity. The seventeenth-century sermons of Varlaam from Moldavia, the 1648 New Testament of Alba Iulia in Transylvania, and the laws of Matei Basarab from Țara Românească and of Vasile Lupu from Moldavia circulated and were used by Romanians everywhere.

The idea of linguistic and cultural unity found scholarly and ideological support in the writings of the Muntenian Constantin Cantacuzino and of the Moldavian Prince Dimitire Cantemir, and were eventually crystalized into a true doctrine in the work of the Transylvanian School and other representatives of the

Enlightenment. This period marked a new stage in the development of the literary language. It was increasingly unified, more organized in its grammatical forms, and had a richer vocabulary, thanks to words borrowed from other languages. Unifying the national language and culture was a general preoccupation of educated Romanians, especially in the early nineteenth century. The struggle for a single literary language and a national culture is thus an integral part of the creation of the Romanian nation.

Romania's *territorial unity*, a reality throughout the ages, should not be understood as some sort of geographic determinism. Geography certainly played an important role in the development of the Romanian people, because of the diversity of the national territory, but in order to understand properly the notion of territorial unity, the geographic factors must be related to economic ones. First of all, in terms of what they produce, the hills and the plains complement each other. Furthermore, the uninterrupted links between the territories on both sides of the Carpathians contributed not only to the development of territorial unity, but to economic unity as well. Economic unity cannot be understood simply as the formation of a marketplace, in the sense of a national economic center for all the territory inhabited by Romanians or a single marketplace for all its goods. Trade implies much more than a specific center. Trade and economic unity mean opportunities for the flow of goods from one of the historical Romanian provinces to another, or from one part of a province to another. Taking the notion of economic unity in this sense, we see that it emerged as soon as products became commodities, and more clearly during the decline of feudalism and the dawn of capitalism, when the commodity economy helped to break down feudal restrictions in each province and artifical frontiers between the provinces.

Goods of all sorts—manufactured wares, handicrafts, animals and farm produce, metals and ores—passed from one country to another even when the authorities tried to prevent the traffic. The map of trading routes linking the three Romanian countries looks like a leaf with veins spreading in every direction. Moreover, there were many more unofficial routes, known to the local populations and used as often as those that were guarded by customs posts. It was these close economic and cultural ties that facilitated Michael the Brave's unification of three Romanian countries under a single political leadership in 1599–1600.

All these factors worked together to produce a national character or spirit peculiar to the Romanian people, which acted as an indissoluble bond throughout the ages. From the dawn of their existence as a people to the present day, all Romanians have shared the same customs, traditions, and religious beliefs (with a few minor variations), as well as the same language. These bonds were so powerful as to inspire awe among foreigners. József Benkö, for example, a Hungarian scholar of the second half of the eighteenth century, wrote that it would be easier to wrest the club from Hercules' hand than to induce the Romanians lightly to abandon their old customs. Similarly, the old unwritten legal code known as "Romanian law" was a single tradition, with small variations, in Transylvania and the other Romanian countries. Finally, there was the Orthodox religion, which the Romanians valiantly defended against the coming of Catholicism and later of the Reformation. The Italian Jesuit Antonio Possevino wrote at the end of the sixteenth century that in spite of threats and dangers, the Romanians remained steadfast in their laws and their Greek rite.

Unity of tradition and spirit found expression in the Romanians' awareness of their national identity. This was first seen in the names the Romanians gave themselves and their language, by which they distinguished themselves from their neighbors and the other people with whom they lived, ethnically and linguistically. Later, this feeling was expressed in the awareness of their common Daco-Roman origins, their ethnic unity, and their aspirations for freedom. Such manifestations of geographic and social awareness, enriched by the knowledge that their group existence would lose its meaning without them, gave rise to a national consciousness. This was evinced as awareness of belonging to the same ethnic stock, of the historical individuality of the nation, of the past, of national sovereignty, of the unity and coherence of the nation, of national prestige, and of the material and spiritual treasures created by the nation as a group. National consciousness was exceptionally important in the fight for social and ethnic emancipation and in the winning of national independence.

Systematic investigation of the development of the foundations of the Romanian nation requires consideration of the slow but steady transformation of the various unifying traits; these were enriched with new characteristics that modified their medieval substance and gave it new meanings. These new meanings had already been seen in the political ideas of Michael the

185

A nineteenth-century Transylvanian village.

Brave and are more noticeable in the eighteenth century. The ideology of Inocenţiu Micu, though still influenced by certain feudal ideas, also prefigures various modern conceptions of national social aspirations and national consciousness, and, moreover, is founded on the historical notions of Romanness and of the continuity of the Romanians in Dacia. The modern meanings of the term "nation" appear still more clearly in that highly significant political document, the *Supplex* of 1791, and in the thought and writing of the Romanian Enlightenment. What makes the modernization of these concepts of nation and national consciousness even more significant is the fact that they reached the peasant masses, who began to talk of the Dacian and Roman origin of the Romanian people. The Romanians necessarily rejected the feudal and conservative sense of "political nation," from which they were excluded. In doing so, they implicitly rejected not only the sense but also the substance of these outdated notions, replacing them with newer ideas of national consciousness and the modern nation. The usage of the term *naţie* ("nation") in Romanian writings of this period constitutes conclusive proof of the evolution to the modern sense of the word. Although here and there *naţie* has the sense of "people" or "ethnic group," the word is used in its modern sense in the work of the most learned writers.

As the nation-forming process reached completion, it was inevitable that internal and external obstacles should be lowered and then swept away. Indeed, in the second half of the eighteenth century the feudal order was undermined by capitalism in agriculture, mining, manufacturing, and trade. Thus it was possible to strengthen economic unity, especially after the Turkish monopoly was weakened in 1775 and then abolished in 1829. Feudal and clerical culture and ideology were gradually replaced by the culture and ideology of the rising bourgeoisie; this was reflected in the Enlightenment ideology of the Transylvanian School, which went beyond political boundaries to concern for the major issues of Romanian origins, continuity, and unity. Thus the potential that had long existed became reality in the second half of the eighteenth century and the beginning of the nineteenth century. The unifying traits of the Romanian nation were clearly drawn, and it should not be surprising that the revolutions in the three Romanian countries in 1848 were very similiar.

As capitalism expanded and the economic and cultural

strength of the bourgeoisie grew, the national movement became more and more powerful. The literary society founded in 1827 by the Muntenians Dinicu Golescu and Eliade Rădulescu, the Transylvanian Aron Florian, and others sought to uplift the Romanian nation through education and the modern spirit of reform. In the 1830s and 1840s there was a noticeable surge of activity in the national movement and the movement for unification. In Lugoj in the Banat, the secret society Constitution was active from 1830 to 1834; its leaders included both intellectuals and tradesmen, and it allied itself with the fight for national liberation. In Transylvania a Romanian-Polish secret society was active around the same time, under the leadership of a Polish emigrant named Adolf David. Among its social goals was the emancipation of the peasants from serfdom; politically, it sought the union of the three Romanian countries in a single independent and democratic republic. The society's membership included leading intellectuals from Ţara Românească and Moldavia as well as from Transylvania, all united around a Romanian version of the French tricolor flag. Meanwhile, the newspaper *România,* published in Bucharest in 1837–38 by G. Hill and Aron Florian, symbolized in its very title a political stand. In Ţara Românească, the national movement was even more active. A group led by Ioan Cîmpineanu proposed a bourgeois-liberal constitution which recorded the desire to unite the Romanian countries—or at least the two principalities on the Danube—into an independent national state.

As the nineteenth century wore on, the national movement became increasingly radical. The revolutionary bourgeois conspiracy of 1840, which was led by Dimitrie Filipescu in collaboration with young Nicolae Bălcescu, Eftimie Murgu of the Banat, and the Frenchman J. A. Vaillant, sought to overthrow the old order by arms; in its place there was to be a democratic republic in which the peasantry would be freed from serfdom and given land. The national movement derived much of its intensity from the strong reaction provoked by the school law that the Hungarian diet passed in 1842. This law provided that Hungarian should replace Romanian in the Romanian schools and churches of Transylvania within ten years. Romanian newspapers and intellectuals raised a chorus of determined opposition to such forced Magyarization. Progressive Saxon intellectuals also were opposed. In 1842, Stefan Ludwig Roth published a pamphlet arguing that the official language in Transylvania had to be Romanian, since it was spoken by a majority of the population and since even Saxons and Magyars were forced to use it to communicate with each other.

The revolutionary struggle to complete the establishment of the Romanian nation was rapidly approaching. Because the Romanian territory was divided into three separate, dependent states, and because there were reactionary forces inside them and three absolutist empires—Ottoman, Habsburg, and czarist—outside, a powerful revolutionary organization had to be forged to lead the fight. The secret society called the Brotherhood, created in Țara Românească in 1843 by Bălcescu, Ion Ghica, and Christian Tell, sought to overthrow the feudal order and achieve national unity; it had links with Mihail Kogălniceanu's liberal-democratic group in Moldavia and with the Transylvanian national movement led by George Barițiu, Timotei Cipariu, and others. The journals *Propășirea* [Progress] in Moldavia and *Magazin istoric pentru Dacia* [Historical magazine for Dacia] in Țara Românească also worked actively for political unity. *Propășirea* was concerned with "the true material and intellectual interests of the Romanians" in order to "create a more lively interest in scholarship and in the nation"; the *Magazin* urged its readers to have "more faith in the future" and to work "wholeheartedly for the political and social reforms that will make us worthy of our rightful position in the great family of European nations." The Literary Society, founded in Bucharest in 1845 through the efforts of Bălcescu and Ghica, was renamed the Literary Association of Romania a year later. It had a five-member organizing committee in Bucharest, which was assisted by committees in Moldavia and Transylvania. This structure, together with the organization's goals and the symbolic inclusion of "Romania" in its name, gave the association the character of a national academy.

The crisis of the old order was rapidly approaching the point of no return. The road to revolution in 1848 was marked by deepening social, economic, and political inequalities and by the transformation of the new national ideology into a force for innovation. Everything contributed to the efforts to overthrow the old order and clear the way for the integration of the Romanian nation into a single independent state. Vasile Pop had proclaimed the principles underlying these efforts in the last decade

Avram Iancu (1824–1872), hero of the Transylvanian Romanians in the revolution of 1848.

before the revolution: "A nation cannot be divided by high mountains, wide rivers, or by political boundaries; it ceases to be a nation only at the boundaries of the language that unites it."

The Revolution of 1848

The socioeconomic, political, and ethnic contradictions in which Transylvania was floundering in 1820s through the 1840s could not be resolved peacefully, for the dominant Hungarian nobility and bourgeoisie rejected every demand made by the serfs and non-Magyar peoples. Moreover, the Romanian serfs were further threatened by various decrees made by the Hungarian-dominated diet in 1842 and 1847. These called not only for the forced introduction of Hungarian in all Romanian schools and, after a certain time, in Romanian churches as well, but also further usurpations of peasant land and an increase in feudal-style obligations. The measures provoked strong reactions, as did, more generally, the reactionary policies of the conservative Hungarian nobility, who were supported by the bourgeois-leaning nobility and by the liberal and conservative parties that represented their interests. The intelligentsia and the Transylvanian Romanian and Saxon press protested with all their strength against the denationalization policy, while the peasantry, especially in the Bihor Mountains, strongly resisted the new laws.

Other European countries also were wracked by social and political discontent. On top of this came famine, caused by a massive drought, which devastated Europe in 1847. The result was that revolution spread over most of the continent.

A few days after the New Year in 1848, revolution broke out in Sicily. The struggle began in Palermo on 12 January and in a few days covered the whole island. The royal army put down the revolt, but the king was nevertheless forced to grant a more liberal constitution in order to restore calm. Ten days after these events, a larger and more consequential revolution broke out in Paris, and the banker's monarchy under the patronage of King Louis Philippe was overthrown. By March revolution had reached still other countries. On 13 March 1848 it broke out in Vienna, with the goal of overthrowing Metternich, one of the pillars of reaction in Europe. The townspeople clashed with the police, barricades were erected, and Metternich was forced to flee the city. On 15 March revolution broke out in Pest. A twelve-point manifesto was published establishing the principles and issues, which included demands for equality of rights for all citizens; abolition of feudal privileges and of serfdom, *robota*, and tithes; constitutional government; freedom of the press and of assembly; and the granting of property to serfs. Similar events were occurring in Berlin. German revolutionaries obtained a promise from the king that a constitutional government would be established, and a bourgeois-liberal regime was brought to power. Meanwhile, revolutionary movements spread to the Habsburg-dominated Italian provinces of Lombardy and Venice.

In the three Romanian countries, the winds of freedom also were blowing. Events were discussed in large meetings and plans for the future were forged. This does not mean that the revolution was, as it were, borrowed. Rather it was expanded; internal conditions were primarily responsible for preparing the way, but there were certain outside influences.

In Transylvania the month of March was dominated by revolutionary activity. Peasants expressed impatient haste to be free of serfdom and the burdens of feudal obligations. There were debates about which path to take in order to restore the rights of which the Romanian nation had been stripped by the dominant Hungarian class and in order to provide a more equitable basis for social relations. Young people wrote and distributed manifestos. The most important was that of 24–25 March, written by Simion Bărnuțiu, the ideologue of the Romanian revolution in Transylvania. It states the essence of the revolution's goals: restoration of rights to the Romanian nation; a national congress to consider Romanian demands; recognition of the Romanian language as an official language; and the abolition of serfdom without any compensation to be paid by the serfs. Hundreds of copies were made and distributed throughout Transylvania.

A number of individuals emerged at this time to organize and direct the revolution—young men, scarcely past their school days. Among these the most prominent were Avram Iancu, Alexandru Papiu-Ilarian, and Ioan Buteanu; they were young lawyers, the sons of peasants or of rural intellectuals. They organized other meetings to discuss the goals and strategies of the revolution. Such meetings were held in Tîrgu Mureș, Blaj, and Cluj, where there were many young Romanian intellectuals, and in Sibiu and Braşov, the most important Romanian cultural and political centers in southern Transylvania. In the Bihor Mountains, meanwhile, the peasants were called to assemblies to prepare for the revolution.

A massive popular assembly was announced for 30 April in Blaj, to discuss events and formulate demands. The meeting was held despite a ban by the Hungarian authorities and was attended by several thousand Romanian peasants and intellectuals. Iancu, Buteanu, and Papiu-Ilarian increasingly became the central revolutionary figures, while Bărnuţiu emerged as a leader who commanded respect from all the others. It was decided to hold an even larger meeting in Blaj only two weeks later. The revolution of the Romanians in Transylvania may be considered to have begun.

The Hungarian authorities retaliated, erecting gallows in villages and sending in armed troops to massacre peasants. The response was just as prompt: the peasantry ceased to obey official decrees and repossessed lands that had been seized from them by the nobility. Romanian militias were formed, and intellectuals made contact with revolutionaries in Ţara Românească and Moldavia, where similar movements were already underway, in order to coordinate their actions and unify their movements and their goals.

In the days leading up to the second assembly, extraordinary agitation gripped the Gubernium in Cluj. The governor ordered the Romanian bishops to permit only protopopes and village delegates to attend the assembly, and he requested the imperial army command in Sibiu to send infantry, cavalry, and artillery. He again ordered the arrest of the revolutionary leaders and the destruction of numerous bridges. But all of the Gubernium's prohibitions, the bishops' circulars, and the measures taken to terrorize the people were in vain. As the day of the assembly drew near, the revolutionary tide was swelled by the return of several Transylvanian professors who had gone to Ţara Românească or Moldavia to pursue their careers, including August Treboniu Laurian, Ion Axente Sever, Constantin Romanu-Vivu, Nicolae Bălşescu, Aron Florian, Vasile Maiorescu, Petre Suciu, and Iuniu Armatu. With them they brought instructions from the Muntenian revolutionaries Bălcescu and Ghica.

By 12 May, tens of thousands of peasants had begun to arrive in Blaj from every corner of the country. Miners and peasants, led by Avram Iancu, came from the Bihor Mountains, representing the most fearless and determined fighters for the Romanian cause. Like a river in flood the peasants came, determined to throw off the double yoke of social and ethnic oppression. No one dared stop them. "It appears that the people have suddenly emerged from a long period of lethargy, and become aware of their strength," wrote a Hungarian observer at the time. "Dressed in their holiday clothes, the peasants arrived in large groups, singing and cheering. Everyone was happy that the end of serfdom was to be initiated at Blaj."

On Sunday, 14 May, a number of revolutionaries from Moldavia were on hand: Gh. Sion, Alecu Russo, Lascăr Rosetti, Vasile Alecsandri, Alexandru Ion Cuza, Zaharia Moldovan, and others. There was a meeting in the cathedral and a memorable speech by Simion Bărnuţiu. "All of Europe," he declared, "is seeing a rebirth of freedom. . . . Even next door in Hungary, great changes have taken place." Substantial new freedoms had been decreed there, he noted, including an end to serfdom. But something else had also been decided—the union of Transylvania with Hungary. "By this union, the Hungarians want to eliminate temporarily Transylvania's privileges, and along with the privileges they plan to wipe out all the non-Hungarian peoples. In this way they want to create a single nation, which will be known as the great and strong Hungarian nation." What then, asked Bărnuţiu, was the Romanians' duty?

> The nation, here assembled in this celebration of freedom . . . must proclaim the freedom and independence of the Romanian nation. The Romanian nation here resolves to throw off the yoke that destroys its character—the yoke of the Hungarian constitution. It solemnly declares that henceforth it will consider itself bound only by laws passed in the country's diet, where it will have rightful and appropriate representation, and it will obey only leaders elected from among its own. The Romanian nation informs the coinhabiting nations that its desire to be constituted and organized as a nation implies no enmity toward other nations; it recognizes the same right for all, and wishes to respect that right in good faith, seeking the respect that comes from justice. No nation, therefore, will allow itself to be subject to another, but there should be equal rights for all.

Bărnuţiu proposed that the assembly take a solemn oath, in the name of the entire nation, never to renounce their nationality, and to defend the nation and work for its survival, honor, culture, and good fortune for all time to come.

On the following day, 15 May, a huge assembly took place in a

The Great Assembly in Blaj, 3–15 May 1848.

field outside Blaj, which from then on was known as Cîmpia Libertăţii, the "Field of Liberty." The likes of this great meeting had scarcely ever been seen before in Europe, according to a Hungarian eyewitness, I. Mészáros. Another description—also from a Hungarian source—was published in *Zur Geschichte des ungarischen Freiheitskampfes* (Leipzig, 1851). "In order to be able to look over the assembly we sat on a hill. An immense multitude stretched out . . . before our eyes, like a large military encampment in the shape of a star. . . . We must report that there was something imposing about the arrangement of this camp. . . . From the center a number of paths led out like rays through the dense throngs . . . and the whole scene had a truly awesome appearance."

Thousands of peasants, deeply moved, listened to speeches. Not only Romanian participants, but also Hungarian, Saxon, and foreign observers noted the exemplary order maintained by the throng. "This vast mass of people," wrote the Hungarian historian Elek Jakab, "which by midday was as large as twenty-five to thirty-thousand, appeared like a quiet sea, on whose surface not the slightest ripple could be discerned." The speakers stressed the glory of the Romans, which was to be reclaimed in the name of the Romanian people; they spoke of the long period of slavery that the Romanians had suffered up to the time of Emperor Joseph. There was also talk of the great burdens that impoverished the Romanians, and of the discrimination suffered at Hungarian, Szekler, and Saxon hands.

Then the assembly formulated specific resolutions, declaring the Romanian nation independent and founded on freedom equal to that of other nations, but reaffirming allegiance to the emperor. An oath was sworn:

> I will always support our Romanian nation by just and legal means and will defend it with all my power against any attack and oppression. I will never work against the rights and interests of the Romanian nation, but will keep and defend our Romanian language and spirit, as well as liberty, equality, and fraternity. On these principles I will respect all nations of Transylvania and ask for equal respect in return. I will not try to oppress anyone, but I will not suffer oppression myself. I will contribute what I am able to the effort to abolish serfdom and to the progress of humanity, the Romanian nation, and our country.

On 16 May, the specific goals of the Romanian revolution were formulated. These were contained in the points of the national petition: independence of the Romanian nation on the basis of liberty, equality, and fraternity; proportional Romanian representaion in the country's diet; proportional Romanian representation among officials in all administrative, judicial, and military departments; acceptance of the Romanian language in legislation and administration; an annual general national assembly; independence for Romanian churches; abolition of serfdom without any compensation to be paid by the serfs; abolition of tithes; freedom of trade and industry; abolition of all privileges and of all customs barriers between Transylvania and the Romanian principalities; guarantees of personal freedom and the right of assembly; Romanian schools at all levels, including a state-supported university; a national guard, to include Romanian border regiments commanded by Romanian officers; a new Transylvanian constitution, based on principles of justice, liberty, equality, and fraternity; and rejection of the union between Transylvania and Hungary.

The significance of the Blaj assembly of 15–17 May does not lie only in the number of participants—about forty thousand—although that number was altogether exceptional for the time; it also lies in the fact that the thousands of representatives of different classes and occupations were able to work together, each group furthering demands based on its particular interests. Thus the peasants asked for the immediate abolition of serfdom without compensation by former serfs and a review of all the land seizures by the landlords. The bourgeoise inserted into the assembly's statement a series of demands aimed at developing their own class: personal freedom and freedom of speech and of the press; sharing of public burdens by all; abolition of all privileges and closing of customs posts on the borders with Moldavia and Țara Românească; establishment and state funding of Romanian schools at all levels; and the payment of priests. The Blaj assembly was a powerful demonstration of bourgeois-democratic antifeudal feeling.

The Blaj assembly had important consequences for the Romanian nation: it strengthened the national consciousness of the Romanian people and sharpened the revolutionary spirit of the masses. For the first time, hundreds of Romanian revolutionaries from all over Transylvania met with those who had come from Moldavia and Țara Românească. The learned Saxon professor and priest Stefan Ludwig Roth, filled with impressions of the Blaj assembly, wrote, "The masses who came to this grand as-

Timotei Cipariu, 1805–1887.

Simion Bărnuțiu, 1808–1864.

August Treboniu Laurian, 1810–1881.

George Barițiu, 1812–1893.

sembly arrived to hear speeches about the abolition of involuntary labor.... In each participant, however little educated he might be, there awoke the thought of nationality. This thought has taken root so deeply that it will never be eradicated by the Romanians' enemies." The thought of uniting the three Romanian countries was spread to a wider group. At Blaj, even among the peasants, voices could be heard calling for union with Ţara Românească, and reports by county officials show that after the assembly the union was discussed by peasants in many communities. "From now on," they declared, "Transylvania is no longer Transylvania, but Romania!"

A large number of Hungarian and Saxon serfs mingled confidently with their Romanian counterparts at Blaj, since their concerns and hardships had been the same for centuries on end. In some places, Romanian and Hungarian peasants held joint meetings upon their return from Blaj. A comparatively small meeting also was held in Lugoj in the Banat on 15 May. Roughly a thousand priests, teachers, and peasants attended. They called for a Romanian national congress and national rights for Romanians; independent churches; the rescission of Magyarization laws and the use of Romanian in churches, schools, and administration; and Romanian officials and military officers.

Only a few days after the Blaj assembly, on 24 May, Moldavian revolutionaries in Braşov who had attended it composed a document known as *Principiile noastre pentru reformarea patriei* [Our principles for reforming the fatherland]. It called for the abolition of feudal obligations; the granting of property to the serfs without any compensation to be paid by them; the abolition of all privileges and the equal sharing by all inhabitants of the burdens of the state; the respecting of the principles of liberty, equality, and fraternity; and the union of Moldavia and Ţara Românească in a single independent Romanian state. The Braşov document is eloquent proof of the intertwining of the revolutionary movements of the three Romanian countries.

In spite of the obvious dangers of such a course, the Transylvanian diet met in Cluj on 29 May without a single Romanian representative and voted in favor of the union of Transylvania with Hungary. Only the radicals associated with the newspaper *Marczius Tizenötödike* [The fifteenth of March] had raised their voices against ignoring Romanian wishes, writing, "In Transylvania, two powers will decide the future of the union: the diet and the Romanian people. The diet represents only a few hundred people, the Romanians all of Transylvania. . . . The union of Transylvania with Hungary without the consent of the Romanians is something we must not even think of undertaking."

Two delegations that had been elected at the Blaj assembly—one to the Transylvanian diet and one to the emperor—returned without results, and the revolutionary movement expanded in consequence. The situation was not improved by the law abolishing serfdom passed by the diet; it was not enforced, and the nobility continued to require peasants to perform involuntary labor. Moreover, no land was granted to hundreds of thousands of jeleri, who thus remained dependent on the landlords. Using a variety of excuses, landlords tried to force their former serfs to continue to work for them. If the peasants resisted, landlords retaliated. On 2 June, for example, a frightful slaughter took place at Mihalţ in the county of Alba; twelve peasants were killed and nine wounded by Szekler border guards summoned by the landlord. Other villages also were punished by military executions, and many peasants were thrown into castle keeps by the nobility. The progressive Hungarian journalist Viktor Erdélyi (Aradi) rightly wrote that

> the dawn of freedom arrived in Transylvania in a rather strange form. . . . The [Romanian] leaders could not meet freely with the people, for the authorities everywhere suspected conspiracies and rebellions. The spring of freedom has been greeted by the lords of Transylvania with acts of terror, with the national guard forcing peasants to work, with the proclamation of martial law, and with beatings, imprisonments, and hangings.

Romanians saw that their only course was to prepare for war. Particularly in the Bihor Mountains, the inhabitants began to arm themselves with scythes and spears.

Another Romanian assembly took place on 27 June in a field near Lugoj. Ten thousand people took part, the overwhelming majority of them peasants from the Banat. Eftimie Murgu was elected president. The assembly sought church autonomy, the introduction of the Romanian language in administration, and recognition of the Romanian nationality.

The outbreak of revolution in Ţara Românească aroused new spirit among Transylvanian Romanians. The Romanian papers in Braşov devoted more than half of their columns to the revolution; the Blaj *Organul naţional* [National journal] likewise greeted the events in Bucharest with enthusiasm, saying that "the hearts of all Romanians are uplifted, wherever in the fatherland they may be." The Braşov papers continued to follow developments, giving extensive coverage to the Muntenian Romanians' proclamation of purpose and describing the "grand celebration" on the "Field of Liberty" in Bucharest.

Once the revolution in Ţara Românească was launched, Bălcescu sent the proclamation and other documents to Eftimie Murgu, his former teacher. Murgu responded, "My brother! I tell you, I wept for joy when I learned of the triumph of freedom in Romania." Moreover, a number of Transylvanian intellectuals went to Romania (as many had already begun to call Ţara Românească) as soon as they were summoned, in order to spread the word of the new constitution among the people and to prepare them for the struggle against domestic and foreign enemies. Plans were made to call a general congress of Romanians in Bucharest to direct the revolution and pave the way for the unification of the Romanian countries.

Meanwhile, conditions in Transylvania worsened. The establishment of commissions to investigate and adjudicate disputes between landlords and peasants were delayed; military executions and hangings continued. The Romanian "chancellists" began to be hunted down. The Romanian national committee was arrested, but then was freed by soldiers of the First Border Regiment. The situation was further exacerbated when the Hungarian authorities organized recruitment into the army. Revolts broke out in several places, and the army was sent in against the peasants. More massacres occurred, including one in Luna in the county of Turda when the townspeople resisted the recruiting commission—headed by the supreme commissioner of the county—with the aid of neighboring villages, saying that the emperor had not put the law into effect. Hussars and members of the Hungarian national guard fired into the crowd, and twenty-two people were killed.

In the face of such events, delegates of the First Border Regiment convened in Orlat in southern Transylvania on 10 and 11 September, together with civilian delegates from the villages in the regimental sector, to protest against the terrorism. In a petition to the emperor, they asked for "the abolition of all feudal personal servitude, the abolition of *robota,* and the abolition of all taxes in kind." At almost the same time, on 13–15 September delegates from the villages in the Second Border Regiment sector met in Năsăud in the northeast, under the leadership of the regimental officers. Those assembled declared that they did not recognize the union of Transylvania with Hungary, since it had been decided without the consent of the Romanians, and that they would not be subject to the Hungarian government. The Austrian Lieutenant Colonel Urban, commander of the regiment, declared the Hungarian government in rebellion, and called on the people to take an oath of allegiance to the emperor.

The crowning event, however, was the third popular assembly in Blaj at the end of September, attended by approximately sixty thousand peasants and intellectuals. The peasants were armed with spears, pitchforks, and rifles, giving the assembly the appearance of an armed camp. A protocol was drawn up, bringing together all the petitions which were to be set before the emperor. These included an end to the terror and introduction of the rule of law; restitution of property stolen from the peasants; release of all prisoners; an end to *robota* and seizures of property; organization of Romanian national guards; rejection of the union with Hungary; the earliest possible opening of the Transylvanian diet, with delegates from the Romanian, Saxon, Hungarian, and Szekler nations in proportion to their numbers; and a provisional Transylvanian government to be elected on the same basis.

The resolutions of this third assembly reflected the bitterness of the masses after a whole summer of arbitrary abuses by the authorities and landlords. Most of the points of the protocol are markedly social in character and express demands crucial to the oppressed peasantry irrespective of nationality. This is the only explanation for the fact that Hungarian and Saxon peasants took part in the third Blaj assembly, as they had in the first two. Indeed, the peasantry no longer had any faith in the authorities, since a full three months had passed since the diet's vote to establish a commission to judge peasant-landlord disputes without any such commissions having been formed. The peasants did, however, trust the Romanian intelligentsia, many of whom were also persecuted.

The third Blaj assembly resolved to raise a Romanian army and to cut off relations with the revolution in Hungary, believing that in this way the principality of Transylvania would become a country with a Romanian leadership and administration, a country in which even the question of land ownership could find a just solution. In the opinion of some Romanian leaders, Transylvania should take the initiative in unifying the three

Romanian countries. No longer having their old faith in the emperor, the assembly addressed a long memorandum to the parliament in Vienna, detailing the situation in Transylvania and asking for support in realizing its demands. Furthermore, at the end of September, a select national committee was formed to act as an executive body for the Romanian revolution. This group organized the Romanian army into fifteen regions, each commanded by a prefect and a vice-prefect. Each legion was divided into a number of troops led by a tribune and a vice-tribune, and each troop was divided into ten centuries led by centurions and vice-centurions.

In October, the latent war in Transylvania burst into open armed struggle. The Hungarian authorities had at their disposal the armed national guard, the Szekler regiments, and the new "Honved" units, while the Romanians, except for those in the Bihor Mountains, were only just learning how to fight in disciplined units. Seizing this advantage, a number of Hungarian leaders sent Szekler troops to villages, arresting and hanging hundreds more Romanians. Nevertheless, the Romanian administrative and military organization made rapid progress. Prefects were named to head the legions: Avram Iancu, Ion Axente Sever, Ioan Buteanu, Nicolae Solomon, Simion Balint, Petru Dobra, and others. These were all young men, ready to sacrifice their lives for the good of the nation. The revolutionaries' first action was to disarm the Hungarian national guard and the nobility, while the Romanian Committee addressed proclamations of peaceful intent to the Hungarians and Szeklers. At the end of October and beginning of November, steps were taken to reorganize the towns and elect new governing bodies for the counties.

The revolution in Țara Românească was suppressed in the autumn of 1848, but the Transylvanians benefited by it, in that leaders such as Nicolae Bălcescu, Gheorghe Magheru, Christian Tell, Ioan Eliade-Rădulescu, and Cezar Bolliac joined them. The newcomers advised the Romanian Committee to get out from under the control of the Austrian command. To accomplish this, given that almost all of Transylvania was controlled by the Romanian legions and Austrian armies, the committee was advised to call a national assembly with the purpose of organizing Transylvania as a Romanian country. The Habsburgs, however, feared the Romanians' strength; General Puchner, the Austrian commander-in-chief in Transylvania, resolved to disarm the Romanian legions.

Around the end of December, the situation changed again, when the Hungarian army entered Transylvania under the command of the Polish General Josef Bem. Bem's army had a large popular base and was composed of a variety of peoples. Having occupied the capital city of Cluj on 25 December, Bem issued a proclamation assuring the populace that he had not come to subjugate the people but to combat despotism. He urged Romanians and Saxons to draw a veil over the past and align themselves with the cause of liberty. As a result, Szeklers, Romanians, and Saxons flocked to join Bem's army, and he was thus able to score several victories and occupy almost all of Transylvania. Unfortunately, Bem's orders, which were supposed to bring peace, were ignored by the Hungarian political and military leaders, who were in many cases linked to the landowners' interests. Hungarian and Szekler nationalists wanted revenge on the Romanians for the devastation and burning of towns with Hungarian populatons, such as Zlatna and Aiud, forgetting the burned and pillaged Romanian villages along the Mureş and the Someş. The commissioner of the Hungarian government, László Csány, declared Bem's amnesty invalid and set up "bloody tribunals" everywhere to punish the "traitors to the country." These courts pronounced thousands of death sentences and confiscations of property.

In April 1849, Bem entered the Banat from Transylvania. On 16 May he announced from Orşova that all of the Banat except the fortress of Timişoara was in Hungarian hands. On 21 May, another Hungarian army liberated Budapest.

After the imperial troops had been driven out, the Hungarian terror continued in one part of Transylvania, while in another— the Bihor Mountains—the bourgeois-democratic Romanian revolution went on. Part of the Romanian legions from the plains joined their fellows in the mountains. Bem would have liked to have reached an agreement with the Romanian forces in order to have a free hand against the Austrian and czarist troops, but the Hungarian leadership, and especially the noble landlords, demanded unconditional surrender by the Romanian armies. They believed that the Romanians, surrounded and without the leadership of Austrian officers, must be defeated easily, and several Hungarian expeditions were sent in. Again the Hungarian troops committed massacres, but they were pushed back by unexpectedly stiff resistance, as women and children joined the men in battle. One after another the Hungarian attacks were

Alexandru Papiu-Ilarian, 1828–1878. General Iosif Bem, 1794–1850.

Bronze medal commemorating the independence of Romania.

rebuffed. The hero of these days of bravery was Avram Iancu, with his lieutenants Simion Balint, Ioan Buteanu, Petru Dobra, and Ioan Axente Sever.

In the winter of 1849–49 and the following spring, a number of Muntenian revolutionaries found shelter in the Bihor Mountains, including Alexandru Golescu-Albu, Ion Ionescu from Brad, George Adrian, and the artist Barbu Iscovescu. Close contact with these men strengthened both the national consciousness of the Transylvanian Romanians and their faith in the future of the Romanian nation. In July 1849, Nicolae Bălcescu spent a few days in Iancu's camp; his talks with the leaders and with the common people deeply impressed the Transylvanian leadership and left an indelible mark on Bălcescu's own consciousness.

In spite of the hostility of some Hungarian nobles, the more progressive and farsighted participants in the revolution of 1848 fought to create a common front of the people opposed to Habsburg and czarist despotism. The Romanan deputies from Crişana, for example, worked tirelessly within the Hungarian diet for Romanian-Hungarian collaboration. Romanian revolutionaries in Constantinople and Paris, exiled after the Turkish and Russian armies had suppressed the revolutions in Moldavia and Ţara Românească, also realized that it would be necessary to form an alliance if they were to serve the cause of the revolution. Hungarian revolutionary groups likewise advanced the idea of a confederation of Danubian peoples to further the common struggle against czarist and Habsburg forces.

The most fervent proponent of this collaboration, however, was Nicolae Bălcescu. Although he recognized the difficulty of his mission, especially after the Hungarian army's atrocities in the Bihor Mountains, he nevertheless tried to convince the Hungarian political leaders that they had to give up the idea of national supremacy if they wanted to ally themselves with the Romanians. Meanwhile, he attempted to get the Romanian leadership to abandon their illusions about help from the emperor. Nonetheless, the Hungarian leaders, even on the eve of czarist intervention in May 1849, would not give up the idea of Magyar supremacy. The Hungarian aristocrats in Transylvania were especially opposed to any concessions, fearing the end of their own rule.

Negotiations with the Hungarian government, therefore, proceeded extremely slowly. Not until 25 June did Bălcescu receive a response, and that was unsatisfactory in terms of concessions to the Slavs and Romanians of Hungary. The deliberately slow pace of the negotiations revealed the Hungarian government's lack of foresight, for the czarist troops had already crossed the borders of Hungary and Transylvania in a number of places on 18 and 19 June. Decisive action was called for. At the end of June, Bălcescu sent two young men to Iancu to advise him to remain neutral between the Hungarians and the Russians, not to come out of the mountains, and to try to persuade Bem to agree to head a Transylvanian uprising without regard to nationality. Bălcescu reckoned that even if the revolution in Hungary failed, the fight against czarism could be carried on with the Transylvanian mountains serving as a center of resistance.

After long negotiation between Bălcescu and the Hungarian government, a Romanian-Hungarian agreement was reached on 14 July. It was signed for the Hungarians by Governor Lajos Kossuth, and for the Romanian exiles by Bălcescu and Bolliac. It is especially significant that this document uses the name "Romania" ten years before the union of Moldavia and Ţara Românească, which proves that the Romanian revolutionaries had not lost sight of their objective of uniting the Romanian countries in a single national state.

On 28 July the Chamber of Deputies passed a so-called Nationalities Law, assuring the Romanians and the Slavic nations of Hungary certain national rights and some degree of national independence and granting freedom to the peasants. Murgu immediately left to communicate the text of the law to Iancu, but because of the advance of the czarist army he could not reach the Romanian camp. The law, passed on the eve of the Hungarian army's surrender, was more symbolic than real.

Bălcescu once more went to the mountains to convince Iancu to recognize the agreement with the Hungarian government and managed to obtain from him a letter to the government which declared that while it was rather late, with the czarist troops advancing in the Mureş valley, to be forging a Romanian-Hungarian alliance, he would remain neutral toward the Hungarian army.

All of these actions to create a common revolutionary front could not block the course leading to defeat. Nevertheless, it is important not to underestimate the significance of the truce between the Hungarian and Romanian troops and of the shared ideas expressed in the correspondence between the Romanian leaders and the leaders of the Hungarian revolution in the summer of 1849. For example, in a letter to Iancu on 21 June, Brigade Commander Jozsef Simonffy sent a fervent appeal under the motto "Liberty, Equality, Fraternity," calling on the Romanians to turn their weapons against their mutual enemy. "The Romanians and the Hungarians," he wrote, "need to be united in brotherhood. . . . Anyone who sows enmity and hate and causes bloodshed between these two sister nations is a traitor to his own nation." Iancu replied on 27 June in a letter addressed to his "Hungarian brothers." What had aroused the Romanians, he wrote, was "nonrecognition of our political nationality and the barbaric tyranny of the Hungarian aristocrats of Transylvania, which the people in this day and age could no longer tolerate, and which would fill any intelligent man with disgust." He regretted the war, he said, for "nature has settled us in one homeland so that we might sweat together to cultivate it, and together enjoy its fruits."

Among the Saxons of Transylvania as well, there was a group of progressive thinkers who were working for unity. Of these one might mention Anton Kurz and the poet Maximillian Moltke. The latter, in his well-known "Siebenbürgen, Land des Segens," exhorted the Transylvanian peoples to understanding and brotherhood.

In the second half of June, Field Marshal Ivan Feodorovici Paskevich, who had put down the Polish revolt of 1830–31, led the czarist army across the borders of Hungary and Transylvania to end the Hungarian revolution. Lajos Kossuth left Hungary and took refuge in Turkey, turning the command of the army over to Arthur Görgey and giving him full power. On 13 August, Görgey surrendered to the Russian army at Şiria in southwestern Transylvania.

Though the revolutions were defeated, the fundamental principles they pursued—the end of the feudal order, the abolition of noble privileges and of absolutism, and the national liberation of oppressed peoples—could not be extinguished. Serfdom, the nobility's exclusive ownership of the land, and certain of the nobility's privileges, like exemption from taxes, were at an end. The three medieval nations were abolished and the Romanians no longer considered merely a "tolerated people." Through the struggles of 1848–49, the Romanian people—in Bariţiu's words—"not only attained an awareness of their national individuality, but also an awareness of their dignity and worth."

11

After the Revolution

The Socioeconomic Structure

AT THE BEGINNING OF JUNE 1848, the diet in Cluj had resolved that the serfs who had *sessiones,* or plots of "urbarial land," should become freeholders of those lands, while landless peasants who worked on the seigneurial reserves—the jerleri and "curialists"—should remain dependent. From the beginning, the situation was complicated by the fact that the "exemption from *robota* and tithes" applied only to the serfs' houses and personal plots of land, and not to the allodial holdings they worked. Suppression of the revolution left many things unsettled, and the nobles interpreted the law in their own favor. The former masters were very reluctant to accept the idea that they must give up forever any claim to the serfs' free labor and, therefore, to their land. With the support and direct connivance of the local Habsburg administrative and military authorities, they perpetrated all sorts of abuses and reinterpretations of the law. To justify their refusal to emancipate serfs, they manufactured excuses like unpaid debts; they claimed "compensation for damages suffered" during the revolution; they contested the applicability of the law to fields, pastures, and forests that until then had been held by the serfs; they doubled the burdens of *robota* for the jeleri and curialists; and they required poor peasants to become sharecroppers on the most unproductive and poorly kept lands.

Under such circumstances, the peasants had no choice but stubborn resistance and the forcible taking of their rights from the nobility. Even in areas with mixed Romanian, Hungarian, and Saxon populations, the peasants united against the feudal class. As before, the movement had its center in the Bihor Mountains, and its leader was the hero of the 1848 revolution,

Avram Iancu. The peasants scored a number of victories. Former serfs and jeleri occupied abandoned estates in Zarand and Hunedoara in southern Transylvania and in Turda and Cluj in central Transylvania, seizing fields and woods and dividing them along themselves. Armed intervention prevented the outbreak of a general rebellion, but it could not force the return of all occupied property. Iancu's arrest only strengthened the peasants' spirit.

Agitation and discontent continued throughout 1851. The fight against the landowners increasingly was combined with that against the Habsburg authorities. A taxation system introduced in the years immediately after the revolution—direct taxes on land, home, and income, and indirect taxes on consumer goods—significantly worsened the peasantry's economic standing. Refusal to pay taxes and open resistance to tax collectors were common occurrences in Transylvanian villages, and occasionally led to real rebellion. In May 1851, for example, there was a bloody riot in the marketplace in Abrud in the Bihor Mountains. On 17 August 1852, Iancu was arrested for a second time, in Cîmpeni, and was jailed in Alba Iulia and then in Sibiu, finally being freed six weeks later.

To quiet the situation, new laws were passed to cover those peasants not affected by the legislation of 1848. New agrarian laws were contained in the imperial patents issued for the Banat, Hungary, Croatia, and Slavonia on 2 March 1853, and for Transylvania on 21 June 1854. The emperor's patent for Transylvania set detailed procedures for doing away with serfdom and for settling land claims; it also established the relations between former feudal masters and their former subjects, and between the latter and the state. In contrast to the 1848 law, it extended emancipation to the jeleri, although they were required to make compensation. The subjeleri (*subinquilini*) were freed without compensation, as were Gypsies both with and without permanent domiciles. The landlords' privileges to operate mills, taverns, and fishing areas remained in force, but their exclusive right to run a slaughterhouse or own a shop was abolished. Pastures, forests, and marshes used only by serfs became their property. To resolve disputes between former serfs and their masters, urbarial courts and provincial land-claim commissions were instituted, as provided in the law of 1848. Formerly feudal property was legislated into private property of the capitalist type.

Even after serfdom was abolished, however, there was marked

socioeconomic stratification among the peasants. According to contemporary statistics, there were about 120,000 day laborers, more than 84,000 full-time agricultural hands, and 28,000 servants, while the total of landowners, large and small, was less than 300,000. In 1857, roughly 60 percent of the peasants owned fewer than 2 ha (5 acres) of land, 24 percent from 2 to 5, 10 percent from 5 to 10, 3 percent from 10 to 20, and 2 percent from 20 to 50. The total proportion of landowners in the population rose to 49 percent, of which 0.9 percent had large estates. Farm workers made up 28.4 percent of the population, and jeleri 40 percent of the population living in villages. By 1861, 173,781 *sessiones (urbariale Ansässigkeiten)* theoretically had been freed from feudal use, or 1,615,574 acres out of a total of 4,680,000 acres of arable land. In the overwhelming majority of cases, however, the amount of land owned was totally inadequate to support a family. Moreover, the jeleri and the serfs from the allodial lands, required to pay compensation out of their own pockets, were materially and socially inferior from the very beginning. Since few jeleri had the means to pay compensation immediately, most were left in a state of feudal dependence.

By 1867, in part because of increased production of commodities, differentiation among the peasants was much greater than in the preceding periods. There was a drop in the number of middle-level peasants, who earlier had formed the bulk of the peasant population; from 1849 to the end of the period of absolutism and through the following liberal regime, their proportion fell to 35 percent. A small portion of the peasantry, some 4 percent, grew rich and hired poor peasants to work for them. Thus the stratum of landless or almost landless peasants increased until it constituted 61 percent of the total peasantry.

Because of the growing hardships, more and more people had no way to earn a living and were forced to emigrate, either to other parts of the Austrian empire or outside it altogether. The census of 1850–51 lists 30,734 persons in Transylvania proper as "absent," while in 1857 there were 54,566 in that category. Emigrants were especially attracted to Moldavia and Țara Românească, where living conditions were better. In 1870, of 16,458 passports issued in Transylvania, 15,867 were for those areas and only 591 for other countries. In any case, most left illegally, without passports. In 1862, roughly 10,000 Szeklers emigrated to Moldavia and Țara Românească from the seats of Ciuc and Trei-Scaune in southeastern Transylvania alone. The majority of emigrants were Romanian, however, not only because they predominated in the population, but because they made up the largest number of landless peasants.

Clearly, then, in doing away with the feudal order the revolution of 1848 had removed the last obstacle to capitalist economic development. The necessary conditions were created for the appearance of a large class of free men with few opportunities, from which the labor force needed by capitalist industry could be drawn. However, Transylvanian industrial development was still hampered by large estates and continued dependence on Austria. In 1850 the imperial government, which represented primarily the interests of the Austrian bourgeoisie, abolished customs barriers, thereby incorporating Transylvania into the imperial customs system and at the same time guaranteeing Austrian industry marketplaces and sources of cheap raw materials. The entry of Austrian goods into Transylvanian marketplaces without payment of customs tariffs was almost disastrous for local industry; only the rich plains regions such as Crișana and the Banat were able to find steady markets for their own products in Austria. In those areas, however, as a result of the grain trade, substantial capital was accumulated and invested, particularly in food processing industries such as milling. One source from 1863 lists some seventy steam mills in Transylvania and the Banat, all started after 1849.

Austria's own economic development, meanwhile, demanded the discovery of new sources of raw materials at the lowest possible price. Again Transylvanian mineral wealth was heavily exploited. Austrians investing in mining not only enjoyed state protection, but also had a labor force available under exceptionally favorable conditions. Tens of thousands of workers, including many women and children, were used in mining, more than in any other Transylvanian industry, although wages were low and working conditions hazardous. As a result, the investment necessary for a given level of production was much lower in Transylvania than in the western regions of the empire. Austrian capital, of course, represented an obstacle to indigenous development, since it emphasized mining and semimanufactures and perennially blocked the way to the manufacturing of machinery.

The fuel requirements of the Austrian railways and the Danube steamers provided an impetus for the rapid growth of coal mining. The coal basins of Transylvania, especially in the Banat and the Jiu valley, were snatched up by the Austrian bourgeoisie after the establishment of the absolutist government, and seven different mining companies were formed during this period. Mining experienced even greater development after the Mining and Smelting Corporation of Braşov began work on Transylvania's first railways, including the feeder line from Simeria to Petroşeni in the Jiu valley. The state railway company, the Staatseisenbahngesellschaft, built smelters, foundries, machine works, a chemical plant, and mills for construction materials. Large quantities of rolling stock and rails were produced. In 1852 there were fourteen steam engines with a capacity of 276 horsepower; by 1863 the number had risen to forty, with a capacity of 1,632 horsepower. Coal production underwent similar growth, from 72,870 tons in 1855 to approximately 204,600 tons in 1867.

With the exploitation of local raw materials and cheap labor, Transylvania's metallurgical industry also burgeoned and created very large profits.

Local capital was invested in the food industry. Large distilleries were established in Cluj, Arad, and Oradea, whose by-products were used as fodder for cattle and sheep. The animals were then easily transported to the major centers of consumption in the western sections of the empire.

The extent to which Transylvania lagged behind other imperial provinces in most industries, however, is quite evident in the statistics relating to factories. Of 2,809 steam engines in the entire Austrian manufacturing industry, Transylvania had only 1.4 percent, with insignificant horsepower. Austrian goods were made in technically well-outfitted factories and were superior to local products, which for the most part came from workshops and small factories.

In the 1850s, attempts were made to convert the textile industry, dominated in the first half of the nineteenth century by large numbers of individual artisans, to mechanized production. With the increased demand for woolen fabrics that resulted from the Crimean War, a number of Transylvanian guilds accumulated capital and tried to establish large-scale factories. These attempts failed, however, because of Austrian and Bohemian competition. Again, while old paper-manufacturing shops— about five of them in this period—were transformed into full-size mills, competition from Austrian paper did not favor their success. In 1856 there were about thirteen glass manufacturing businesses, all of them on the scale of small factories. Faced with competition from glass imported from Austria and Bohemia, they had either to cease production or become small workshops of only local importance. Nevertheless, the industrial working class grew, the proportion in the general population reaching 2.8 percent in 1857. To protect their interests, workers organized into mutual aid societies.

Since production by Transylvanian factories was relatively low, trade in their products was not especially well developed. Transylvania's trading partners, taking all manufactured goods and agricultural products into account, included the other countries of the Habsburg monarchy and Romania. The Romanian trade was vitally important, since only in that country could local products be sold. In order to increase this trade, Transylvanian commercial groups campaigned for an extension of the railroad through Braşov to Predeal in Romania.

Transylvanian exports to Moldavia and Ţara Românească rose steadily after the revolution, in 1851 reaching 10,352 tons, in 1852 26,547 tons, in 1853 30,729 tons, and in 1854 22,730 tons. Import and export data for 1851 break down as follows: of the total value of imported goods—21 million florins—animals represented 46.3 percent, animal products (hides, tallow, wool, and so on) 39.1 percent, grain 6.3 percent, and other 8.3 percent; the total value of exports was approximately 15 million florins, of which textiles represented 41.6 percent, metal products 9.7 percent, clothing 7.6 percent, and other 26.2 percent.

As commerce and industry grew, the Transylvanian bourgeoisie also increased, until it constituted about 6.3 percent of the total population in the early 1850s; the professional class represented 2.6 percent. Of the total Transylvanian population in 1857, Romanians constituted 62.5 percent, Hungarians and Szeklers together 27.6 percent, Saxons 9 percent, and Jews 0.9 percent.

Political Orientation

The aims and desires of the Romanian people, which had emerged clearly during the revolutionary turmoil, were brutally put down by the absolutist regime reimposed by the Habsburgs in late 1849. Transylvanian autonomy was extinguished, and the country was reduced to a mere imperial province run by a military governor. Civil authority was subordinated to the military, which ruled with military courts and emergency decrees. Forced Catholicization was in effect everywhere, though it provoked reactions both from the Orthodox Romanians and from the Lutheran Saxons and Reformed Hungarians. In November 1849, separate provinces were formed from Serbian Voyvodina and the Banat. The seat of the latter was Timișoara, while the Voyvodina was ruled directly from Vienna. Western regions of Transylvania—Arad, Bihor, Sătmar, and Maramureș—were incorporated into Hungary.

The Romanian delegation that had arrived in Vienna while the revolution was still in progress was forced to realize, after three years of fruitless petitions and memoranda presented to the court and the imperial government, that its persistence was in vain. The Romanian representatives sought the creation of an autonomous province from the imperial territories with Romanian majorities—the principality of Transylvania, the Banat, Crișana, Maramureș, and Bukovina; the Romanian language would be used and the administrative officials would be Romanian. However, this plan was never seriously considered. Many Romanians recognized the truth of a contemporary witticism to the effect that the nations which had remained loyal to the emperor had received as a reward the same thing meted out to the Hungarians as a punishment.

In order to prevent the Romanians in Transylvania from expressing sympathy and solidarity with their brothers across the Carpathians—sentiments which were considered extremely dangerous to the Habsburgs—various emergency measures were taken. Among these were the press control committees established in accordance with the press laws of 1851 and 1852; the only materials which could be published were those contained in official news bulletins. The Transylvanian press was thus stifled by Austrian censorship. Nonetheless, the trans-Carpathian bonds were unbreakable. Writers from Moldavia and Țara Românească contributed to progressive publications, both Romanian and Hungarian, in Transylvania. Pro-union propaganda in the Transylvanian press (both overt and disguised) found a receptive audience, for the masses' desire for unification, although suppressed by Habsburg absolutism after 1849, lived on. Numerous reports sent by local civilian and military authorities to the Viennese court in 1857 and 1858 attest to the unrest among Transylvanian Romanians. A report in April 1857, for example, drew the court's attention to the unification issue, saying that the movement had caused such turmoil in Moldavia and Ţara Românească that it had to have repercussions among Romanians in the neighboring Austrian provinces, and particularly in Transylvania, since all of the Romanians had the same ethnic background, spoke the same language, and professed essentially the same religion.

In 1857, poor harvests, losses suffered by stockbreeders, and treasury proceedings against those unable to pay their taxes intensified the desire for unification. Two years later, the head of the district of Orăştie reported to Internal Affairs Minister Alexander Bach that the discontent of the poor peasantry and the desire for unification with Ţara Românească and Moldavia were so strong as to endanger the existing social order. Not only the Romanian but the Hungarian and Saxon industrial and commercial bourgeoisie were equally dissatisfied. An Austrian police report concluded, realistically, that "there is not a party or a social group that would consider the current state of affairs as a benefit of the empire and worthy of support. On the contrary, so great is the discontent that public opinion could only be a cause for concern in the event that trouble erupted. Nowhere are there conservative elements loyal to the government."

The double election of Alexandru Ioan Cuza as prince of Moldavia on 5 January 1859 and as prince of Ţara Românească on 24 January 1859 brought into being the new state of the United Principalities—which two years later became Romania. One of the most perceptive observers of the Romanian people, Alexandru Papiu-Ilarian, expressed a truth worthy of attention when he wrote that "the Romanians of Transylvania look only to the Principalities. . . . When Cuza was elected prince, the enthusiasm of the Romanians in Transylvania was perhaps greater than in the Principalities." The Viennese court, however, was confronted with an even greater danger to the integrity of its empire.

After the Austrian army was defeated near Magenta and Solferino in the summer of 1859, disturbances increased inside Transylvania. The Romanian masses fought side-by-side with the Hungarian, Saxon, and Serbian populations against the local imperial authorities, and in many places they were driven out and their directives ignored. The Romanian bourgeoisie in Transylvania, the Banat, and Bukovina also increased its resistance. The regime was subjected to blunt criticism; liberty for the peoples of the country and restoration of the autonomy of

Romanian-inhabited territories were openly discussed. On a number of occasions, Cuza in Romania made allusions to plans for unifying Transylvania with his country. Newspapers received from Romania during those months emphasized the necessity for a national state; this was "the Daco-Romanian idea."

Romanian political representatives, together with Hungarian and Saxon leaders from Transylvania and the leaders of other nationalities with the Habsburg empire, took advantage of the crisis in the court in 1860 to present their ideas about reorganizing the monarchy in a federal form to the Reichsrath. The Romanian deputy from the Banat, Andrei Mocioni, supported reorganization. He called on the monarchy to abandon its Germanization program and to stop identifying its interests with those of the privileged classes and peoples. Instead of this unreasonable policy, he said, the court "should take as the foundation of its reconstruction and consolidation the interests of all peoples and nationalities and the principle of the equality of all political, national, religious, and cultural rights." This could be achieved only if modern states were and continued to be based on "individual nations, with their general interests of culture, civilization, and prosperity."

Mocioni eventually emerged as the defender of the interests of all of the people of the monarchy, supporting the idea of equality and of an empire reorganized on the basis of national territories with considerable autonomy. According to his view, such a plan meant that all of the monarchical institutions should be based on the principle of equal national rights; that the administration of justice should be simplified and less expensive; that education at all levels should be in the language of the people; and that there should be religious freedom and equal support of all churches by the state. Mocioni's proposals aroused the opposition of the Austrian and Hungarian aristocracy and bourgeoisie, one of whom characterized them as "Garibaldian tendencies" which would destroy the monarchy. The Romanians, Czechs, Ruthenians, and Slovaks, on the other hand, greeted his ideas warmly. The principles of equality and self-determination also were supported by Andrei Şaguna, the Romanian Orthodox metropolitan.

The proposals were not accepted. The Reichsrath resolved that the Habsburg monarchy would be organized without regard to the wishes of the various peoples. The Romanians of the monarchy would be divided among four provinces, even though they occupied contiguous areas in the eastern end of the monarchy.

Bukovina was to be part of Galicia, Crişana and Maramureş of Hungary, and the Principality of Transylvania was to be ruled directly from Vienna. It was the question of the organization of the Banat, however, that created substantial turmoil. The court sent Count Alexander Mensdorf-Pouilly to decide the region's fate. Should it remain autonomous, or, as the Hungarian aristocracy demanded, should it be incorporated into Hungary? To protest against this whole procedure, Andrei Mocioni called a national assembly of Romanians in Timişoara, which in its sessions of 18 and 19 November 1860 resolved that the Banat and the Serbian Voyvodina should be autonomous. As a reply to Mensdorf-Pouilly's statement that "the province is not in any condition to be able to organize and administer itself," Mocioni presented the monarchy with a petition from the Romanians with over twelve thousand signatures, asking that "if it cannot be constituted by itself, the province and its Romanians should be incorporated into Transylvania, as it has been in the past." The proposal was rejected, and the Banat and the Serbian Voyvodina were incorporated into Hungary. This decision provoked much anti-Habsburg agitation. In Arad, Lipova, and Reşiţa, imperial insignia were torn down, while in Lugoj, Romanian, Hungarian, and Serbian flags were raised.

The struggle to regain autonomy for the Banat continued in the Hungarian diet. Mocioni pointed out the injustice of ignoring the region's 600,000 Romanians and subjecting them to the rule of 40,000 Hungarians. He also corresponded with the Romanian leaders in Transylvania, proposing that they seek approval for a national congress of all of the Romanians in the Austrian empire, "who can no longer stay divided into several provinces, tricked and exploited by foreign privileged classes, but must be united into a body politic, with its own national territory and its own political organization."

The court rejected the Romanian request, although it did promise autonomy for Transylvania, including a separate diet and recognition of the Romanian nation there. At the same time, however, applying the principle of divide and conquer, it decreed the annexation to Hungary of Crasna, Solnoc, Zarand, and Chioar, territories with a large majority of Romanian inhabitants. The populations in those areas expressed their discontent in assemblies in the spring and summer of 1861. In a statement presented to the emperor, they emphasized the fact that their regions formed "an integral and inseparable part of Transylvania."

The court nevertheless went ahead with the annexations, costing the autonomy of territories with a population of about 240,000, of whom some 75 percent were Romanian.

Romanian leaders from the Banat, Crişana, and Maramureş initially reacted with passive resistance, refusing to participate in the Hungarian diet or the Reichsrath. Later, however, they elected deputies in the hope that they could defend the "national demands" in the diet. The nineteen Romanian deputies elected in Hungary and the Banat did exactly that. However, the diet was thought to "demand too much from Vienna" and was dissolved in August 1861. Romanian leaders from the Banat and Hungary then increased their efforts to call a Romanian national congress. They wanted "to constitute all the Romanians in the monarchy into a body politic, headed by a monarch and with the character of a Romanian nation." The new prime minister, Anton Schmerling, rejected both the demands of the Hungarian leaders and the Romanian proposals, thus keeping the nation divided.

The Romanians of the Principality of Transylvania, meanwhile, were also in turmoil. Bishop Andrei Şaguna emerged as a leader of the fight to assure the broadest possible Romanian participation in political life. A delegation was chosen to go to Vienna and request that the emperor issue a special diploma guaranteeing the political rights of the Romanian nation; the principle of equality of the Romanian, Hungarian, and German languages; the autonomy of Transylvania; proportional representation of the Romanians in the constituent assembly to form the diet; and the convocation of a Romanian national congress. The national congress was to play a role analogous to that of the national assembly in Blaj in 1848; it was to study in detail those questions of national interest that would be discussed at a multiethnic conference to be held in Alba Iulia and in the future diet, so that the Romanian delegates might in every case act with the full support of the masses who had elected them as representatives.

For their part, the Romanian bourgeoisie began early in 1861 to be concerned with the careful organization of the Transylvanian administration and with municipal and county reorganization. They met in a national conference in Sibiu from 13 to 16 January 1861, and those present resolved to take the following stands: affirmation of the political existence of the Romanian nation; preservation of Transylvanian autonomy and the political equality of the Transylvanian peoples; and recognition of the

Romanian nation and its proportional representation in the Transylvanian diet. The conference protested the staggering injustice of the chancellor of Transylvania, who had fixed the number of representatives to the multiethnic conference at 24 for 139,218 Hungarians, 8 for 116,375 Saxons, and 8 for 1,354,550 Romanians. These demands were also presented to the conference in Alba Iulia on 11 February 1861. The purpose of this conference was to arrive at some consensus among the Romanian, Hungarian, and Saxon nations. However, differences of opinion were so sharp that conflicts between the Romanian and Hungarian leaders were difficult to avoid. The Hungarian representatives wanted to bring back the arbitrary resolutions of 1848, including the union of Transylvania with Hungary, while the Romanian representatives demanded a law that would recognize the equal rights of the Romanian nation with other nations and the exercise of those rights in proportion to their contribution to the support of the state.

The Hungarian leaders from both Hungary and Transylvania had no real understanding of the strength of the Habsburg monarchy, believing it to be so enfeebled that its fall was imminent. To an important extent, this opinion was furthered by the circle of exiles, led by Lajos Kossuth, who were preparing to intervene against the monarchy. However, the Hungarian leaders were unaware of the weakness of Kossuth's organization, and they also foolishly expected support from the great powers. Thus the Hungarian leaders in Transylvania continued to insist that the Transylvanian diet be abolished and its deputies be sent to the diet in Budapest. Romanian leaders openly protested against all attempts to incorporate Transylvania into Hungary and intensified their efforts to elect delegates on various levels who would represent Romanian interests. This tactic also was espoused by the majority of the Saxon delegates, led by Konrad Schmidt. Assemblies were organized in all counties to demonstrate popular support.

The emperor, confident that the Romanians would cooperate, called a Transylvanian diet for 1 July 1863 in Sibiu. The Romanians were infused with hope. This was an important test, an opportunity to demonstrate their political maturity. The results were better than expected. "The Romanians went to the polls as they go to church," contemporary observers noted. The peasantry's political awareness was proved in these elections: all their votes were cast for their own candidates. The result was the election of 48 Romanian deputies, 44 Hungarian and Szekler deputies, and 33 Saxon deputies, as well as 11 regalist deputies for each group. Obviously proportional representation had not yet been achieved, but the situation was significantly improved.

However, the Hungarian deputies, with the exception of the regalists, refused to participate in the diet. The Romanian and Saxon representatives then proceeded to pass a series of very important laws guaranteeing the autonomy of the Principality of Transylvania and its independent development. Equal rights for the Romanian nation were passed into law, as were equal rights for the country's three languages. Other significant laws included those concerning the supreme court, the administration of laws, and the election of deputies to the Reichsrath. The equality of the majority Romanian nation with the coinhabiting nations and the introduction of the Romanian language in administration and justice—actions which had been obstructed for centuries by the privileged classes—were proclaimed, though they survived for a short time only. The Romanian press emphasized these events, noting that "if 1848 marked our rebirth as a people, 1864 has made us into a nation."

Another achievement was the religious unification of all the Orthodox Romanians of the monarchy, an extremely important accomplishment given the circumstances of the time.

The period 1859–64 may thus be considered a successful one in the long struggle for Romanian rights: Transylvanian autonomy was reestablished and expanded, and the religious unity of the Orthodox Romanians of the monarchy was achieved. However, the true goal, the formation of a single officially recognized body politic of the Romanian population in the monarchy, still was out of reach.

Although the Austrian monarchy's political situation had improved between 1861 and 1864, the danger hanging over it had not entirely disappeared. Austrian authority was endangered by the growing strength of Prussia, on the one hand, and by the struggle of the subject peoples for liberation on the other. Liberation movements continued unabated through the period 1861–64, while the rapprochement between Prussia and Russia enabled Bismarck to wage a war against Denmark for the duchies of Schleswig and Holstein. Austrian involvement in this war proved fatal for the monarchy.

As early as 1863, Emperor Franz Josef proposed to Count György Apponyi, a representative of the Hungarian aristocracy, that he develop a plan for an understanding between the Viennese court and the Hungarian dominant classes. Count Apponyi presented the emperor with a memorandum proposing a "coordinate dual monarchy" between Austria and Hungary. By assuring the interests of the Hungarian ruling classes in a dual system, the emperor hoped to save the Habsburg monarchy. In the spring of 1865, Ferenc Deak, a major representative of the Hungarian bourgeoisie and landowners, announced a plan for an understanding with the dynasty, a loyal collaboration to consolidate the empire. A short time later the secret negotiations were replaced by official ones, and in the autumn of 1865 an agreement in principle was reached.

When the leaders of the Romanian national movement heard of the discussions between the two sides, they intensified their efforts to save Transylvanian autonomy. The political and legislative reorganization of Transylvania which had been passed by the Sibiu diet was abruptly halted on 1 September 1865 by an imperial rescript abolishing the diet and convoking a new one in Cluj. According to the decree, the right to vote was reserved to the nobility and to those who paid a direct tax of eight florins. By thus reviving the law of 1791, the court sought to guarantee the election of a diet which would carry out its plan to eliminate Transylvanian autonomy.

The imperial rescript provoked great agitation among the Romanian leaders. One group, whose interests were linked to the court's, consisted of state officials and a part of the high clergy, especially the Orthodox clergy, who had just managed to have their bishopric raised to the level of a metropolis; these argued in favor of accommodating to the situation and participating in the Cluj diet on the basis of the old law, even if in reduced numbers. The majority of the Romanian leaders, however—professionals led by George Barițiu, I. Măcelariu, and Ioan Rațiu—favored passive resistance, and proposed boycotting the elections.

The leaders of the Romanian national movement in the Banat and Hungary also became very active after they learned of the negotiations between Vienna and Pest on the dual monarchy. They tried to talk with the Hungarian leaders in the diet, hoping to get the diet to approve a general nationalities law guaranteeing the development of separate nations while also respecting the historical traditions of Transylvania and Croatia. They fought to preserve Transylvanian autonomy, emphasizing its history and its Romanian majority. Deputies from the Banat and Hungary did their best to obtain what they could. Immediately after a commission proposed the development of a nationalities law, the Romanian deputies suggested that the law "should be written so as to take into account all the country's nationalities in proportion to their numbers." Although the proposal was rejected, the Romanian deputies, in their efforts to influence the members of the commission and of the whole diet, did manage to emphasize equal rights for the nationalities and their separate traditions and customs.

Around the same time the Romanians of Transylvania composed a substantial memorandum, which was issued on 31 October 1866, urging the preservation of the historical identity of the Grand Principality of Transylvania as it had been decreed in the Diploma Leopoldina and affirmed by the Pragmatic Sanction and by Article Six of the diet of 1791. The natural consequence of such recognition would be the reopening of the Transylvanian diet, in accordance with the provisions of the election law passed by the diet of Sibiu.

The emperor ignored the memorandum. Those who had written it knew its fate in advance; nevertheless, they presented it for the sake of "the honor and reputation of the nation." It was published, in its entirety or as excerpts, in many contemporary newspapers, and it had a significant impact in Transylvania. Some 2,500 copies were printed and distributed to the farthest corners of the province.

Cultural Activity

Cultural activity in the years immediately after the revolution of 1848 clearly mirrored the conditions in social, economic, and political life. Tendencies toward a democratic culture, oriented toward lifting the masses from ignorance and illiteracy, were opposed by the conservative culture preserved by the nobility and that part of the bourgeoisie allied with it. In this struggle, those areas controlled by officials serving the interests of the dominant classes—education, for example—continued to be dominated by conservative ideas; in other fields, such as creative activity in the arts and sciences, and in various clubs and societies, a more democratic way of thought prevailed. This more progressive thought actually represented a continuation of the ideology of 1848; indeed, many of its adherents were themselves revolutionaries at that time: Avram Iancu, Simion Bărnuțiu, Alexandru Papiu-Ilarian, August Treboniu Laurian, Eftimie Murgu, George Barițiu, Pavel Vasici, János Bolyai, Ferenc Mentovich, Fr. Krassner, and others. All of them, historians, philologists, philosophers, biologists, and mathematicians alike, campaigned actively for social progress through culture.

The principles of natural law and the rights of peoples were the main legal and philosophical concerns of Iancu, Bărnuțiu, Murgu, Barițiu, and other leaders of the 1848 revolution. Confident of the power of legal arguments to advance their struggle for equal rights, they worked for the establishment of an academy or faculty of law for Romanians. Iancu's only wish was for the good fortune of his nation; Bărnuțiu's conception of equal national rights was that no nation "should be master of another," but that there should be "equality for all." The elimination of enmity between peoples was a major idea of Murgu and Barițiu, who fervently denied "that there is any hatred between nations," arguing instead that hatred exists only between "oligarchs and privileged classes."

The natural sciences witnessed significant progress in the period following the revolution of 1848. Works of a merely descriptive character gave way to analytical studies, though in the absence of specialized journals, many such studies had to appear in newspapers and general journals. Many physicians and biologists—Vasile Pop, Pavel Vasici, Atanasie Șandor, and Ioan Poruția, as well as Eduard Bielz and K. Fuss, or Miklos Szilagy and Josef Greissing—made noteworthy studies of physiology, epidemiology, surgery, balneology, zoology, and botany. Most of their work was based on or influenced by Darwinian ideas. Farkas and János Bolyai, father and son, did distinguished work on non-Euclidian geometry and complex numbers.

History and philology continued to play a leading role in Transylvanian intellectual life, particularly since they had a long tradition and were closely linked to political issues. The implications of work in history, language, and literature for the troubled political life of the time were many and varied. Thus it is entirely natural that the political leaders were also the most dedicated researchers in these fields. Among the Romanians were August Treboniu Laurian, George Barițiu, Alexandru Papiu-Ilarian, Timotei Cipariu, Iosif Hodoș, Ioan Russu, Andrei

Mureşanu, and Gavril Munteanu; among the Hungarians were László Kövári, Elek Jakab, János Arany, János Kriza, and Miklos Josika; among the Saxons were G. D. Teutsch and Josef Haltrich.

Historical studies of the period leading up to the revolution of 1848 and the years afterward, based on documentary evidence and on the authors' own experiences, were published; works on the Romanian, Hungarian, and German languages and on ethnography and folklore also appeared. These years also saw the publication of various journals dealing predominantly with history and philology.

Most of the notable Romanian historians, philologists, and biologists were also the principal founders and organizers of important cultural associations and clubs. Foremost among these societies certainly was the Association for Romanian Literature and Folklore in Transylvania, or Astra. This institution was founded in Sibiu in 1861, after long and persistent efforts by Romanian leaders. Astra's goal was set out in its constitution: to aid in "the progress of Romanian literature and the culture of the Romanian people in its various branches" through books, articles, prizes, and scholarships. Its membership came from Romania and Bukovina as well as from Transylvania. Thus Astra was actually a cultural (and political) society for all Romanians. It was involved in the arts and sciences, but especially history, philology, and ethnography. Its activities were organized into three sections: philology and literature, history, and science. Branches existed in all of the major Transylvanian towns, and its general meetings were full-fledged scholarly conferences, with hundreds or thousands of participants from Transylvania and Romania. *Transilvania*, Astra's journal, was the most important historical and philological publication in the Romanian language in Transylvania. Romanian cultural societies modeled after Astra were founded in Marmureş and Arad, but their influence was not as great.

Hungarian culture in Transylvania was represented primarily by the Transylvanian Museum Society and its journal, *Erdély muzeum* [Transylvanian museum] played a major role in guiding work in various fields. Its main activities, however, were in history and ethnography, and it founded an important historical archive. A similar role was taken in Saxon culture by the Society for Transylvanian History and Culture, founded in 1841, and its journal, *Archiv des Vereins für Siebenbürgische Landeskunde.* Like Astra and the Transylvanian Museum Society, it was primarily concerned with history and philology, and only second-arily with other fields; it too founded a valuable historical archive.

Even so, it must be said that, as in the social and economic spheres, cultural development was relatively restricted, for po-litical conditions in the absolutist regime—and even under the more liberal government that followed it—were hardly favor-able. The successes achieved were the result of working to over-come difficulties and hardships, and did not attain the level pos-sible under the more generous conditions of freedom and official support.

12

The Consolidation
of Capitalist Society

DURING THE SECOND HALF of the nineteenth century and the early part of the twentieth, Transylvanian society continued to develop slowly toward capitalism. It did so in spite of the obstacles created by the Viennese court's protectionist policies and the Austro-Hungarian dual monarchy compromise, which robbed Transylvania of its autonomy and forcibly united it with Hungary. Population increased: in 1870 the total population of Transylvania (in its most inclusive sense) was 4.4 million, of which over 60 percent were Romanians. In 1880 there were 4,281,417 (53.4 percent Romanians; 24.8 percent Hungarians; 21.8 percent others); in 1890 4,714,738 (52.1 percent Romanians; 26.1 percent Hungarians; 21.8 percent others); in 1900 5,218,908 (50.7 percent Romanians; 28.4 percent Hungarians; 20.9 percent others); and in 1910 5,263,602 (53.8 percent Romanians; 31.6 percent Hungarians; 14.6 percent others). Thus there was an increase of about 2.7 percent from 1880 to 1890; of over 9.6 percent from 1890 to 1900; and of only about 0.85 percent between 1900 and 1910. This represents a slow growth in the first decade (1870–80), a very slow growth in the next two decades, and no growth at all in the last.

The different nationalities also experienced unequal rates of growth. Though the Romanians formed a majority of the population, between 53 and 60 percent, their number grew by only 314,450 between 1880 and 1900. The combined Hungarian and Szekler population, on the other hand, which formed something over 24 percent of the total, grew by 529,403 in the same period. The explanation for this difference lies in three clear and well-known phenomena of the time: the "denationalization" of the Romanians, the falsification of census records by the authorities, and the counting of Jews as Hungarians because they reported

Hungarian as their language. Yet in spite of the falsifications and denationalization, the Romanian population maintained its majority throughout the whole period from 1870 to 1910, constituting between 53 and 53.6 percent of the population, while the Hungarians, Szeklers, and Jews together accounted for between 24.8 and 31.6 percent, and the Germans around 10 percent.

Of the whole population, something like 15 percent lived in towns and 85 percent in villages. Two-thirds of the rural population was Romanian, while in the urban population the Romanians represented only a quarter of the total; there were official curbs on Romanian settlement in towns.

Agriculture and Rural Property Structure

In the late nineteenth and early twentieth centuries, agriculture throughout the Austro-Hungarian Empire underwent a capitalist transformation, although the degree depended on the particular region. There was increasing use of paid labor, improved machines, and a growth in acreage under cultivation, while products became commodities. Patterns of property ownership, however, were viciously unfair. While 884,638 peasant farms—99.22 percent of the total number of properties—represented only 60.02 percent of all farmland, there were 6,953 large estates—0.78 percent of the number of properties—which owned 39.98 percent of the land. This contrast is especially striking when we realize that the average size of the property of the poor peasants was 1.99 hectares, while the size of the large estates over 500 hectares averaged 1,900 hectares. The economic dominance of the landowners, who held huge tracts of land in a majority of the countries and provinces of the empire, led to capitalist development on the Prussian model. The process was slow, but crushing for the peasants.

This situation grew out of the remnants of feudalism that survived the abolition of serfdom in 1848. By robbing the peasants of part of their land, combining properties, and resettling peasants, landowners were able to create large estates. The governmental policy of support for large holdings was even more pronounced after the dual monarchy was formed in 1867. The goals of the 1867 agreement included protection of large estates and strengthening the dominant classes against the masses; in the new empire the Austrian and Hungarian bourgeoisie and landowning classes, with the help of the army and of their own political power, tried to maintain the left-over feudal power of large estates. As capitalist development proceeded in agriculture in general, and on the large estates in particular, capitalist forms also appeared to some extent on peasant farms. As a result, differences arose among the peasants, producing a numerically insignificant but economically powerful stratum of wealthy farmers (*Grossbauern*) at one extreme and, at the other, the overwhelming majority of the poor peasantry, the agricultural proletariat and semiproletariat, who represented three-quarters of the total number of peasant farmers.

In the distribution of peasant land, the Transylvanian situation was similar to that in the countries that made up Czechoslovakia, and almost identical to Croatia and the coastal regions. The farms of poor peasants (up to 5.77 ha) represented 71.88 percent of the total number of peasant farms, but only 29.52 percent of the total area. The middle-level peasantry, with 26.82 percent of the total number of farms, held 60.26 percent of the land area, while the rich peasants, who were only 1.3 percent of the total, owned 10.22 percent of all peasant land. This picture would be incomplete without adding the fact there was also a large group of poor peasants, agricultural hands, and day laborers who were completely or almost completely without property. Only 6.5 percent of the farmhands (*argați*) and 14.7 percent of the day laborers had their own tiny plots of land; the rest of the village proletariat and semiproletariat—roughly 88 out of 100 families—had no land whatsoever.

The striking inequity of land distribution in the multinational Austro-Hungarian Empire was matched by the equally unjust fact that the great majority of large landowners were German and Hungarian, while the majority of the poor peasants came from the other nationalities, even though these other nationalities formed a large majority of the general population. According to the census of 1910, in Hungary proper 91.4 percent of the owners of estates over 500 hectares were Hungarian and only 8.6 of other nationalities, while of the poor peasant farms, 61.7 percent belonged to Romanians, Czechs, Slovaks, Serbs, Croats, Ukrainians, and other nationalities, and only 38.3 percent to Hungarians. In general, the larger the estate, the more likely it was to be owned by a member of the dominant nations.

The greatly disproportionate distribution of land along ethnic lines was true in Transylvania as well. According to the census of 1910, Romanians had 70.5 percent of the proletarian and semiproletarian farms in Translyvania, as against 18.9 percent Hungarian and 5.1 percent German; of the poor peasant farms, 69.4 percent were Romanian, while 18.9 percent were Hungarian and 6.2 percent German. Moreover, 58.3 percent of the landless farmhands and 56.7 percent of the agricultural day laborers were Romanian. Hungarian landlords owned 61.4 percent of all estates of between 50 and 500 hectares, as against 20.3 percent for Romanians, and 85.7 percent, as against 5.7 percent, of all estates over 500 hectares. Of the 1,023,660 Romanian farmers who were heads of households, better than one-half owned less than 2.5 hectares of land, and a good portion had no land at all. More than three-quarters (roughly 80 percent) of the Romanian rural population belonged to the categories of poor peasantry, semiproletariat, and proletariat. Thus the economic base of the Romanian rural population in Transylvania was both extremely restricted and at a disadvantage compared to the Hungarian and German rural population. This is also seen in the fact that in 1918 the Hungarian and German populations had an average of 3.5 hectares per capita, while the Romanian population owned barely 1 hectare apiece.

A considerable percentage of all property was thus concentrated in the hands of a few landowners, while at the same time there were millions of peasants who either had no land or who had small plots insufficient to feed their families. Along with this inequality, and closely related to it, were social and ethnic inequalities. The majority of the peasantry belonged to the oppressed nationalities and the majority of the large landowners to the dominant ones. Moreover, the landowners, in close collaboration with the bourgeoisie, were staunch defenders of the status quo, opposed to any social progress, bound in thousands of ways to the backward and outdated old order, and proponents of reactionary policies. Against this background, the modernization of agriculture slowly proceeded.

Gradually, however, the quality and variety of machinery used increased. Not only the large landowners, but also the rich peasants—and in some cases even the middle-level peasants—recognized the benefits of machinery: it both guaranteed better quality agricultural work in a shorter time and reduced the amount of paid labor. Obviously, on a farm too large to be worked by one family, the amount of paid labor was inversely proportional to the amount, variety, and quality of machinery used. The agricultural machinery of the period may be grouped into three categories: 1) machines drawn by animals or worked by men; 2) machines driven by steam; 3) and machines driven by electricity. In the first category we may include straw cutters, balers, winnowers, milk separators, and so on. These were found primarily on large estates, then on medium-sized farms, and lastly, but rarely, on peasant farms, and even then only on the larger ones, ten to fifty hectares in area. In general the peasant with a small holding did not have the means to acquire such equipment, and in any case its use requires a larger area for maximum economic return. Machines driven by steam and electricity—steam tractors, threshers, plows—were found almost exclusively on large estates.

The increase in the use of machinery can be attributed to the need for increased agricultural production. The improvement of agricultural machinery by the Americans—primarily threshers, but also reapers and planters—made larger volume and cheaper production possible. In America, the area under cultivation grew by 300 million acres between 1870 and 1900; because of this competition from overseas, European farmers were forced to introduce such machines as well.

In Transylvania, at the beginning of the twentieth century, 99.22 percent of all the farms were peasant-owned, but they possessed only 45.89 percent of the machinery, while the large estates, 0.78 percent of the farms, owned 54.11 percent. The consequences of this state of affairs are obvious. Little peasant farms, unable to afford advanced agricultural technology, worked ploddingly with old equipment; middle-sized and large peasant properties, using some machinery, were able to achieve more productivity and better quality; but the large estates with their motorized equipment reached the highest levels of production and superior quality. As a result, small properties could only sell their inferior products at low prices and were thus ruined by the competition; the peasants from such farms either became part of the agricultural proletariat or abandoned the land altogether, emigrating or moving to town in search of work. Middle-level peasants, especially those owning ten to twenty ha of land, were able to survive with some difficulty. The large peasant farms not only withstood the competition, but often even increased their acreage through purchases of new land.

Still another factor contributing to the impoverishment of the peasantry was the increase in taxes. Property taxes were more burdensome for the peasants and for small properties in general than for large ones. Indeed, the regressive tax system provided lower tax rates on larger holdings; again very large estates benefited most.

As the urban population grew in the late nineteenth and twentieth centuries and as industry developed, there was an increasing tendency for specialization in agriculture. This was seen both on large estates and on peasant farms, as individual landowners specialized in industrial crops such as fiber plants, or in vegetable farming. This led to an increasing division of agricultural labor and a growth in trade between producers of different agricultural products. This period saw a rise in the production of hemp and flax, as well as in sugar beets, textile and oil-producing plants, and vegetables. Most agricultural work on these larger farms was done by permanent or temporary hired labor. As the use of free hired labor increased, so did the importance of "intensive" agriculture—that characterized crop specialization—more varied crop rotation, and so on at the expense of "extensive" agriculture, which remained on more backward properties and on small peasant farms.

In those regions where the development toward capitalism was most advanced, by the turn of the century tenant farmers (arendaşi), who rented land from large landowners and acted as middlemen between the owners and the farm workers, were common. These tenant farmers, in order to achieve higher production and bigger profits, made increasing use of hired labor and machinery.

Several things must be kept in mind as we consider this phenomenon. The large tenant farmers worked substantial acreage, often thousands of hectares. Having the necessary capital or credit, they could afford the mechanized equipment they needed, which would pay for itself very quickly. Thus the large tenant farmer contributed to the introduction of new technology and the production of commodities. Generally, a large tenant farmer would take part of his rented estate and divide it into small parcels or lots which were then sublet to the local peasantry. This arrangement was particularly useful in the case of certain crops, such as corn, sugar beets, potatoes, sunflowers, tobacco, and vegetables, since these required hoeing and special care for which there was not always appropriate machinery. The peasant subtenants normally gave the tenant farmer a portion of the harvest, and were often obliged to donate a number of days of free labor as well.

The difficult situation of the peasants in general, and especially of the poor peasants, was one of the principal reasons for the worsening of relationships between the peasants and the landowners and local authorities. Discontent and agitation had become so general that they were a major public concern. The Romanian National party (RNP), for example, in its national conference on 10 January 1905 in Sibiu, decided to abandon passive resistance and enter parlimentary activity, thus building on its 1881 platform. It sought the granting of adequate land to farmers through the sale of state property on favorable terms; further, it sought a minimum property guarantee, forest-use laws that were fairer to the people, and a modification of progressive taxes so as to provide exemption for subsistence-level incomes and to abolish taxes on indispensable foodstuffs. The Social Democratic party (SDP) of Hungary and its branches, meanwhile, were propagating the idea of an end to all social and ethnic discrimination. The creation of socialist organizations in the villages, resulting from links between the peasants and active radical elements of the SDP, intensified the peasant movement to break up the landowners' estates.

Because of oppression, the population seemed to be constantly in motion. But internal migration did not solve the peasants' fundamental problems, and many of those who had little or no land sought opportunities in foreign countries, especially the United States. Those who left included capable, energetic people, with a will to face the unknown. In the first five years of the twentieth century, 12,000 Romanians from Transylvania alone emigrated to America; in the period from 1905 to 1909, the figure rose to more than 70,000.

Another form of peasant protest was seen in harvest strikes, which were especially widespread in the decade from 1900 to 1910. Some were successful in that the harvesters gained an increase in the amount of grain they were paid and an increase in wages paid in money. In many places there were disturbances and even open rebellions by poor peasants and agricultural proletarians, the most important being in Bihor in northwestern Transylvania and in the Banat.

Industry and Finance

Economic and industrial development proceeded erratically in the late nineteenth and early twentieth centuries. The crisis of 1873, which dragged on until 1879, disturbed the straight line of Transylvania's development, as did the customs war waged between Austria and Romania from 1886 to 1891. The latter was an attempt by the Habsburg authorities to limit trade between Transylvania and Romania through extreme protectionist tariffs, which resulted in a serious disruption of Transylvanian trade relations. The competition from the crown countries of Austria and Bohemia, which resulted from the customs union between Austria and Hungary, created a further obstacle to free development.

Consequently, mining and metallurgy continued to play a leading role from 1867 to 1914, for ores and metal products were a necessity for the empire. The gold mined in the Bihor Mountains and the northwestern sections of Transylvania (Baia Mare and Baia Sprie) placed Transylvania among the leading gold-producing countries in the world. From 1,429 kilograms in 1868, production rose almost 70 percent in thirty years, to 2,427 kilograms. The production of silver, however, fell during the same period by about 25 percent, from 9,511 kilograms to 7,099 kilograms, because most countries abandoned the bimetal gold-silver standard and silver prices fell in response to increased silver production in North America. The drop in copper production was even greater, from 400 to 54 tons, following the closing of the mines around Oravița in the Banat because of competition from cheaper Austrian ore. On the other hand, salt production rose 26 percent, from roughly 136,000 tons in 1868 to 172,000 tons around the end of the century. This growth stemmed from the introduction of steam engines.

We should also note the relation between the huge development in coal mining and the development of the iron and steel industry, given impetus by railway construction, around Hunedoara and in the Banat. Coal production reached 240,000 tons in 1868, the most important coal deposits being those in the Banat, but by the turn of the century, the Jiu Valley in southern Transylvania had surpassed the Banat, producing 800,000 tons to the Banat's 460,000. The total Transylvanian production was thus over 1.2 million tons. Iron ore production grew from 70,000 to 500,000 tons per year, while the annual production of cast iron grew from 35,000 to over 200,000 tons. In 1900 over 70,000 tons of steel were produced. The steel mills at Reşiţa in the Banat were the first in southeastern Europe and in the Austro-Hungarian Empire to introduce, in 1868 and 1869, the Bessemer process. The Reşiţa works also gradually expanded their metallurgical and machine shops, producing parts for metal bridges, rails, steam engines, farm equipment, and narrow-gauge locomotives and cars.

Much of the financing of Transylvanian industry was done through the twenty or twenty-five credit institutions and twenty-four to thirty savings banks, with a combined capital of 4.6 million gold florins. The foundations of the Romanian bourgeois credit institutions were also laid down during this time, the most important of these banks being the Albina in Sibiu. It had assets of 300,000 gold florins, and primarily served the needs of agriculture through loans to farmers. Other Romanian banking institutions with the same purpose were founded in a number of towns: the Ardeleana bank (Orăştie); the Victoria bank (Arad), second in importance after the Albina; the Timişana bank (Timişoara); the Somşana bank (Oraviţa, Dej); and the Economul bank (Cluj). Despite official obstacles, the number of Romanian banks reached 72 in 1899, with total assets of over 50 million gold florins. The Romanian banks represented about 15 to 20 percent of the total capital, the most numerous and powerful banks being those of the Hungarian bourgeoisie (over 50 percent of all capital), and then the German ones (25 to 30 percent).

The capital invested in mining, steel, and other metallurgical industries was for the most part foreign. The coal and iron mines in the Banat were owned by STEG, the state railway company, but with massive investment from France, Belgium, and England. The mines in the Jiu Valley were taken over by another company with Austrian capital, the Braşov Mine and Foundry Corporation. These same two Austrian companies also dominated the iron and steel industry. STEG owned a number of foundries and steel mills in the Banat and in Hunedoara. The mining and metallurgical industries thus came to be controlled by cartels, which raised prices anywhere from 15 to 40 percent up to the eve of the First World War, and favored Austria and Hungary in their sales practices. During the last two decades of the nineteenth century and the first two decades of the twentieth, however, Austrian and Hungarian capital fell under the control of German, French, Belgian, and British monopolies.

Light industry grew around local raw materials, and as a result various branches of the food, paper, textile, and lumber industries were the best developed. Since capital requirements were not so high, most of the investors were Transylvanian merchants. However, increasing profits attracted foreign capital into light industry as well, and little by little it came to predominate. This made possible the creation of businesses with assets three to four times greater than those in the earliest stage, which illustrates the process of concentration in light industry as well.

In the textile and chemical industries, competition by Austrian products suppressed technological progress, and the paper industry, for example, lost substantial ground compared to the period preceding the dual monarchy. Of fifteen mills operating at midcentury, only five survived in 1890. The glass and sugar industries suffered in the same way. Competition from Austrian and Hungarian products was especially stiff during the customs war with Romania; unable to take advantage of their traditional links to the territories south and east of the Carpathians, many Transylvanian industries—cotton spinning and weaving (especially in Braşov), leather, wood, paper, and ceramics—were hit hard, and in some cases destroyed. Not much progress was made even in mechanization of production until the First World War.

In the food and construction material industries (including lumbering), there was somewhat more mechanization. Large-scale production based on machinery became the rule. The number of steam-driven mills doubled, and the total horsepower of the machinery used increased tenfold. The sugar industry was represented by two rather large refineries, one in Bod, near Braşov in southeastern Transylvania, and one in Tîrgu Mureş in eastern Transylvania; however, these did not meet the demands of domestic consumption.

Part of the demand for clothing was met by cottage industry in textiles, which was very well developed, especially in southern Transylvania, a major sheep-raising region. Cloth and peasant clothing were made and sold at the fairs and markets of Transylvania and Romania.

As industry developed, there were corresponding changes in the structure of Transylvanian society. The ratio of rural population to working-class and urban population shifted in favor of the latter. In 1868 there were 114,000 workers—24,000 in mining, 80,000 in manufacturing, and 10,000 in commerce and transportation; by the eve of the First World War, their number had risen to 200,000. The normal phenomenon of concentration of workers in larger economic units also occured: more than 39 percent of all workers were in businesses with over five hundred employees just after the turn of the century. Another phenomenon to be emphasized is the increasing size of the industrial proletariat in the strict sense of the term; these workers were concentrated around a few powerful centers of the mining and metallurgical industries. For example, STEG alone had over 11,000 workers in 1880; Brașov Mine and Foundry had around 2,300. In a few towns—Timișoara, Arad, Cluj, Sibiu, and Brașov—the number of workers was as much as 45 percent of the "active" population—that is, that portion of the population with its own income.

The workers' living conditions were the same as those found in any country where capitalism was developing. Until 1872, no legal limits were placed on the working day; a law passed in that year confined itself to setting a limit of sixteen hours a day, with breaks totaling two hours. The eight-hour day existed only in the state mines, and only for underground work. A regulation in 1884 required that workers be permitted to go to church on Sunday; there was no talk of a day of rest. The right to strike was not recognized. Furthermore, there were extreme inequalities in wages, both from one place to another and between men and women and children. Women and children in general were paid less than the minimum wage level for men. Wages were also subject to serious fluctuations in times of crisis. Health care, accident protection, and social security were unknown. Industrial accidents claimed hundreds of workers' lives each year.

To defend their rights, workers organized, first into aid and assistance associations, and later into more comprehensive vocational organizations. Between 1867 and 1869, in Sibiu and Brașov, so-called Romanian Artisans' Fellowships, associations of masters, journeymen, and apprentices, were formed. In 1871 a similar association was founded in Cluj and Turda, and still others under the influence of the First Internationale in larger towns in the years that followed. In addition to work-related demands, workers also formulated political goals: universal suffrage in parliamentary elections and in those for county, town, and village councils; unrestricted freedom of association, assembly, and speech; freedom of the press; abolition of the standing army and its replacement with a general arming of the people; equality of rights for all the nations of the empire; abolition of indirect taxes and introduction of a progressive tax on income;

and abolition of clerical orders and the use of church property for educational purposes. When their demands went unheeded, the workers organized numerous strikes, asking for an eight-hour work day, higher wages, and an end to the inhuman treatment to which they were subjected by the mine operators. All the repressive means possible, including the army, were brought to bear against them.

New life was given to the Transylvanian workers' movement following the establishment of the Second Internationale in Paris in 1889. One of the earliest important actions based on the Internationale's directives was the first celebration of May Day in 1890, under the banner of international worker solidarity in the fight for the eight-hour day. There were large demonstrations in all the more important towns, including Timişoara, Arad, Oradea, Cluj, and Braşov, and in industrial and mining centers like Reşiţa, Oraviţa, Drencova, Bocşa, Dognecea, Petroşeni, and Baia Mare.

Against this background, the SDP of Hungary was formed, with a platform that included freedom of the press and of assembly, universal suffrage, passage of laws on worker safety and health, free schooling, and replacement of the standing army by general arming of the people. The first local Social Democratic organizations were founded in Arad and Cluj in 1891; others followed in Braşov and Orăştie. By 1898 the SDP had an organizational network that covered all of Transylvania, and in the early twentieth century the number of local branches had increased considerably. One of the direct consequences of the new activity in the workers' movement was a substantial strengthening of the workers' press.

The leadership of the Hungarian SDP, however, under the influence of the Austrian Marxists Otto Bauer and Karl Renner, recognized only the right to cultural autonomy of the subject nations of the empire and opposed national liberation struggles and the right to self-determination. For this reason, Social Democrats of the subject nations organized their own separate branches of the party. On 24–25 December 1905, in Lugoj, the first independent convention of the Romanian branch of the Hungarian SDP took place. Organizations of Romanian workers were founded in a number of places in Transylvania, while in areas where there were fewer Romanian workers, Social Democratic and union organizations included Romanian, Hungarian, and German workers together. Ties with the workers' movement in Romania, strengthened by the presence in Transylvania of individuals who had been expelled from Romania, also played an important role.

The Austro-Hungarian Dual Monarchy and Romanian Political Autonomy

The dual monarchy compromise was a formula by which the Viennese court could prop up the Austro-Hungarian Empire, and this compromise managed to prolong the agony of dissolution for half a century. At the time, this compromise represented a victory for the Hungarian landowners and bourgeoisie. The Romanian masses and bourgeoisie, however, did not passively accept the dual monarchy. The Romanian delegation in the diet in Pest fought earnestly to salvage what they could of Transylvanian autonomy. Meanwhile, major antiunification activities were unleashed in various parts of Transylvania.

Against this background the important memorandum known as the Blaj *Pronouncement [Pronunciament]* was drafted. The product of long debate among the Transylvanian Romanian political leaders, it expresses the basic ideas of the struggle of a Romanian bourgeoisie from 1848 to 1867, and is a vehement protest against the forced incorporation of Transylvania into Hungary. It was developed at a meeting in Blaj on 15 May 1868, which was attended by roughly 60,000 peasants from most parts of Transylvania. The *Pronouncement* was a mass protest, demonstrating that the great majority of the population of Transylvania considered the forced union with Hungary a historic injustice. It was in fact a protest and a memorandum at the same time. Even though it did not call for the peoples' resistance to the local agencies of the empire, it nevertheless took a determined stand against the Austro-Hungarian pact. It exercised a significant influence, particularly on the Romanian people in the Principality of Transylvania, but also in the other Romanian provinces of the empire, thus underscoring their unfailing adherence to the principles of the revolution of 1848.

In composing their protest, the Romanian bourgeoisie reached another conclusion, greatly important both at the time and in later years: the court's negative attitude toward the many memoranda it received must be exposed to the world by appeals addressed to civilized Europe. The *Pronouncement* had to be published and thereby made known to all who were interested in such issues. The support expressed in the popular assembly gave the movement mass backing. This solidarity, in a time when the nationalities law was coming into effect, was extremely important. The Hungarian dominant classes wanted a law that would wipe out the economic, social, cultural, and political distinctions between the various provinces that had been incorporated into Hungary. They fought to guarantee equal rights with the Magyar people and individual development of those regions with non-Magyar majorities. But the diet, ignoring these demands, passed a bill introduced by Ferenc Deak, which recognized a single nation—the Hungarian nation—that included "nationalities."

The situation called for new methods. More and more, the leaders of the nationalities accepted the idea that they would achieve their aims only with the support of the masses and the help of pan-European public opinion. But there were two conflicting views. The *activists*, led by Metropolitan Andrei Saguna, supported continuing the fight in parliament, while the *passivists*, led by George Barițiu, argued for refusing to participate in parliamentary affairs. It was the latter idea that gradually won over the majority of the Romanians.

Around the same time, Romanian leaders in the Banat and in Hungary began to act. Although for a while they supported the old activist tactics, they were also involved in working out their own approach to the fight for national liberation. At the beginning of 1869, Alexandru Mocioni wrote an open letter to the Romanians containing guidelines for the proper political attitude of Romanians in the Hungarian state. He emphasized the importance of the national struggle and that its "political program must be the concern of the masses, and must be understood by them."

A public assembly was called in Timișoara for 7 February 1869. About five hundred Romanian intellectuals from the Banat were present. Also participating in the assembly was a delegation from the Serbian national committee from Novi Sad, led by Svetozar Miletić. Journalists came from Pest, Vienna, and Prague. After fruitful discussions, the conference resolved to found a political party dedicated to solidarity with other nations having the same interests; support for the struggle for Transylvanian autonomy; opposition to the nationalities law led by all legal means; support for the Croatian national efforts to achieve autonomy; and adoption of the principles of liberation and democracy in all spheres of public life. The establishment of the Romanian National party (RNP) of the Banat and Hungary was a first step toward closer collaboration with Transylvanian Romanians, while respecting their tactics and favoring the autonomy of the principality, and also with the Serbian and Croatian delegations. It is significant for the closer links among the Romanian, Croatian, and Serbian national movements that at the Serbian conference at Becicherecul Mare on 28 January 1869, one of the positions taken by the representatives was "defense of Transylvania's territorial integrity on the basis of its common law."

An urgent need began to be felt for a meeting of the Romanian political leaders in Transylvania as well, in order to discuss all issues and form a single political viewpoint. Such a meeting was held on 7 March 1869 in Miercurea. The call to the meeting, published in a variety of newspapers, announced the discussion of two topics: the establishment of a Romanian National party; and the establishment of a unified view on the coming election for the diet in Pest and on defending the national and political interests of the Romanian people. About three hundred Romanian leaders from all over Transylvania took part. Passivist tactics were adopted, which did not imply withdrawal from political life, but meant only that the struggle for Transylvanian interests would not be carried out in the parliamentary framework. Having decided on passive resistance, the meeting then established the RNP of Transylvania, to be led by a central national committee based in Sibiu.

The organization of the Romanian bourgeoisie into parties signaled a new phase in the fight for national liberation. The activists, by participating in Hungarian parliamentary affairs, managed to keep Hungarian public opinion focused on the nationality issue. The fact that the Romanian delegation presented the diet with detailed analyses of the material, cultural, and political situation of the Romanians of the empire, and demanded equal rights, also forced the government to remain involved in the issue. The work of the passivists had even more important consequences, despite the fact that the RNP of Transylvania was banned by the Hungarian authorities. Its leaders continued their activity semilegally in meetings and electoral groups. They succeeded in mobilizing the masses to political action in cities and counties, protesting against the incorporation of Transylvania into Hungary.

One result of this multifaceted activity was the strengthening of the masses' consciousness of the political issues of the day, both domestic and foreign. Such awareness is shown, for example, by the messages sent to the diet by the residents of a number of villages protesting the German invasion of France, and indeed, by the general discontent with imperial policies.

The proclamation of independence by Romania and the victorious war that ratified that proclamation provided even greater impetus for the national struggle of the Romanians within the Habsburg empire. Thousands of volunteers from Transylvania, Bukovina, and the Banat, despite official restrictions and prohibitions, left for the front; they crossed secretly into Romania and were assigned to various military units. In towns and villages of Transylvania and Bukovina, committees were formed to help the wounded. Press reports alone name 350 such committees, led by the most noteworthy residents of their towns, in Transylvania; many others were formed in Bukovina. The Hungarian and Austrian authorities, worried by the enthusiasm shown by the Romanian population for supporting the war and helping the wounded, banned the aid committees. Nevertheless, they continued to function, collecting large sums of money and other contributions for the Romanian army. The appeals made by the various committees invoked "blood ties," "brotherhood," "bonds of spirit and culture"; they emphasized the fact that the victory of the Romanian armies was a victory "for the entire nation, no matter how widely scattered in the world it may be." Impressive national solidarity was seen among all "in whose breast beats an impassioned Romanian heart," those "who are fighting for the glory and the future of the Romanian folk," bound "by close ties of blood" which "will never be broken but by death itself." Inspired by a vision of the historic significance of the war, Romanian peasants, workers, artisans, merchants, intellectuals, and students in Transylvania and Bukovina collected hundreds of thousands of crowns and hundreds of pounds of pillow stuffing, cloth, clothing, shoes, food, medicines, and bandages. Issue after issue of Transylvanian newspapers contained commentaries praising the army of the brave Romanians, who were accompanied by "the best and most fervent wishes of your brothers across the Carpathians."

The *Memorandum* Movement

The independence of Romania and the proclamation of the king-dom of Romania in 1881 enhanced its influence and prestige in the subjugated Romanian provinces. Thus on 12–14 May 1881, a short time after the proclamation of the kingdom, a national conference of Romanians from Transylvania and the Banat met in Sibiu to discuss uniting their activities and national parties. After much discussion, the conference agreed that the two parties should amalgamate as the RNP of Hungary and Transyl-vania. The unified party platform covered the most significant issues of the day for the Romanian nation in Transylvania, the Banat, and "Hungarian regions" in the fight to regain Transyl-vanian autonomy; the use of the Romanian language in adminis-tration and justice in all areas inhabited by Romanians; the ap-pointment of Romanian or Romanian-speaking officials in those same areas; the modification of the nationalities law; the exten-sion of the right to vote; and the fight against national oppres-sion. Vincențiu Babeş expressed the thoughts of all those present when he said, "We are and feel ourselves to be members of a Romanian family of eleven million people."

Another significant decision made by the Sibiu national con-ference was to draft a comprehensive "Memorial" which clearly analyzed all aspects of the Romanians' situation and which was given the widest possible publicity. It was printed in Sibiu in 1882 in Romanian, Hungrian, and German. A French version also was prepared and printed in Bucharest with the support of a number of important men. The "Memorial" presented a critical analysis of imperial, electoral, press, and agricultural laws under the dual monarchy. The conclusion was unequivocal: "Never under any circumstances will the Romanian nation be able to make peace with the dual monarchy system."

The national movement saw a great deal of activity in 1884. First of all, there were reactions to the denationalization law for the schools, which provoked serious protests in the diet and in the press and popular demonstrations in several Transylvanian towns. In addition, it was the hundredth anniversary of Horea's Uprising, and thus an occasion to recall a century of suffering and to resolve to put an end to it. In the service of this idea, the newspaper *Tribuna* [Tribune], founded by Ion Slavici, began pub-lication in Sibiu in April 1884. It was to distinguish itself through its steadfast and courageous defense of the Romanian national cause, of national culture, economic development, and national unity. The newspaper's base of support was the masses, and it directed its efforts toward the improvement of the cultural and economic situation. Under the influence of more radical currents of thought, younger, braver members were brought to the head of the national movement: Ioan Rațiu, a lawyer in Turda, became president; Gheorghe Pop, who came from Băsești and was a landowner around Sălaj, became vice-president; Vasile Lucaciu, a priest from Sisești (Satu Mare), became secretary-general.

Beginning in September 1884, in party meetings, in the press, and in private and public discussion, the drafting of a new "purely political" memorandum to expose the oppression of the Romanians by their Hungarian rulers gradually became the most important issue of the day. A mass movement took place in Romania and in the foreign-dominated Romanian provinces, organized in support of the struggle for unity and including soldiers and their officers, teachers, peasants, and small merchants. These circumstances produced a Garibaldian plan for freeing Transylvania, the work of Ioan Axente Sever, the brave prefect from the revolution of 1848: in an eight-day lightning operation, with the help of the Romanian army and rebel forces in Transylvania (especially in the Bihor Mountains), Transylvania would be set free.

The League for the Cultural Unity of All Romanians, founded in Bucharest in December 1890, played an important role in preparing both Romanian and foreign public opinion. Its announced goal was "to support the continued consciousness of solidarity, on the basis of national culture, of the entire Romanian people." Under the league's influence, the Bucharest *Student Memorandum* was composed, which exposed to the world "the oppression of the non-Magyar and non-German nationalities." The careful documentation and sober, dignified language made a favorable impression. The press devoted considerable attention to the *Memorandum* in France, Belgium, and England. Student organizations in Paris, Brussels, and other French and Belgian cities discussed it eagerly and guaranteed it a wide audience, while the English politicians William Gladstone and Edmond Fitzmaurice, a former foreign secretary, responded favorably.

At the interparliamentary convention in Rome in 1891, after hearing the report of the Romanian political leader Nicolae Fleva on the injustices suffered by the Transylvanian Romanians, the Italian delegate Renato Imbriani proposed a motion concerning "the right of all people to national unity." The motion was seconded by Menotti Garibaldi, Giuseppe Garibaldi's son, and was accepted by all the delegates except those from the Austro-Hungarian Empire. This attracted the attention of the Italian press, which fervently defended the Romanian cause and provoked a demonstration of support in which over twenty thousand people participated.

Public opinion was now prepared. In January 1892, the National Conference of the RNP in Transylvania resolved to present the *Memorandum* to the court in Vienna. New oppressive measures by the Hungarian government were already posing a more serious threat to the Romanian nation. The press law, stricter in Transylvania than in Hungary, sought to throttle free written expression, and the Transylvanian election law was likewise more oppressive than the Hungarian. The poll tax was much higher (84 florins) in Transylvania, where the majority of the population was Romanian, than in Hungary (16 florins); it was also higher in rural areas, where the majority of the population consisted of Romanian peasants, than in the towns, where the Hungarians were a majority.

The nationalities law, moreover, was not consistently enforced. A proposal by the Romanian, Slovak, and Serbian deputies to establish the principle of equality of all the nations of Hungary and to recognize the historical nations—Hungarian, Romanian, Serbian, Slovak, Ruthenian, and Saxon—was rejected. Other similar measures presented to the diet over a period of some thirty years—to recognize the languages of the nationalities in administration, justice, schools, and the diet, or the right of representatives of the nationalities to both high and low public offices—were also all rejected. The unequal treatment of the nationalities was also evident in economic life. Hungarian landowners and bourgeoisie attempted by every means to eliminate or limit as much as possible the participation of non-Magyar peoples in the economy of the country, thereby assuring their own cultural and political dominance. The continued inequality of land distribution just as flagrantly continued to favor Hungarian large landowners over Romanian peasants.

The *Memorandum* concluded that the only way to end social and ethnic oppression was for the Romanian nation to be recognized as having equal rights with the dominant nations. In fact, the *Memorandum* represented the wishes and desires of the entire Romanian nation: this was the way it was intended by its backers, who presented it to the emperor in the name of all the Romanians of Transylvania, and was also the way it was taken by the people. A committee was formed by Romanian students from Transylvania and Bukovina living in Vienna to welcome the Memorandists. The Austrian Social Christian party, led by Dr. Karl Lueger, also put on a rousing welcome for them, joined by Slovak, Serbian, and Croatian representatives.

The *Memorandum* was rejected by Emperor Franz Josef I, and those who presented it were the victims of official reprisals. In reaction, an exceptionally large and strong protest movement emerged simultaneously in Romania and various other European countries. Big meetings were held in all the towns of Romania. The League for the Cultural Unity of All Romanians put out a special newspaper, with the significant title *Turda* (Ioan Rațiu's hometown), which drew a parallel between the assassination of Michael the Brave on 19 August 1801 and the events of 1892. The Romanian socialists declared their solidarity with the Romanians in Transylvania, "brothers with the same origin and the same language." The movement in Bukovina also grew; in March 1892 the RNP of Bukovina was formed, based on the statement of principles published on 14 May 1891 in the Romanian newspaper *Gazeta Bucovinei* [Bukovinian gazette]. It favored preservation of the autonomy of Bukovina and of its historical and political identity; the development of Romanian culture; an increase in the number of Romanian-language schools; the introduction of Romanian in administration and justice; the protection of the rural economy; and good relations between the Romanian people and other peoples.

The prospect of the formation of a single Romanian state was very worrisome to the Hungarian government. Prime Minister Sándor Wekerle, in order to prove his patriotism and put himself beyond suspicion (he was a Magyarized German) began legal action against the whole committee of the RNP and other Romanian political leaders. On the other hand, the Romanian cause was espoused by international public opinion. The Belgian newspapers *La réforme* and *L'indépendance belge* denounced the state of affairs in the empire and the oppression of the nationalities. The well-known French journalist Félix Lesseur published an article in the Parisian *La République française*, exposing once again the oppression of the non-Magyar nationalities, and still other internationally known papers joined the general chorus, including the *Journal des débats, La Justice, Corriere della Sera*, and the *Neue Preussische Zeitung*. The interparliamentary convention in Bern declared its solidarity with the Romanian struggle, and the well-known English politician Fitz-James defended the Romanian cause with conviction.

Such was the general atmosphere in the months leading up to the trial of the Memorandists. In March and April 1894, before the trial began, the turmoil and agitation attained impressive proportions—not only in Transylvania, Romania, and Bukovina, but in foreign countries as well. A 5 March meeting at Oxford, England, was especially significant in its size and in the renown of its participants. The meeting was chaired by the great philologist and Romanist W. R. Morphill, and those in attendance included such well-known professors as T. W. Bridges, S. Ball, A. H. Carlyle, and W. Spooner. Morphill's speech was a paean to the Romanians of Transylvania, whom he described as a people of noble origin speaking a Latin language. He exposed the persecution to which they had been subjected, which, however, had not kept them from developing "as vigorously as they could." He expressed the feeling of those present that the Romanian people of Transylvania should achieve national autonomy, and regretted that the Hungarians treated the other nationalities so inhumanely. His speech was received with lively applause. Around the same time, part of the French press and a number of French politicians and leading journalists, including Emile Flourens, a former foreign minister, D. Lorbac, director of the newspaper *Le Nord*, and Félix Lesseur also declared their support for the Romanian cause in Transylvania.

These demonstrations of solidarity and support were a real aid and encouragement to the Memorandists awaiting trial. Even more supportive were the many enthusiastic demonstrations in Romania. On 19 April, there were more than twenty meetings in cities, towns, and even villages all over Romania. Over one hundred and thirty speeches were made by scholars, politicians, peasants, and artisans. Hundreds of thousands of people from all social classes participated.

The opening day of the trial, 7 May 1894, was awaited with great anticipation by both the Romanians and the Hungarians. Students and intellectuals assumed the task of going through the villages to encourage the defendants to keep their faith, and to assure the presence of a large crowd in Cluj on the day of the trial, while everywhere meetings were held to protest the oppressive policies of the Hungarian government and to express solidarity with the Memorandists. Peasant participation was massive, and telegrams of support signed by dozens of people flowed into the Committee of the RNP.

The Romanian political leaders' trip to Cluj was a triumphal march. At every large station they were met by crowds bringing flowers and singing national songs. The popular demonstrations were not discouraged by official intimidation, by long distances, or by the rain. As a result, 7 May was no ordinary day in Cluj. According to some witnesses 25,000 people were there; according to others, there were 30,000 or even 40,000. Such a demonstration, according to contemporary reports, had not been seen since the assembly on the Field of Liberty on 15 May 1848. Young people distributed manifestos declaring "for all the world to hear" that the *Memorandum* was the work of the entire Romanian people. A delegation was elected to present the complaints and wishes of the Romanian people to the emperor; it consisted of three peasants chosen from three corners of Transylvania to represent symbolically the entire people. As the trial proceeded, other reports told of nighttime village meetings in which there was talk of rebellion if the accused were found guilty. Those on trial thus had faith that they had the wholehearted support of the entire Romanian people, men and women, young and old. All the regions inhabited by Romanians were in a state of revolutionary turmoil, which the contemporary writer Jancsó Benedek, no friend of the Romanians, likened to the events of 15 May 1848 in Blaj.

The Cluj trial showed once again that the solidarity of the Romanian people extended beyond political boundaries. A National Student Committee was formed in Bucharest on 24 May, which published a newspaper called *Tinerimea Română* [Romanian youth] to expose oppression and to express solidarity with the Memorandists. In addition to students, a number of well-known figures collaborated on the paper, such as the historian and philologist Bogdan-Petriceicu Hașdeu, the historian Vasile Alexandrescu Urechia, and the writers Alexandru Vlahuță, Barbu, Stefănescu Delavrancea, Cincinat Pavelescu, Radu Rossetti, and Theodor Sperantia. The Romanian socialists declared their solidarity with the Romanians in Transylvania in their efforts to achieve a "united Romania that would include all the nation's sons," in the words of *Lumea Noua* [New world];

this would follow the "deliverance of all Romanians," wrote the *Evenimentul literar* [Literary news], and be "founded on the right of each people to rule and govern itself." The newspaper *Munca* [Labor] also argued for the deliverance of all peoples, and especially "for the deliverance of all Romanians"; it also presented a stinging indictment of the authorities.

An appeal signed by all members of the Romanian Academy was addressed to all cultural institutions and men of scholarship in Europe, asking for their support in "this just cause" of the Romanians in Transylvania, which, they said, was "a general cultural cause." The Cultural League addressed itself to European public opinion, condemning the Magyarization and the punitive measures being taken against the Memorandists. In a meeting in Bucharest on 4 June, an appeal and manifesto bearing 423,837 signatures was addressed to Europe at large, in which the "citizens" of Romania exposed the policy of denationalizing the Romanians in the Austro-Hungarian Empire, a policy backed by school laws, political associations, the Magyarization of names, resettlements, and trials of journalists and newspapers.

The trial of the Memorandists sent a shock wave through western Europe. French, Italian, Belgian, and English newspapers reported and condemned the trial; their columns bore the by-lines of such well-known and authoritative writers as Emile Flourens, Georges Clemenceau, Ernest Lavisse, Henri Gaidoz, Roberto Fava, and many others. In the Italian parliament, nine deputies led by Imbriani proposed that the parliament send a note of support for the peoples who were fighting and suffering for their independence, and the measure was approved. In Paris, the renowned French historian Ernest Lavisse presided over a meeting at the Sorbonne on 11 May, at which the learned philologist and historian of the Romanians, Emile Picot, gave a long speech exposing the evils of the dual monarchy. The student committee of the University of Lyons sent the accused Memorandists their sympathy and support, assuring them that the justice of their cause would triumph; it was no longer possible, they said, to put down their cause by the sword. Similar sentiments were echoed by French students at the University of Geneva and Serbian students at the University of Graz. Yet another example of the display of European support was furnished by the 146 telegrams, letters, poems, essays, and articles sent to V. A. Urechia, the president of the Cultural League, from France, Italy, Spain, Belgium, and Switzerland alone. These were signed by such well-known politicians as Clemenceau, Flourens, Lafargue, Jules Simon, and M. Maressiltag, professors such as Lavisse, Cesare Cantù, and Picot, writers like Giosue Carducci, Francisc Mistral, Le Conte de Lisle, Émile Zola, and Sully Prudhomme, and journalists such as Fava, Henri Rochefort, and Lesseur.

Intensification of Confrontation

That the defendants of the Cluj trial ultimately were convicted and imprisoned in no way weakened the struggle for self-determination and national unity. Expressions of solidarity, signaled by letters and personal visits, continued after the trial, and were manifested further by the student convention held in Constanţa on 10–13 September 1894. It was attended by representatives from all over Romania and Transylvania and from other countries as well. On this occasion the national flag, which at a demonstration in Predeal a year earlier had been divided among delegates from Transylvania, Moldavia, and Ţara Românească, was joined together once again. The Transylvanian student representatives declared that Romanians would know no peace until the tricolor waved triumphant everywhere on Romanian soil.

The national general assembly in Sibiu on 26 November 1894 voted to call a conference of nationalities to establish a common plan for promoting the interests of each people, and in response a crowd of Romanian, Serbian, and Slovak peasants, artisans, intellectuals, and journalists attended. The plan for allying the Romanian, Slovak, and Serbian national parties, presented by the Romanian Ştefan Cicio Pop, was unanimously adopted. The conference passed resolutions relating to the alliance of nationalities' common effort in their political struggles, and mutual and reciprocal support of the individual nationalities' goals. Two more large meetings of the allied nationalities subsequently took place in the summer of 1896. One of the meetings was held in Vienna and was presided over by Dr. L. Psenner, the president of the Austrian Social Christian party; the other, chaired by Emile Flourens, a former French foreign minister, met in Paris on 11 July. Both attracted considerable publicity and support.

However, the Hungarian landowners and bourgeoisie ignored the new spirit and general discontent. They continued to pass laws to guarantee their economic, political, and cultural dominance. When, late in 1897, the diet in Budapest passed a law Magyarizing place names, public protest meetings were organized in many Transylvanian cities, which drew not only city-dwellers but also peasants from neighboring villages. Once more the Romanians from Bukovina, whose political program for developing an awareness of their national and civil rights had been better formulated, declared their solidarity with the Romanians of Transylvania.

Given this situation, it was necessary for the RNP to revise its tactics. A group of younger members argued that it was again time for parliamentary activism, a tactic which would provide "tangible evidence of the growing political maturity of the Romanian people." A new forum for arguments in favor of this policy was needed; early in 1897, the *Tribuna Poporului* [People's tribune], edited by Ioan Russu-Şirianu, was founded for this purpose in Arad.

As oppression grew worse, the Romanian bourgeoisie was increasingly kept from participation in economic life and prevented from buying land; antipeasant laws were toughened, and the nationalities laws affected more and more spheres of everyday activity. In response, the revolutionary and democratic movement became radicalized. A wave of strikes gripped Hungary between 1903 and 1907. The effect of the strikes was increased by a number of harvest strikes—or rebellions—by poor peasants between 1903 and 1905 in Arad, Bihor, Satu Mare, Sălaj, Timiş, and Torontal. All were brutally put down by the authorities. Socialists, the bourgeoisie, and the bourgeois press came to the defense of the workers and peasants in county meetings and publicly criticized abusive laws, in particular the school laws that sought the abolition of the Romanian church schools.

The political committee of the RNP was renewed and rejuvenated. In 1905 the party's political goals were reformulated to include recognition of the Romanian people's political identity and guarantees of its ethnic and constitutional development; the use of Romanian in the army; an end to denationalization efforts; enforcement of laws on equal rights for the oppressed nationalities through the use of their own languages in administration, justice, and schools; full autonomy for all religions; election of officials from among the local population; universal suffrage; the right of assembly and free association; freedom of the press; a minimum property guarantee; reform of the tax system to take taxpayers' financial status into account; granting of land to peasants, where possible, from state property; and laws against the exploitation of workers by employers. An active election campaign was waged on the basis of this platform, and eight Romanian deputies, one Serb, and one Slovak were elected to the diet in Budapest. These ten deputies formed the nationalities caucus, which was led by the Romanian deputy Teodor Mihali. The caucus's manifesto proclaimed the political rights of the masses in general and of the oppressed peoples in particular, and reaffirmed their unshaken conviction that the general interests of all peoples urgently demanded "the most radical reforms."

As the RNP's platform was very close to that of the SDP on certain points, collaboration between the socialists and the nationalists became possible and even necessary. The bourgeoisie assumed the leading role in political life, but there were common problems that transcended class distinctions and the interests of any particular social group—for example, the winning of general democratic rights and the national unity of the Romanian people. These causes were also espoused by the manifestos published on the occasion of the Bucharest jubilee exposition in 1906, which celebrated the fortieth anniversary of the kingdom. Throngs of intellectuals and peasants from Transylvania, the Banat, and Bukovina went to Bucharest to express their support for unity, both by their mere presence and by the many demonstrations that took place in the capital during the jubilee.

Romania's attraction for all Romanians was "inconceivable," in the words of the Hungarian deputy István Bethlen, who stated in a speech in the diet in Budapest on 10 April 1907 that, in the eyes of Romanians from Austria-Hungary, the importance of the Hungarian state had diminished on the day the Romanian state had come into being. The leaders of the Hungarian government, however, did not understand. They increased and intensified repressive measures. Gyula Andrássy proposed a bill to introduce Hungarian as the training language in all military units, while Albert Apponyi's school law sought the introduction of Hungarian in the nationalities' religious schools. These measures aroused great concern; protests were repeatedly raised in the diet and in public meetings by representatives of all of the nationalities.

In addition to the outcry at home, there were protests by Romanian students in Vienna, Berlin, and Paris, and by Romanians in America, who identified with the struggle of their "parents and ancestors" who were shedding blood to preserve their language. The great Russian writer Leo Tolstoy and the prominent Norwegian writer and politican Björnstjerne Björnson added their voices to the chorus; the latter exposed the duplicity of Count Apponyi, who presented himself as a champion of peace and harmony at international conferences even while declaring war on children at home.

The socialists among the oppressed nationalities of the Austro-Hungarian Empire supported the right to national self-determination, with each nation having the right to decide its own fate and to govern itself independently. National unification also was the goal of a new newspaper called *Românul* [The Romanian], published in Arad under the direction of Vasile Goldiş. The paper's principles were based on the manifesto *Către Români* [To all Romanians] and on the editorial in the inaugural issue: propagation of ideas of unity; strengthening of links to other Romanian newspapers; and national solidarity, the supreme duty of Romanians in the empire. Similar strivings were apparent at the general meeting of Astra in Blaj in 1911, when that prestigious association celebrated its golden anniversary. Thirty thousand delegates from the various branches all over Transylvania were present, as well as intellectuals and politicians from Transylvania, Bukovina, and Romania. Thus the conference took on the aspect of a general convention of all Romanians.

It was not by coincidence, but by deliberate plan, that at the same time the Cultural League organized large-scale patriotic celebrations at the so-called Romanian Arena in Bucharest. Over 150,000 people, mostly peasants from Romania and the areas under foreign domination, responded to the call. The thread that ran through the Bucharest demonstrations again was the idea of the unification of all Romanians, and of their gravitating toward Bucharest, "the capital not only of Romania, but of all that is Romanian."

In the midst of the continual turmoil, Franz Ferdinand, the heir to the Habsburg throne, who hoped to strengthen the authority of the crown with his innovative ideas, decided to grant equality to all the nationalities. He was convinced that the dual monarchy compromise of 1867 had been a disaster, and he declared that once he ascended the throne he would grant substantial administrative autonomy to all nationalities and would replace the dual monarchy with a supranational federal system. His plans, however, never went beyond a theory designed to extricate the empire from its crisis, and events rushed on unchecked.

The great European powers entered on an insane race to invade new territories. Austrian manufacturers were especially eager to see a military conflict unleashed, and other industrial and commercial monopolies were similarly interested in acquiring new marketplaces for their products. This identity of interests culminated in the outbreak of the Balkan Wars in the autumn of 1912. Turkey was defeated, but disagreements arose among the anti-Ottoman allies—Serbia, Bulgaria, and Greece—over their wartime spoils. The conference of European diplomats in London, in December of that year, tried without success to settle the situation in the Balkans. Romania, said Romanian Prime Minister I. I. C. Brătianu, had to be prepared "to receive our brothers in Transylvania without opposition from anyone; in achieving this end Russia can be of no help." Independent and opposed to the Austro-Hungarian plans, Romania intervened in the Second Balkan War in the summer of 1913, playing an arbitrating role in the peace talks in Bucharest that August. Under pressure from public opinion in Romania and Transylvania, Romania's foreign policy gradually diverged from that of the Central Powers, from which it derived no benefits, and moved toward that of the Allies.

These circumstances were even more favorable to initiatives toward Romanian unification. The Romanian press in Transylvania and Romania openly and boldly supported it; the Hungarian press, of course, opposed it, but recognized the movement's power. Scholars and politicians encouraged the idea through their writings, and activity in support of unification became more and more widespread, more and more open. There was a moving demonstration of national solidarity in mid-September 1913, when the Romanian aviator Aurel Vlaicu crashed on his symbolic flight over the Carpathians. New newspapers with militant names appeared: *Lupta Noua* [The new struggle] in 1912; *România Mare* [Great Romania] in 1913. Public demonstrations like those organized by the Cultural League were openly directed against Austria-Hungary and supported the Romanians of Transylvania. A "grand peaceful demonstration" on Victory Boulevard in Bucharest "ended the patriotic event, which augured the storms of spring." Indeed, the spring of 1914 brought the storms of war.

13

The Birth of Unified Romania

THE THREAT OF WAR hung in the air. The world was aware of the rapidly approaching danger. Yet World War I, for all the misery that accompanied it, hastened the end of such anachronistic political entities as the czarist empire and the multinational Austro-Hungarian Empire. That, in turn, brought closer to fulfillment the oppressed peoples' aspirations toward political unity.

The imperialist powers, playing along with the monopolies and militaristic interests, competed in preparing the war. An excuse was sought for setting off the powder keg; it was found in Sarajevo on 28 June 1914, when Archduke Franz Ferdinand, the heir to the Habsburg throne, and his wife Sophia were the victims of an assassination plot by young Bosnian nationalists.

The Outbreak of War

On 24 July 1914, the Austro-Hungarian and German governments delivered an ultimatum to Serbia. Because certain provisions would have meant the total subjugation of Serbia to Austria-Hungary, the ultimatum was rejected. Four days later, the Central Powers declared war on Serbia, and then on Russia and France, the two principal Allied Powers. Germany then violated Belgian territory and England declared war on Germany on 5 August.

The Habsburg government immediately took steps to militarize Transylvanian life, abolishing such basic civil rights as freedom of the press and of assembly and assigning trials previously in the jurisdiction of civil courts to military tribunals. The flower of the country's youth was sent to the front. However, recruiting efforts differed between Hungarians and other nationalities, and in Transylvania the proportions were heavily weighted: over 52 percent of all soldiers from Transylvania were Romanian; only 26 percent were Hungarian. Of the Romanian soldiers, 92.4 percent were sent to the front; only 7.6 percent were assigned to support units. Hungarian teachers from state schools were declared unfit for service and left at home indefinitely, while Romanian teachers from religious schools were mobilized. Consequently, Romanians from the empire struggled under a fearful burden, for they were required to fight for a foreign cause even amid the fair hope of liberation.

The Central Powers failed in their plans for a lightning war. The Austro-Hungarian army suffered serious defeats on the eastern front at the hands of the Russians, just as the German armies experienced severe losses on the French and Russian fronts. The Central Powers, counting on the support of King Carol I and conservative circles, began to pressure Romania to enter the war, invoking the treaty of alliance. The Allied Powers equally were trying to attract Romania, promising help "so that the territories in Austria-Hungary inhabited by Romanians might be united to the Romanian crown."

The Romanian masses and Romanian public opinion in general favored taking action to undermine the Austro-Hungarian monarchy and to achieve unification. The press expressed the opinion that if a plebiscite were held, "the principal point that would be accepted with wild general enthusiasm would be the unification of all Romanians into a large and powerful state." However, Romania did not yet enter the war on either side. The Crown Council, meeting in Sinaia on 3 August 1914, decided that Romania should follow a "policy of national instinct"—a period of neutrality and subsequent cooperation with whichever powers recognized Romania's right to rule the provinces of the Austro-Hungarian Empire inhabited by Romanians. Romanian politicians saw this course as providing a necessary breathing space in which plans could be made for national unification. No longer content with "autonomy," they wanted to see the formation of "powerful states within ethnic boundaries"; the union of Transylvania with Romania was considered not only "imperative" for the interests of the Romanian people, but also "a prerequisite to social and political evolution and therefore in the interests of progress and humanity as well."

The Romanian people shared this opinion. They were, as the Austro-Hungarian envoy in Bucharest, Ottokar Czernin, put in his reports in September and October 1914, ready to "go to

Transylvania." Similar statements are found in King Carol's private diary from that autumn, and in the secret report that the king presented to Germany's Kaiser Wilhelm II. He speaks in the report of "continual demonstrations" and of "such great agitation throughout the whole country that even the leaders have been swept up into the current. Former ministers, teachers at universities and upper schools, indeed all segments of society have today but a single goal: Transylvania." Czernin's troubled report to the foreign minister in Vienna expresses the same feeling. The slogan "We want to go to Transylvania" was said to be the order of the day. In Bucharest, street demonstrators shouted "We want Ardeal!" and called for the removal of the king, who was considered the main obstacle to the realization of this goal. The Cultural League, meanwhile, based its whole program on the struggle to unify Romania, and took a new name, League for the Political Unity of All Romanians. A new League Committee was elected in a special convention in December 1914; it included Vasile Lucaciu, an unyielding fighter for unification who had come to Romania from Transylvania, as president; Barbu Ştefănescu Delavrancea, a well-known playwright, as vice-president; Nicolae Iorga, the eminent historian, as secretary-general; Simion Mîndrescu, another Transylvanian and a well-known Germanist, as treasurer; and the important and influential Nicolae Filipescu, Take Ionescu, Constantin Istrati, Ionaş Grădişteanu, and Octavian Goga as the members-at-large. The League's demonstrations in the capital and other cities attracted people from Transylvania, Bukovina, the Banat, and, of course, from Romania. Similar activities were carried on by the National Campaign the Transylvanian League, and the Unionist Federation, as well as by the Association of Bukovinians and Transylvanians in Bucharest, which was composed of Romanians who had fled from Transylvania and Bukovina. All these groups and societies, through direct appeals and other forms of pressure, tried to get the government to join the war for national liberation, and at the same time they made public appeals to all Romanians to take up the struggle.

Under these circumstances, it is entirely natural that the radical viewpoint gained prestige and influence in Transylvania and Romania. In January and February 1915, there were impressive demonstrations organized by the League in Bucharest and by the National Campaign in Brăila. University faculties passed resolutions pledging allegiance and commitment, while nonetheless acknowledging the sacrifices that Romanians would have to make to achieve union. The student body in Bucharest passed an appeal containing a solemn vow to fight against anyone, at any cost, for the same great ideal. A convention of Romanians from Austria-Hungary living in Romania met in Bucharest and voted in favor of Romania's entry into the war.

In turn the Central Powers intensified their efforts to attract Romania. A solution to the problem of the Romanians in Transylvania was a necessary prerequisite to success; thus Gottlieb von Jagow, the German chancellor and foreign minister, stated, "The German government, desiring to support the demands of Romania, resolves that Romania should occupy Bukovina at once, and should be given all of Bessarabia and the Timoc Valley, while Transylvania should receive a political status like that of Croatia." A conference was organized in Vienna, attended by von Jagow's close adviser Matthias Erzberger and by Aurel C. Popovici, Vasile Goldiş, and Iuliu Maniu, the representatives of the Romanians in Transylvania. The Transylvanians presented the following demands: national autonomy for the twenty-three countries with Romanian majorities; confederation-style relations between Transylvania and the other provinces of the empire; and a separate government, a national army, and an independent bank for Transylvania. These Romanian demands seemed excessive to the Central Powers, and the conference ended without result. Through their spokesman Constantin Racovski, the socialists then called for the proletariat to take advantage of the new circumstances to achieve union. The government responded by bringing new repressive measures to bear on educated and politically active residents of Transylvania. Some were drafted and sent to the front; others were jailed or interned in concentration camps on the charge that they had spread propaganda among the peasants and soldiers in favor of uniting Transylvania with Romania. But these measures were in vain, as many other soldiers deserted and crossed to Romania, while written manifestos calling for the union of Transylvania with Romania appeared everywhere.

The first half of 1916 saw even bolder offensives in favor of union. The newspapers made clear that not only intellectuals but also millions of peasants understood that "the joining of Transylvania to Romania is in the interests of their own existence." The Transylvanian Romanians were in an enthusiastic mood, and the authorities feared a movement against the monarchy, especially in face of unrest among the working class. The most important manifestation of this discontent was a miners' strike in the Jiu Valley in the summer of 1916, involving over ten thousand Romanian, Hungarian, and other workers. More than four hundred miners were arrested and jailed; ten were sentenced to death, and a large number were sent to the front.

The military situation on the various fronts in the summer of 1916 spurred the hopes of those who were fighting for the national cause. The great German offensive against the French army collapsed at Verdun, the Germans being forced by English tanks to withdraw to the Somme. The Italians achieved successes in Gorizia, on the Isonzo River, which eased the pressure on the Verdun front. The Russian army inflicted severe losses on the Austrians in Galicia, the Saloniki front was successfully resisting Bulgarian attacks, and the German fleet was bottled up in numerous ports.

About the same time, on 28–29 June 1916, the Conference of Nationalities met in Lausanne. Organized by the Union of Nationalities, which had been founded in 1912, the conference discussed the relationship between the national principle and a durable peace, resolving that "nationalities [based] on common origins, language, or tradition, or which result from the association, freely agreed to, of more than one ethnic group, have the right to decide their own affairs." The legitimate basis for the existence of states should be sovereignty manifested by the freely expressed desires of the population. There should be no annexations or transfers of territory contrary to the interests and desires of the population.

The Allied efforts to win Romanian cooperation now intensified. Romania was reminded that to remain neutral would mean giving up her national mission and make inevitable the loss of her opportunity for the union of all her "children." Thus an agreement was reached on Romania's territorial demands, and on 17 August a treaty of alliance was signed by Romania, Russia, France, England, and Italy. In return for an Allied guarantee of the integrity of her current frontiers and recognition of her right to unite with the Romanian territories in Austria-Hungary, Romania agreed to declare war on Austria-Hungary and to break all relations with enemies of the Allies. The signatories also agreed not to conclude any separate peace and that a peace treaty should unite the Romanian territories with Romania; Romania was guaranteed the same rights as the other Allies to take part in peace negotitions. The treaty of alliance was accompanied by a Russo-Romanian military pact making the countries equal partners. This treaty was the first international recognition of the union of the Romanians in a single state, of Romania's territorial integrity; it provided international recognition of the ethnodemographic principle.

Romania's Entry into the War

Once the treaty of alliance and the military pact were signed, Romanian military preparations quickened enormously, since the agreement gave the country only ten days to declare war on the Central Powers. On 26 August, a decisive meeting of the Crown Council took place, attended by all members of the government, the presidents of the Senate and the Chamber, the former prime ministers, and the heads of the political parties. Prime Minister Brătianu declared that Romania could no longer remain neutral without permanently compromising her future. Rather, she was duty-bound to pursue the ideal of unity, for there might never again be such favorable times; in order to achieve unity, Romania must side with the Allies. Brătianu's declaration was supported by the great majority of those present, all of whom based their arguments on the higher interests of the nation.

The die was cast. King Ferdinand's proclamation of the same day informed the country of the decision to enter the war and the goals that called for this decision. Romanians everywhere were gripped with enthusiasm at the word of Romania's entry into the war of national unification. Singing stirring national songs, Romanian soldiers—peasants, workers, and many intellectuals—prepared for battle.

Romanians in Transylvania also greeted the proclamation with great joy, even though they were well aware of the hardships they would face as a result. Desire for unification—which could now be seen more clearly on the horizon—was stronger than fear of the sacrifices that would have to be made. Some ten thousand Romanians were taken from their homes and sent to Hungary, where many were used in mines and factories. The notorious "cultural zone" was created in southern Transylvania along the border with Romania, in the region of Brașov, Făgăraș,

Sibiu, Hunedoara, and Caraş-Severin. The authorities closed 311 Romanian religious schools in this area, leaving 477 teachers without a livelihood. Many local peasants were moved elsewhere. Yet more peasants and intellectuals were interned in concentration camps or thrown into prison.

The enthusiasm of Transylvanian Romanians at the sight of the Romanian army cannot be described. As the soldiers entered Braşov, according to contemporary reports, "all the Romanians in town went out before them with flowers and speeches; the likes of such fiery animation had never been seen before." The enthusiasm, moreover, was backed by concrete action. Thirty thousand young Transylvanians presented themselves to military commanders asking to be accepted as volunteers. Even a few Hungarians were swept up in the enthusiasm and offered a warm welcome to the Romanian army. The reverberations were felt in Bukovina, where in the face of pitiless official terror calls were made for autonomy—the first step toward union with Romania or with Transylvania. In Bessarabia the newspaper *Cuvînt moldovenesc* [Moldavian word] expressed the wish for the union of Bessarabia and Romania. The same sentiments and ideals also inspired the Romanians in America, the great majority of whom came from Transylvania. In Cleveland, Ohio, for example, the Romanian paper *America* proclaimed its faith in the eventual achievement of unity through the concerted efforts of all the national forces.

The Romanian army was caught between two fronts—the Transylvanian one led by General Eric Falkenhain, and the southern one under the command of General August Mackensen—and, without aid, was forced to withdraw from Transylvania after battles lasting forty days. As the army retreated, many young intellectuals from the southern districts of Transylvania—reportedly as many as twenty thousand—left for Romania, fearing the punishments being prepared for them. Those who did not retreat were arrested and interned in concentration camps or jailed. Many of them either lost their lives in prison or died later from the treatment they had suffered there. A group of 257 intellectuals, workers, and peasants were tried for espionage and condemned to death. Most went through the trial with dignity.

Following the withdrawal from Transylvania and the defeat on the southern front, Bucharest was occupied by the Austro-German armies on 6 December 1916, the troops bringing with them the future presumptive king of Romania, Prince Wilhelm of Hohenzollern. Two-thirds of the territory of Romania was thus occupied by the Central Powers, and was pillaged and robbed without mercy. The government and administration were forced to retreat to Moldavia. Nevertheless, the most courageous and farseeing of the political leaders of Transylvania and Romania did not succumb to despair. The Romanian prime minister repeated the idea enunciated in the Crown Council of 17 August 1916, reaffirming his hope for unification of the territories inhabited by Romanians. Nor did the people lose faith: when signs of light appeared on the horizon, moral strength—a true force in this period—and then military strength were reborn.

In December 1916, President Woodrow Wilson of the United States addressed a message to the warring powers in which he proclaimed the need to solve the problem of nationalities. Though Wilson did not make concrete proposals, his gesture served to bolster hope among the nationalities of the Austro-Hungarian Empire, who never for a moment abandoned their aspirations and continued to express them as circumstances permitted. One such expression was desertion from the Austro-Hungarian army by Romanian soldiers, who would cross to Romania and join the Romanian army. In 1916 the number of Romanian deserters reached the rather considerable figure of 38,869. Any who were captured were sentenced to death. This climate of opinion, together with military defeats suffered on various fronts by the armies of the Central Powers, led to a growing conviction that Austria-Hungary should be dismembered. Some groups within Austria-Hungary and Germany themselves began to express a desire for peace. The Allied Powers, however, rejected the peace proposals, declaring that the struggle would continue until the principle of nationalities and the existence of small states were recognized. Allied plans included the restoration of Belgium, Serbia, and Montenegro; the freeing of occupied territories in France, Russia, and Romania; reparations; the reorganization of Europe to respect the rights of the nationalities; the liberation of the Italians, South Slavs, Romanians, and Czechoslovaks from foreign domination; and liberation of the peoples under Turkish rule.

The Austro-Hungarian Empire began a general collapse. The future of the monarchy seemed very dark. The new emperor, Karl, who was crowned in December 1916 after the death of the aged Franz Joseph, attempted at the eleventh hour to salvage what could be salvaged. Influenced by Empress Zita, a known

Germanophobe, and by the Deutsches Haus political society, Karl made plans to federalize and even democratize the empire. Another decisive factor in the unfolding of events was the entry of the United States into the war on 6 April 1917; the weakness of the Central Powers and especially of Austria-Hungary at this point was very evident.

Such was the background for a meeting of a group of Romanian prisoners in Darnitsa, near Kiev, on 26 April 1917. Organizing themselves into a powerful volunteer corps, the Romanians—officers, noncommissioned officers, and enlisted men from Transylvania and Bukovina—took an oath to fight with all their strength for the emancipation of the country and the unification of Transylvania with Romania. In their declaration of 26 April, they announced their resolve to sacrifice their lives in the fight to "unite all the Romanian people and all the Romanian territory of the Austro-Hungarian Empire in a single and undivided, free and independent Romania." Their goal was the formation of "a single Romanian national state . . . based on the most progressive democracy." Signed by about five hundred delegates in the name of the roughly thirteen thousand Romanian prisoners in Russia, the declaration was then distributed to the Allied governments, the Romanian state press and newspapers, and to Czech, Serbian, Polish, and Ruthenian national organizations in Russia.

The words were followed by action. Tens of thousands of Transylvanian and Bukovinian volunteers headed for Romania to experience their baptism of fire and the greatness of sacrifice. The enthusiasm aroused by the arrival in Iaşi of the first detachments of volunteers early in June expressed the importance of the event, "the beginning of the climax in the achievement of national unification." The first batallion of volunteers left for the front on 1 August 1917. They joined the Romanian army under the command of Generals Alexandru Averescu and Eremia Grigorescu and contributed to the great victories over the German army commanded by the storied Marshal Mackensen in Mărăşti, Mărăşeşti, and Oituz. These defeats shattered Mackensen's plans to occupy Moldavia, take Romania out of the war, and divide it. The battles of summer 1917 and the historic victories of the Romanian troops can be compared to the great encounters of Verdun, Marne, Isère, and Isonzo; they were decisive for the future of Romania and the development of national unity.

The actions of the Romanians in Transylvania were significantly influenced by the military successes of the summer of 1917, as well as by demonstrations of support for national unity by various political groups, the masses in Romania, and the volunteers from Transylvania and Bukovina. There were also demonstrations of support by emigrants in various Allied countries, notably France, England, Italy, and the United States, where a climate of opinion favorable to self-determination and national unity had been created. As a result of the campaigns by emigrants of various nationalities from the Austro-Hungarian Empire, the United States, little by little, changed its position. The Putney Report of June 1917 proposed a compromise solution to the nationality problem: the creation of an independent Yugoslav state (though without the Slovenians, who were regarded as linked to the Habsburgs); the union of Trieste and Istria with Italy and Fiume with Austria; the independence of Bohemia, but without the Slovaks; the union of Transylvania and the Banat with Romania; and the restructuring of Poland to exclude large minority groups.

In the second half of 1917, there were exceptionally important changes not only in the battlefield situation, but in the social and political arenas as well. The war, with its retinue of suffering, had deepened the discontent of the oppressed social classes; sizable demonstrations for peace and bread were organized by workers and peasants from the factories and the fields. Everywhere—at home and on the front—there were strikes and antiwar demonstrations. Civil unrest intensified when the socialist revolution in Russia emerged victorious in the days from 25 October to 7 November. The establishment of worker-peasant power in Russia served as an example and a signal for the masses in other countries as well. Large strikes broke out in Germany, with workers from every city participating, demanding food, freedom, immediate peace with no annexations, and the establishment of workers' councils. Demonstrations with the slogan "End the War" were organized by Viennese workers. The Hungarian proletariat demonstrated in force for peace and against István Tisza, the leader of the Hungarian bourgeoisie and landowning class. In Transylvania, at a number of large peoples' assemblies in several cities and working-class centers, the working masses petitioned the government for an increase in wages and food rations, universal suffrage, and the recognition of workers' organizations. There was peasant resistance everywhere to troop levies and conscriptions and to labor assignments on large estates. Actual rebellions against the authorities and the militia occurred in a few villages.

Union with Bessarabia

On 20 October 1917, the Romanian Military Congress met in Chişinău, Bessarabia. Five hundred delegates participated—officers and enlisted men, representing 250,000 Bessarabian Romanian soldiers, the sons of peasants and of intellectuals—and proclaimed the autonomy of Bessarabia. The congress further resolved to establish a national council and convene a Bessarabian constituent assembly as quickly as possible. The National Council met on 21 November. The entire population of the province was represented, both the Romanian majority and most of the minorities. On 2 December 1917, a resolution was passed creating the Federated Democratic Moldavian Republic.

Events both east and west now moved with dizzying speed. In the United States, President Wilson set his Fourteen Points before Congress on 8 January 1918; these included the Allied program for dealing with the political and economic problems of Europe. The reaffirmation of the principle of justice for all peoples and nations and the right of all, weak or strong, to live equally free and secure, meant the implicit affirmation of the right of national self-determination. Influenced by the October socialist revolution and by Wilson's Fourteen Points, the entire proletariat of Austria-Hungary was gripped by great agitation, which, in January 1918, led to a movement for a general strike. The strike spread to cities in Bohemia, Hungary, and Transylvania, where thousands of workers were "eager and ready for anything," including immediate revolution. Strikes then spread to Germany, where workers demanded immediate peace, a change of government, election of workers' councils, freeing of political prisoners, and improvement of supplies. Romanian emigrant communities undertook intensive campaigns for unification in the Allied countries. In Paris, beginning in January 1918, Romanian emigrants in France published the newspaper *La Roumanie*, described as an "organ for Romanian demands and rights" and edited by Paul Brătăşianu. This paper performed an invaluable service in preparing French, English, and Italian public opinion for the course of Romanian unification.

Meanwhile, hungry and war-weary, some Austro-Hungarian troops revolted. These uprisings even achieved the scale of actual rebellions as, for example, the one staged in early February 1918 by Italian, Czech, and Romanian soldiers at naval bases on the Adriatic. This revolt sought both rights for military personnel and national liberation for oppressed peoples through the signing of a peace and the granting of the right of self-determination.

Thus the proclamation of the independent Moldavian republic gave greater force to the desires and efforts of the entire Romanian people for unity. The manifesto of the Central Committee of Moldavian Students in Bucharest, addressed to the whole population between the Prut and the Nistru (Dniester), concluded, "Long live the freedom and unity of all Romanians." This idea was taken up again by the same committee, the young people proclaiming as an article of faith that "the deliverance of our people is in the union of all our sons into a single country." Meanwhile peoples' councils (zemstvas), in meeting after meeting, expressed the same feelings and desires. Faced with these crises, the Romanian government accepted armistice negotiations with Germany and Austria-Hungary. The Peace of Bucharest, by which the country's riches and a good part of its territory was taken over by the Central Powers, was signed on 7 May.

Protests against the enslaving treaty broke out everywhere. The RNP in Transylvania met in secret to decide on a plan of action. The workers' movement protested in the press and in public meetings. Another protest was the resolution of the Bessarabian National Council of 27 March–9 April, which declared, "From this day forward and forevermore the Moldavian Democratic Republic is united with its mother Romania." It called for respecting the rights of minorities; universal, equal, and direct suffrage with secret ballot; personal freedom, as well as freedom of the press, of speech, of religion, and of assembly; and all the community freedoms that would be guaranteed in the constitution.

Preparations for Success

The spring of 1918 saw the turning point of the war. The temporary successes of the Central Powers were canceled out by the Allied victories, particularly after the arrival of the American armies in Europe. Socialist political parties took up the banner of peace, democracy, and national independence. The Interallied Socialist Conference met in London on 21–23 February 1918 to agree on a course of action. Representatives of French, Italian, and English socialists were there, as well as Serbian, Romanian, and Polish representatives who had taken refuge in the west. The conference approved a memorandum calling, among other things, for the right of peoples to national independence. Formation of the Socialist Committee for Understanding between Oppressed Nationalities was decided on; the committee was headed by Albert Thomas, who stated that the existence of multinational empires was incompatible with the right of nations to self-determination. On 2 and 3 March, Yugoslav representatives met in Zagreb and adopted a resolution declaring the Slovenians, Croatians, and Serbians a single nation and demanding the right of self-determination.

The Romanians, too, continued their struggle at home, while the immigrants and the diplomatic mission kept up their work in America. The Romanians of America, of whom the majority—roughly two hundred thousand—were from Transylvania and the Banat, met in a convention in Youngstown, Ohio, on 10 March and approved a motion, later presented to President Wilson, expressing "unshakable faith" in the emancipation of all small nations, which could then unite with the Romanian kingdom and the four million Romanians in the Austro-Hungarian Empire. To continue the fight for unification, the Romanian National League, headed by Vasile Stoica, and the National Committee, headed by Epaminonda Lucaciu, son of Vasile Lucaciu, were created. In March, the National Committee organized large demonstrations in Chicago, Indianapolis, and other cities, where thousands of Romanians marched the streets with Romanian and American flags, calling for the union of Transylvania with Romania. Legions of Romanian-American volunteers began to organize to participate in the fight against the Central Powers. Through such activities and editorials in their newspapers *Romania* (published in Chicago by the brothers Paul and Gogu Negulescu) and *Libertatea* (published in Cleveland by Ioan Moța), the Romanians in America succeeded in winning over American public opinion and such large and prestigious newspapers as the *Washington Post* and the *New York Times*. Many congressmen, too, joined their forces, including the former president Theodore Roosevelt, who gave several speeches in support of the independence of the Slavs and the Romanians; Secretary of State Robert Lansing and Undersecretary Polk assured the Romanians that they understood the circumstances which had forced Romania to make peace with the Central Powers.

Public opinion in France and in the other Allied countries also became more and more openly opposed to maintaining the Austro-Hungarian Empire. An important step was taken at the Allied conference in London in mid-March, at which it was officially recognized that Romania had been "drowned in the torrent of domination" of the Central Powers, and that the treaty that had been signed under such circumstances would not be recognized. The Anglo-Romanian Society, led by Lord Robert Cecil, the archbishop of Canterbury, the historian and politician James Bryce, and such authoritative writers as Henry Wickham Steed and Scotus Viator (Seton Watson) played a significant role in forming English opinions.

An equally important step in dealing with the problem of oppressed nationalities in the Austro-Hungarian Empire was the convention of those nationalities held in Rome on 8 April. Senator Francesco Ruffini presided, and representatives of the Allies and the nationalities served as vice-presidents. The convention resolved that "every people proclaims its right to constitute its own nationality and state, or to unify in order to win full political and economic independence." The Austro-Hungarian Empire, "the instrument of German domination," was declared the basic stumbling block to national aspirations and rights. Consequently, the convention declared "the necessity of common struggle against the common oppression," until each people had won total independence and political unity. From Capitoline Hill, for all the world to hear, a sanctioned international forum had proclaimed the right of peoples to be constituted in free sovereign national states. The moment was not only solemn, but significant: no one and nothing could stop the realization of those aspirations. Indeed, they would be fulfilled before the year was out.

The resolutions of the Rome convention were recognized by the Allied political leaders—Italian Prime Minister Vittorio Emmanuele Orlando, French Prime Minister Georges Clemenceau, and American Secretary of State Lansing. Lansing, in his 10 May memorandum to President Wilson, urged open support of the revolutions for national independence in the empire and active cooperation by the United States in order to "wipe Austria-

Hungary from the map of Europe as an Empire" and to "divide it among the nationalities which make it up."

On 30 April, in Paris, the National Committee of Romanians from Transylvania and Bukovina was formed under the leadership of the great inventor and engineer Traian Vuia. It was resolved to enlist Romanians from France in the Allied armies in order to contribute to the liberation of Transylvania and the unification of Transylvania with Romania. A periodical entitled *La Transylvanie* was published to further the cause. Vuia's committee did succeed in forming a legion of officers, student pilots who had come from Great Britain to Paris. A few French volunteers also joined. The organization of this legion in France provided an impetus for Romanian prisoners from Transylvania and the Banat in Italy, who numbered more than eighteen thousand by the end of 1917, to organize a similar group. They vowed to "fight side-by-side with the Italian army, against the Central Powers and for union with Romania." Enthusiastic demonstrations of solidarity with the Romanian people were organized in Rome, in which major political figures took part. Letters and telegrams expressing support and agreement were sent by individuals who could not participate, including Orlando, the president of the Council of Ministers, who expressed his admiration for "the courage of the Romanian army" and his faith in the achievement of a unified Romanian state.

The Hungarian authorities in Transylvania responded to all of these activities as they always had, with stiffer laws and stricter supervision of schools, teachers, and priests. Military courts continued to sentence groups of peasants to death or to many years of imprisonment on charges of high treason for having worked for the unification.

Such internal causes, together with military ones, hastened the fall of the dual monarchy. The French-English-American counteroffensive early in June, led by Marshall Foch, could not be stopped. Seeing that the end was near, the oppressed nationalities tried to avoid being caught unaware by the course of events. The Romanians and Czechs met several times in Vienna to discuss economic and political problems. By September, the fall of the Central Powers was a matter of days. The German foreign minister, Hintze, faced with the military failures, proposed opening diplomatic negotiations through the queen of Holland and the king of Spain. Count Stefan Buriau, the Austro-

Hungarian foreign minister, meanwhile, proposed convening a conference of all the belligerent powers in order to stop the hostilities at once and establish a basis for peace. His note was rejected by those to whom it was addressed. Once her armies suffered new defeats in Italy, all that remained for Austria was to surrender. Beaten on all fronts and shaken internally by national liberation movements, the Habsburg empire had no choice.

The Proclamation of the Right of Transylvanian Romanians to Self-Determination

As the Habsburg monarchy fell apart, the Romanian political leaders were constantly moving, seeking ways to achieve their great purpose. On 24 September 1918, the Executive Committee of the Romanian National Party decided to resume militant activities and to reestablish contact with the leaders of the Social Democrats. It was decided that representatives of the two parties should meet on 6 October and begin organized collaboration through the creation of the Romanian National Council. These early October days also saw the establishment in Paris of the National Council for Romanian Union, headed by Take Ionescu and recognized by the Allied Powers as the representative of Romania's interests.

Against this backdrop, representatives of the Romanian National Party met in Oradea on 12 October, including Vasile Goldjs, , Stefan Cicio Pop, Aurel Vlad, Ioan Suciu, Alexandru Vaida, Teodor Mihali, Aurel Lazăr, and Ioan Ciordaş. Noting that time had vindicated the Romanians' centuries-old demands for full national liberty founded on the natural right of every nation to decide and control its own destiny, the meeting declared that "the Romanian nation of Hungary and Transylvania" claimed its right "to decide on its own position among free nations" and to establish relations with other free nations. Denying the right of the Hungarian parliament and government to consider themselves representatives of the Romanian nation and to represent its interests at the peace conference, the Romanian nation declared that this right belonged solely to delegates elected by their own national assembly. Any decisions taken and agreements made without the approval of those elected by the national assembly were declared null and void, committing the Romanian nation to nothing.

The Oradea resolution, representing the proclamation of the right of the Romanian nation to self-determination, was virtually equivalent to a declaration of the independence of Transylvania from Hungary. Nonetheless, the declaration also advanced the idea of convening a national assembly. The conference elected an action committee to put its resolutions into effect, but the fact that the committee was composed of representatives of a single party weakened its claim to be a national representative. Consequently, on the initiative of the Romanian socialists, the collaboration between the two parties was substantially strengthened. This was especially evident when the Romanian Social Democrats, at their convention on 13 October, proclaimed, through Ioan Flueraş, that the right of self-determination was a right of all peoples.

In any case, neither the emperor's negotiations with the representatives of the nationalities nor the imperial manifesto of 16 October which announced that the empire would be reorganized and that Austria would become a federal state in which each nationality would become a political community within its own territory could save the empire. Peoples were called on to collaborate in this "great task" through their national councils, so that the empire might be reborn after the war as a "Federation of Free Peoples," but this appeal was fruitless. The nationalities would no longer be fooled by empty promises, and what they were offered was far short of what they were demanding.

Meanwhile, President Wilson's 18 October response to the Austrian government's note of 4 October had a paralyzing effect. The American president declared the Austro-Hungarian Empire dissolved. The Czechoslovak government was recognized as a belligerent party which alone had the right to speak in the name of the Czech and Slovak peoples; the right of the Yugoslavs and Czechoslovaks to form independent national states was recognized. However, the Romanians in Austria-Hungary were not included among those peoples recognized as having the right to form a national state. On the same day, Hungarian Minister-President Wekerle's declaration announcing the end of the dual monarchy was made public, although independent Hungary would continue to recognize a personal union with Austria— that is, only through the person of the emperor, as king of Hungary. The common government was maintained, however, with

Gyula Andrássy named as common foreign minister and palace minister.

These writhings were like the agony of a creature beyond help. Soldiers of the nationalities deserted the front in groups. Czechs, Slovaks, Hungarians, Austrians, and Romanians headed home, lining the roads and crowding the trains. In the big cities, especially in the two capital cities of the empire, the population, suffering from shortages of all kinds, wanted an end to this unbearable state of affairs, and the discontent could no longer be put down by force of bayonets. Soldiers' and workers' councils were formed, in secret at first, more openly later on. These groups, together with masses of the people, demanded peace at any price, freedom, and a socialist republic.

On 18 October, the very day of President Wilson's negative reply to Austria-Hungary's peace offer, Alexandru Vaida, the representative of the Executive Committee of the RNP, presented the Oradea declaration of 12 October to the Budapest parliament, together with a long speech. Vaida rejected the notion of "nationality," demanding the status of "nation" for the non-Hungarian and non-German populations of the empire. As one of these peoples, the Romanian nation assumed the right to decide its own destiny. His speech amounted to a manifesto concerning the right of the Romanian nation to control its own affairs. It was heard with amazement by some, disapproval by others, and was enthusiastically approved by the Slovak representives and a few Hungarian deputies from the radical party. In truth, the 12 October declaration was a historic moment of both practical and programmatic importance. All the decisions of the second half of October and November were based on this declaration and made in the name of the principles set forth in it. The crowning achievement was the great national assembly in Alba Iulia on 1 December and its proclamation of the unification of Transylvania with Romania. It was especially significant in that the Romanian Social Democrats espoused the declaration without reservations.

The day after Vaida's speech, 19 October, the Slovak deputy Ferdinand Juriga followed the Romanian lead and made a similar declaration on behalf of the Slovaks. The Petru Maior Society of Romanian students in Budapest, led by Dumitri Antal, took courage from Vaida's speech and addressed an appeal to Romanian students at the universities in Vienna, Budapest, and Cluj, and at the theological seminaries in Blaj, Oradea, Lugoj, Arad, and Caransebeş, urging them to support the struggle begun by the RNP. In an article entitled "Brothers, We Are with You," the Romanians of Bukovina proclaimed their unreserved agreement and solidarity with the Transylvanian Romanians' resolution. The Society of Freeholders and Former Boyars of Bukovina called for union with the Romanians in Transylvania, Maramureş, the Banat, Crişana, and Romania. *La Roumanie*, the newspaper of the Romanian emigrants in Paris, emphasized that the Romanians were not a nationality, but a nation, and that the right of the non-Hungarian nations to organize themselves freely was an international question, a matter of honor for all mankind.

In these last days in October, the outcome of the war and of the peace was decided. On 23 October, President Wilson sent his third note to Germany, this time seeking discussion on an armistice. At the same time the commanders of the Allied western front, summoned by Marshall Foch, met in Senlis on 25 October to work out the decisive plan of action. The imperial government made one more desperate attempt to obtain a settlement. On 28 October, Foreign Minister Andrássy proposed a separate peace with each of the belligerent parties; the United States, in reply, made peace negotiations contingent on recognition of the right of self-determination for the peoples of Austria-Hungary. Once these conditions were accepted, the imperial government proposed an immediate armistice on all fronts so that peace talks could begin.

About this time the Italians won a major victory at Piave, a battle in which the Cloşca regiment of the Italians' Romanian Legion took part. On 30 October, Vittorio Veneto was occupied. Franchet d'Esperey, meanwhile, advanced victoriously into the Balkans with the southern army. Turkey signed the truce of Mudros on 30 October, and on 1 November the Allied armies were in Belgrade. The Lammasch government, which had been brought to power in Vienna on 28 October, and the Provisional National Assembly of the Autonomous State of German Austria, which took the place of the old Assembly of the Empire, could no longer keep up with the situation. Workers and soldiers, organized in councils, demanded peace, proclamation of a republic, removal of the government, and the emperor's arrest, and a general strike occurred.

The demonstrations in Vienna and acceptance of the peace conditions by the Austrian government gave fresh strength to the independence movements in the empire. In Hungary, the situation was controlled by the workers, petty bourgeoisie, and army. The Hungarian National Council formed on 25 October under the leadership of Mihály Károlyi. The council promised removal of the central government in Vienna, a separate peace, universal suffrage by secret ballot, rights for nationalities, agrarian reform, and independence for Hungary while maintaining its boundaries. On 28 October, the Czech National Committee proclaimed national independence. Two days later, the Slovak National Committee proclaimed the union of the Slovaks and the Czechs. Thus was born the independent state of Czechoslovakia. Simultaneously, identical movements were taking place in the southern Slavic provinces. On 29 October, the Croatian National Council (Sobor) in Zagreb proclaimed separation of Croatia from Austria-Hungary and creation of the independent Yugoslav state.

In the wake of all these incidents in the former provinces, the Provisional National Assembly of the Empire was convened on 30 October. The assembly handed over its power to the State Council, which formed a social democratic government headed by Karl Renner. On 3 November, the Habsburg empire signed the Villa Giusti armistice, the coup de grâce for both the empire and the dynasty.

The landslide rolled on with devastating strength. The bourgeois-democratic revolution in Hungary was victorious. On 1 November, the People's Republic was proclaimed, with Mihály Károlyi as president, and the next day complete independence from Austria was declared.

Revolution in Transylvania and Bukovina

Events in Transylvania and Bukovina paralleled those unfolding in other territories in the dying Austro-Hungarian Empire. A large political assembly was held in Cernăuți on 27 October, whose purpose was to declare itself a constituent assembly and to elect a national council as the representative body of the Romanians in Bukovina. The new assembly's first resolution concerned "the unification of all Bukovina with the other Romanian countries in an independent national state, in complete solidarity with the Romanians in Transylvania and Hungary." The assembly then elected a national council with full powers to represent it at the peace conference.

The thirtieth of October 1918 was a date of especial importance and significance. On this day Romania reentered the war on the side of the Allies and against the Central Powers, in order to annul the Treaty of Buftea-Bucharest, which in any case she had never ratified. Romania also hoped to regain her international position stipulated in the treaty of alliance of August 1916, and to assure herself of a place at the peace table. On the same day, the Romanian National Council was constituted, which was to assume and exercise governmental functions in Transylvania for about a month. The council was announced by the newspaper *Adevărul* [Truth] under the significant headline, "The Revolution Triumphs. The Romanian National Council Is Formed."

The Romanian National Council was formed on a basis of parity, with six representatives each from the RNP and the SDP. From the former were Teodor Mihali, Vasile Goldiş, Alexandru Vaida-Voievod, Ştefan Cicio Pop, Aurel Vlad, and Aurel Lazăr; from the latter were Ioan Flueraş, Iosif Jumanca, Enea Grapini, Basiliu Surdu, Tiron Albani, and Iosif Renoi.

In Vienna, a National Committee of Romanians in Transylvania and a Romanian Military Senate were formed on 31 October. The committee was led by Iuliu Maniu, who had returned from the front, and the senate by General Ioan Boieru. The senate informed Romanian officers that the peoples of the former Austro-Hungarian Empire henceforth were organized on a national and democratic basis, and that from that day forward they belonged to the National Committee, the only authority to which they owed obedience and allegiance.

This clarification was critically needed, since events of the last ten days of October had signaled the start of the bourgeois-democratic revolution in Transylvania and Bukovina. It began in Arad, where the actions of the masses were described as "agitation and revolution" by the newspaper *Românul*. On 31 October, a "colossal action" took place in Timişoara, involving a general strike and a demonstration on the city's streets for a democratic republic. The revolution spread wildly to other towns and working-class centers in the Banat, and one contemporary newspaper wrote that "all the Banat is in flames." Oradea, too, was gripped in revolutionary turmoil. A general strike brought out all the workers in the city. The three thousand soldiers garrisoned there organized a mass meeting on 31 October, at which they called for the proclamation of a republic.

After the meeting the soldiers spread out through the villages, taking their revolutionary ideas with them. The miners in northern Transylvania also called a strike on 1 November, and a state of siege was established in the city of Baia Mare.

The revolution spread everywhere in the mining centers of the Jiu Valley. In Braşov workers' demonstrations ended with the formation of a workers' guard, whose job was not only to watch over factories but also to keep order in the town. In the Bihor Mountains there was violent turmoil; miners formulated demands and organized strikes, such as one in Zlatna on 31 October. There were similar upheavals in Sighişoara, Tîrgu Mureş, Făgăraş, and Sibiu. Villages, too, were involved. Revolts and uprisings occurred in late October and early November in many villages in a number of Transylvanian districts. The causes are easily understood—the misery caused by the war, first of all, but especially the abuses by the authorities in the requisitioning and distribution of food. Peasant revolts broke out simultaneously in several areas. Mayors, notaries, guardsmen, and landowners were attacked and run out of town, or in some cases arrested or robbed.

Clearly a new political era was in the making in Transylvania, and it necessarily involved a new political-administrative organization. The Central Romanian National Council was established for this purpose, and since the people, through their political organization, had invested it with power, it possessed both moral and political authority. The council reorganized itself in order to discharge its responsibilities more effectively, with Ştefan Cicio Pop as president and George Crişan as secretary-general. It was recognized as the supreme executive forum.

On its very first day of power, the Central Romanian National Council created a central military organization, the Romanian National Military Council, which was responsible for keeping order and calm and for securing lives and property. The National Council and the Military Council exercised their powers through subordinate regional and local organizations, Romanian national councils, and Romanian national guards.

The complex political issues needed immediate public clarification, which came on 2 November in the Romanian National Council's *Appeal*. This document informed the "Romanian Nation" of the right of nations to free action and equal rights; it asked the people and the soldiers to have patience and love for their nation, which had joined the ranks of free nations, so that it might show itself worthy of the trust of other nations; and it asked trust in the National Council, which had been recognized by the people's great power and which represented the entire Romanian people in Transylvania. It listed five imperatives of the moment: 1) cooperation on the part of all good people, regardless of nationality or ethnic background, to maintain order; 2) protection of lives and property; 3) obedience to the advice of the men sent by the National Council; 4) organization of the local national guards, which were open to all men of good character, without regard to nationality or ethnic background; and 5) refraining from looting. All Romanians were called on to give aid to the council so that the "fine young Romanian nation" might present its best face to the world, "unsullied, in all its splendor." Reparation was being made for centuries of injustice; the government and defense of Transylvania were being assumed by representatives of its majority nation, the Romanian nation. It was the next-to-last act of the great historical process which Romanians had hoped for and worked for century after century. For the fulfillment of this dream, the most valiant sons of the Romanian people—common people and intellectuals— had fought and sacrificed themselves. With the final acts of unification of the Romanian national state, all the branches of the Romanian nation would at last be united in a single country.

All of the actions of the following days were intended to guarantee and consolidate the historic conquest. The establishment of national councils in each district were intensely patriotic occasions, although the calls summoning people to the constituent assemblies asked for calm, peaceful coexistence with the other nationalities, the forgetting of old wrongs, and the forgiving of those who had committed them. Festive assemblies took place everywhere, indoors or in the open air, and thousands of people from all over the districts, towns and villages for which they were being held participated. National flags heightened the occasion; the solemnity of the opening ceremonies was emphasized when the national anthem was sung in chorus by all present. Each constituent assembly closed with a unanimous oath to "defend with all their faith the common good and the life and property of every person, without regard to language and beliefs; to live in peace and understanding with one another—Romanian, Hungarian, Saxon, and any other nation; and to obey peacefully the Romanian National Council. This advice was followed by those to whom it was addressed. The bourgeois-democratic revolution in Transylvania was not a bloody one. A few exceptional acts aside, events generally proceeded peacefully.

National guards, executive organs subordinate to the national councils, were established at the same time as the councils. Within a few days, every district, town, and village in the twenty-three districts inhabited by Romanians had such a guard to secure order, life, and property. The guards' powers were set by the Central Romanian Council: they were to reestablish and maintain order, but also to instruct and enlighten the people, so that they might be worthy of the rights and freedoms they had won, and to prove to the people that after so much suffering they would have justice, would be rewarded for all that they had endured, and would be given land. The supreme commander of the national guards was Major Alexandru Vlad, commander-in-chief of the Romanian National Guard in Arad, Lieutenant Romul Rimbaş, adjutant, Lieutenant Cornel Albu, secretary, and a number of advisers. The Arad command was in charge of the district national guards, while the town, village, and local guards were responsible to the district guards.

Through the Romanian National Council in Arad, and through the district and local national guards and national councils, Romanian government was introduced throughout Transylvania, but union with Romania continued to be the ultimate goal. On 5 November, encouragement for unification arrived from Washington. The United States' government and President Wilson approved of "the desires for unification of the Romanian people everywhere" and cast their support to the Romanians so that they might earn their political and territorial rights. They promised that the "integrity, liberty, and independence of Romania were one of the points of honor for the Allies" and that the Allies would support the "national demands of Romania." Meanwhile Romanian emigrants emigrants kept up the pressure throughout the turbulent days of November. In Paris, the National Council for Romanian Union firmly demanded the dismemberment of Austria-Hungary into independent national territories, on the principle of self-determination of peoples. This demand had an immediate result when Raymond Poincaré, the president of the French Republic, addressed to the council the wish "for the prompt realization of national unity for France's friend Romania."

At the same time revolution broke out in several places. In Kiel the navy revolted, and the revolt spread widely. Soldiers' and workers' councils were formed; a million to a million-and-a-half German soldiers deserted; princes and dukes abdicated. In Bavaria, the schoolteacher Kurt Eisner proclaimed a republic. As early as 31 October, the German chancellor advised Kaiser Wilhelm II to abdicate, thinking it would bring easier terms for peace; the abdication did occur on 9 November. A Council of Commissioners of the People was formed, consisting of six members and headed by the moderate Social Democrat Friedrich Ebert. In Berlin the republic was proclaimed.

In response to the Allied ultimatum, a delegation led by Government Minister Matthias Erzberger was formed to negotiate the terms of the armistice. The armistice was signed in Rhétondes, on 11 November 1918, at 5:20 A.M. in Marshall Foch's railway car. As a direct result of the signing, Austria's Emperor Karl abdicated on the same day, and the following day the Reichstag proclaimed German Austria a republic. There was hope, nourished by the Social Democrats, Otto Bauer and others, of uniting Austria with "its German big brother"—Germany— on the basis of the Herderesque "community of destiny" (*Schicksalgeneinschaft*). But the slaughter that had cost ten million their lives and scarred and multilated twenty million others had ceased; everyone could have faith in tomorrow.

All these events were important, though not decisive, in the historic resolutions of 9 and 10 November, in which the Romanians in Transylvania resolved to take over the actual administration of the territories they inhabited. On the tenth an ultimatum was presented to the Hungarian National Council, telling the Hungarian government to publish a manifesto proclaiming the sole authority of the Central Romanian National Council over all institutions and governing bodies in the regions with Romanian majorities. In turn, the council guaranteed public order and security for lives and property. If the ultimatum were rejected, the council would announce to the Romanian people, the country, and the whole world that the Romanian people had been prevented from exercising its right to determine its own destiny, and the Hungarian government would bear responsibility for the consequences. A joint commission was to set terms for the transfer of power. Negotiations took place in Arad between the Romanian and Hungarian delegations on 13 and 14 November, but they were doomed from the start. On the fifteenth, the Romanian National Council met to consider the situation, and called for a great representative assembly to proclaim the union of Transylvania with Romania. The assembly was to include representatives of all electoral districts; of the churches, led by bishops of both faiths; of cultural and economic organizations; of the press, which would inform the world of the great event; and of peasants and workers.

The Call to the Alba Iulia Assembly

Once the priniciples of the representative assembly were decided on and the path to be followed was set, specific measures had to be taken quickly. The very day after the failure of the Arad talks, the Central Romanian National Council, as the embodiment of the "sovereign will of the Romanian nation" in Transylvania, announced to district, local, and municipal councils the "regulations for the selection of delegates to the national assembly." These stipulated that within twelve days delegate elections should be held in all districts inhabited by Romanians for "the Great Romanian National Assembly" which was to be convened in a short time. The elections were to proceed according to the "principles of universal suffrage." The assembly was "to embody, in as suitable and appropriate a way as possible, all our democratic strata" and to be the essence of all those groups— intellectuals, peasants, workers, businessmen, and industrialists—who would designate their representatives "in an atmosphere of fraternal understanding."

The pace of events quickened. New national councils and national guards were constituted in various parts of Transylvania; new demonstrations took place under the same unfailing banner, the union of Transylvania with Romania. The Council for National Unity in Paris and the Romanian diocese in the United States sent a memorandum to President Wilson, outlining the harsh life of the Romanian people in Transylvania and presenting the necessity for the union of Transylvania with Romania, which would "create in Eastern Europe a democratic country, in which brotherhood, equality, and political, economic, and religious freedom would rule over all its citizens without regard to nationality." On 18 November the Great Council of the Romanian Nation in Hungary and Transylvania (as the Romanian National Council was still known) published a manifesto addressed to "the peoples of the world" and printed in Romanian, French, and English. After exposing the oppressive practices of the "ruling class of the Hugarian people" and the Hungarian government's refusal to recognize the Romanian people's right to self-determination, the manifesto bound the Romanian nation—"the embodiment of the most advanced democracy"—not to oppress other peoples, to guarantee full national liberty for all, and to organize its own free and independent state on democratic foundations, guaranteeing equality to everyone. On this basis, the Romanian nation announced to the peoples of the world its resolve to create "its own free and independent state on the territory it inhabits."

Material preparations were now complete. The call to the Great National Assembly in Alba Iulia was published on 20 November. This "historic assembly," as one of its organizers rightly characterized it, was truly representative of the nation. Not only were there delegates from all institutions and social classes, but the selection of Alba Iulia was extremely appropriate. Alba Iulia was one of the most important cities of Roman Dacia; it was the center of the first union of the Romanian lands under Michael the Brave; it was the place where Horea, Cloşca, and Crişan, the leaders of the great peasant revolt of 1784, were martyred, and where Avram Iancu, the hero of the revolution of 1848, was imprisoned. It was a city of the greatest and deepest significance in the history of the Romanian people in Transylvania.

The ten days between the issuing of the call and the Great National Assembly itself were the most joyful and emotional in the history of the Romanians in Transylvania. Demonstrations and statements of support for unification were seen everywhere there were Romanians. The significance of these demonstrations is shown by the statements of the many municipalities and villages, bearing hundreds of thousands of signatures of men and women, young and old. It is shown, too, by the text of the oath of the "community of the Romanian people," which stated that the Romanian people "on its own initiative, neither forced nor induced by anyone, here gives expression to the burning desire which inspires the heart of every Romanian, and declares that its unshakable desire is to be joined together with the Romanian territories in Hungary, Transylvania, and Maramureş in the Kingdom of Romania."

The Romanian socialists again stated their positions. Ioan Flueraş, the representative of the Romanian Central Committee of the SDP, gave the Great National Council in Arad a clear presentation of the position of the working class, seeking guarantees in the new Romanian state. Just as clearly, the representatives of the RNP in the Great Council acknowledged the legitimate rights of the socialists: they had an important mission and were to constitute a powerful, flourishing force in the new state, since the new governing bodies would represent all classes and respect the rights of all nationalities. Satisfied with this response, the socialists stated that, despite efforts of certain foes to sow ill will between the Great Romanian National Council and the Romanian SDP, "there was perfect agreement." This, according to the socialists, was the logical consequence of the "socioeconomic structure of the Romanian people"; they expressed their faith that the working class would find "maximal guarantees" of realizing its ideals in the framework of broad democracy.

The Cernăuți Assembly
and the Union of Bukovina with Romania

As the Transylvanian Romanians were preparing to leave for Alba Iulia, the Romanians in Bukovina were meeting in Cernăuți. The National Council of Bukovina, following the resolution of the constituent assembly of 27 October, convened a Congress of Bukovinian People for 28 November. At the time it was announced that discussions had been held with representatives of the Poles, Germans, and Jews of Bukovina on their attitude toward the resolution to unify Bukovina with Romania. They had unconditionally approved the union with a guarantee of freedom of education. Preparations for the congress were complete by 27 November, and it opened on the morning of the twenty-eighth. "It was a clear late autumn day," as I. Nistor recalled decades later, "when those attending the congress headed in animated groups toward the metropolitan palace in Cernăuți." There were 105 official delegates, as well as "several thousand representatives of every nation and every social class from all parts of Bukovina."

The president of the National Council, Dionisie Bejan, opened the congress with a moving speech emphasizing its mission to "bring to fulfillment the aspirations that our people have nourished and kept alive . . . for a century and a half." Iancu Flondor was elected chairman and presented the motion declaring Bukovina to be an integral part of Moldavia. The motion stated that the Romanians of Bukovina, together with their brothers in the rest of Moldavia, "have defended the existence of the race throughout the ages"; that Bukovina had been arbitrarily torn from the body of Moldavia; that the Romanians of Bukovina had endured much oppression by "foreign masters"; and that they had not lost hope of liberation. Now that the hour of liberation had come, and all the nations of the Austro-Hungarian Empire had won "their right to decide freely for themselves," Bukovina's first thoughts went toward Romania. Therefore "the General Congress of Bukovina, embodying the supreme power of the land and invested with legislative power, in the name of national sovereignty," resolved "the unconditional union in perpetuity of Bukovina—in its old boundaries at the Ceremus, the Colacin, and the Dniester—with the kingdom of Romania. Stanislav Kwiatowski, the Polish representative, and Alois Lebouton, representing the Germans, acknowledged the right of the Romanians in Bukovina to unite with Romania, and thus supported the resolution. In this way the congress, with the unanimous vote of thousands of participants, representing millions of inhabitants, resolved to reunite Bukovina with Romania, thereby righting yet another historic injustice.

The Union of Transylvania with Romania

As the assembly in Bukovina completed its work, great throngs from all over Transylvania were approaching Alba Iulia to fulfill the voters' certain mandate. The 1,228 official or elected delegates arrived: at the train station, an honor guard waited in proud colors. They presented the honor salute, the triumphant voice of the trumpet blending with the powerful harmonies of the national anthem sung by eager young people.

On Sunday morning, 1 December, the town wore a festive appearance. In the main square, decked out with tricolor flags, a seemingly unending procession of people dressed in holiday clothes and cockades began about seven o'clock. In columns four abreast and in groups of one or two hundred, singing national songs, they filed in front of the building where the members of the Great National Council were lodged. At eight o'clock, solemn Te Deums were celebrated in the two Romanian churches, after which the delegates proceeded to the Casino Hall, which would henceforth be known as Unification Hall. At ten o'clock, to cheering and stormy applause, the prelates and members of the Romanian National Council mounted an improvised platform. First to speak was Ștefan Cicio Pop, the president of the Central Romanian National Council, who in stirring words emphasized the importance of that historic moment. Gheorghe Pop from Băsești, the eighty-year-old president of the RNP, was elected chairman of the assembly. The most triumphant moment, however, was reserved for Vasile Goldiș. In closing his speech, Goldiș offered a resolution of unification: "The National Assembly decrees the union with Romania of the Romanians in Transylvania, the Banat, and Hungarian lands, and of the territories they inhabit." The hall replied with thunderous applause.

Under the terms of the resolution, the territories united with Romania would preserve their autonomy until a constituent assembly elected by universal suffrage could meet. Full national liberty and equal rights were granted to all coinhabiting nationalities, including the right to education, administration, and justice in their own language; to belong to legislative bodies and to participate in the government of the country in proportion to their numbers; to full religious liberty for all faiths; to a strictly democratic regime in all spheres of public life; to direct, equal, and secret suffrage for all persons of both sexes over twenty-one years of age; to freedom of the press, association, and assembly; to free dissemination of ideas; to radical agrarian reform that would give peasants the possibility of creating properties that could be worked by a family; and to the same rights and privileges for the industrial working class as those established by law in the most advanced industrial countries of the west.

The National Assembly expressed the hope that the peace conference would create a community of free nations along the same lines, so that liberty and justice might be guaranteed impartially to all nations large and small, and war might be eliminated as a means of regulating international relations. The assembly welcomed the liberation of those nations of the Austro-Hungarian Empire that had been freed so far—Czechoslovakia, Yugoslavia, Austria, Poland, and Ruthenia—and consecrated the memory of those Romanians who had shed their blood for the sake of achieving the national ideal. The National Assembly also thanked the Allied Powers that had fought to save civilization. In speeches that followed, by Iuliu Maniu and, in the name of the working class, Iosif Iumanca, other arguments and ideas were presented to round out the view that the unification process was in accordance with historical law. Finally, in order to conduct public affairs constitutionally, the assembly elected a Grand National Council, a provisional representative legislative assembly composed of 212 members.

Although the union of the Romanian provinces with Romania had been decided, the representative assemblies and the temporary governments continued to perform legislative and executive functions until political and administrative unification was complete. In Bessarabia the legislature was called the Council of the Country; it was presided over at first by Ion Inculeţ and later by Constantin Stere and Pan Halippa. Executive powers were exercised by the eight-member Council of Directors, headed initially by Daniel Ciugureanu and then by Petre Cazacu. In Bukovina legislative powers were exercised by the National Council, led by Dionisie Bejan, and executive powers by a fourteen-member administration led by Iancu Flondor. In Transylvania, a Great Council with legislative powers was instituted, with Gheorghe Pop de Băseşti as president; this group elected an executive body known as the Administrative Council, which had fifteen members and was led by Iuliu Maniu.

One at a time, King Ferdinand issued royal decrees proclaiming unification with the three Romanian provinces: Bessarabia on 27 November, Bukovina on 18 December, and Transylvania on 24 December. Under the terms of provisional organization decrees, public services remained under the authority of provincial governments, while matters of foreign relations, army, railways, post office, telegraph, telephones, financial matters, customs, public debt, and general state security were to be handed over to the Romanian government. The newly united provinces were represented in the central government by ministers without portfolio.

Unified Romania

The second half of December 1918 and the first half of 1919 was a period of clarification and refinement of the Romanian union, both at home and abroad. Taking a realistic view of the situation, the national minorities—the Germans in Bessarabia, the

Poles and the Germans in Bukovina, and the Saxons, Swabians, Slovaks, Szeklers, and some of the Hungarians and Ruthenians in Transylvania—saw that they would have to come to terms with the new social and political situation. In Bukovina, at the congress of 28 November, Stanislav Kwiatowski and Alois Lebouton spoke for Poles and Germans and recognized "fully the unimpeachable rights of the Romanian people to their lands south of the Dniester in general and Bukovina in particular." The first concrete act of support for the resolution of the Great National Assembly of Alba Iulia was that by the Saxons of Bucharest. Meeting in Transylvania Hall on 8 December, the Saxons greeted the union of Transylvania and Romania "with great joy and satisfaction." They recognized the resolution of 1 December, considering it favorable to the cultural and national development of all minorities in Romania, including the Saxon minority. They therefore urged their ethnic group to follow their example.

And, indeed, the Germans of both Bessarabia and Transylvania did follow. In a convention on 7 March 1919, those of Bessarabia unanimously voted to recognize the act of 9 April 1918; in Transylvania, after consultations on New Year's Day of 1919 between representatives of the Administrative Council and the Saxon National Council of Transylvania, a convention of Saxons met in Mediaş on 8 January. Those assembled voted unanimously to recognize the union. A manifesto was published announcing to the Saxon population the decision of "annexation to the kingdom of Romania" and conveying "to the Romanian people fraternal greetings and cordial best wishes on the occasion of the fulfillment of their national ideals."

Following the Saxons' example, the Swabians of the Banat, through General Philippe Berthelot, sent a declaration to the peace conference in Paris, accompanied by a memorandum requesting the annexation of the Banat to Romania, since the Swabians wanted to be together with the Romanian nation, which was related to the French nation.

The most realistic of the Szeklers recognized the realities; József Tóthfalusi, the reformed priest of Tîrgu Mureş, asked his bishop to contact the Administrative Council in Sibiu.

In the midst of these readjustments, the Romanian socialists, in order to quiet doubts about their position, again issued statements at the SDP convention held on 19 and 20 January 1919 in Sibiu. They declared themselves "in complete agreement with the stand of the Social Democratic delegates who, in accordance with the wishes of the entire Romanian people, voted at the National Assembly in Alba Iulia for the union of all Romanians." The Social Democrats defended their view on the basis of the fundamental historical principle and natural law, saying that "the union of the Romanian people in a single independent state is a historical necessity, based on the right of free action of all peoples."

In March the Jewish community also took a position. In Bucharest on 31 March, a meeting of Transylvanian Jews living in the capital passed a resolution stating that "in recognition of the act of Alba Iulia of December 1918, we support, with great satisfaction and from our hearts, the programs outlined in that act." They explained their position by noting that the provisions for national liberty in the Alba Iulia resolution assured them of equal rights in political, cultural, and religious life.

Early in May, the new Hungarian government acknowledged the fundamental Romanian claim to Transylvania and the Banat, but sought in return that the Romanian government avoid involvement in Hungary's affairs. On 8 June, a general conference of the entire German population of Romania met in Sibiu. It was there decided to form a single German political organization, which declared that the Germans wished to be faithful citizens of the new Romanian state; in the summer of 1919, the Slovaks likewise recognized the union. The Swabians of the Banat hastened to declare their support for the union at a national assembly in Timişoara on 10 August. This assembly wanted to show the world that "it is a question first of all of the categorical desire of the unanimous assembly that the Swabian people be united with the Romanian people, whose civilization is superior, whom the Swabians love and respect, and to whom the Swabians feel bound by the origin of many of their sons of common Latin origin." Second, the assembly declared, a century of living together with Romanians had taught the Swabians to appreciate their "true worth," and "the experience of recent years" had strengthened the Swabians' conviction that "only through union with Romania could they be offered sufficient guarantees of their existence and their progress."

Thus, by late by 1919, more than 80 percent of the Transylvanian population had agreed to the unconditional union of Transylvania with Romania. The resolutions of union and support, freely made in popular assemblies, invested the act of union with a plebiscitary character. Faced with this undeniable reality, the rest of the Hungarian population gradually modified its stance concerning the Alba Iulia resolutions, especially as the principles of equal rights for national minorities approved in Alba Iulia were put into effect. In the elections for the constituent assembly in November 1919, based on universal, direct, and secret vote, deputies were elected by the national minorities, including the Hungarians. The Hungarian representatives circulated a manifesto addressed to the Hungarian population of Transylvania in November 1919, urging support for the union with Romania. The Hungarian National Democratic Party of Transylvania, founded in 1919, began active campaigns to convince the Hungarian population to participate actively in the political life of Romania. With the way thus cleared, the representatives of the Hungarian National Party at the assembly declared their full support for the Alba Iulia resolutions and their commitment to convince all the Hungarian population to participate actively in the political life of Romania. The Ruthenian deputies from Maramureş joined in this support.

No one may doubt, then, that the union with Romania of the Romanian territories in the Austro-Hungarian and czarist empires was achieved on the basis of contemporary legal principles. Delegates were chosen in accordance with the electoral laws in force, via universal suffrage, by electoral districts with recognized political organizations, and with societies and associations set up and recognized by them. The delegates were provided with credentials, written empowerments giving them the right to vote in the deliberations. Moreover, they had a precise mandate from the voters to decide in favor of union. The unification, therefore, was unquestionably legal. Finally, in the case of Bukovina and Transylvania, the unification act was rendered even more valid by the presence of the multitudes at the Cernăuţi and Alba Iulia assemblies.

14

Great Romania

The Paris Peace Conference

THE SO-CALLED WORLD PARLIAMENT that met in Paris for the peace conference of January 1919 struggled to find equitable solutions for a war-torn world, new, fairer arrangements to protect it from a new catastrophe. When Raymond Poincaré, the president of France, opened the conference on 18 January, it faced staggering tasks: to draw new national frontiers; to guarantee food to the populace; to restore economic life in most of Europe; to bind the wounds of war; to assess reparations; to stabilize the European political and military balance; to prevent violations of international law; and to create the League of Nations, whose mission was to provide guarantees of political independence and territorial integrity to all states, large and small.

Matters proceeded slowly and with difficulty, because of the different and often conflicting ideas and interests of the five great powers, France, Britain, the United States, Italy, and Japan. The statements of a conference historian, that "it is easier to destroy than to construct" and that "we need wise men and prolonged efforts to establish peace in place of war," proved very true. It was more than five months before representatives of the Allied Powers and of vanquished Germany finally signed the Treaty of Versailles, on 28 June 1919, in the Hall of Mirrors of the Sun King. On the basis of the general framework of the treaty, other special treaties were concluded: with Austria at Saint-Germain on 10 September and 18 December; with Bulgaria at Neuilly on 27 September; with Hungary at Trianon on 4 June 1920; and with Turkey at Sèvres on 10 August 1920.

The Romanian delegation to the Paris conference consisted of I. I. C. Brătianu, the president of the Council of Ministers, Nicolae Mișu, the Romanian envoy in London, Victor Antonescu,

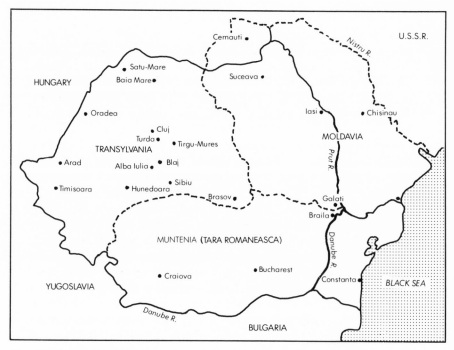

Twentieth-century Romania.

Romanian envoy in Paris, General Constantin Coandă, Alexandru Vaida-Voievod, Nicolae Titulescu, and Ioan Cantacuzino. The Romanians called for recognition of the unification of 1918 on the basis on the treaty of August 1916 between Romania and the Triple Entente (Allies), which provided for equal Romanian participation in the peace talks. This point of view was supported before the conference by the American secretary of state, Robert Lansing, the French foreign minister, Étienne Pichon, and the British foreign minister, Arthur Balfour, on the basis of the resolutions of Chişinău, Cernăuți, and Alba Iulia.

Nevertheless, there were difficulties. First of all, interested smaller states had not been apprised of the text of the treaty with Germany, and they had been given a totally inadequate proportion of the war damages to be paid by the Germans. Romania, for example, which had suffered material losses of 31 million gold lei in addition to an enormous human toll, was to receive 1 percent. A second difficulty arose during the discussions of the conditions of the Treaty of Saint-Germain. While the treaty recognized the union of Bukovina with Romania, it also contained certain clauses which would mean outside interference in Romania's internal affairs. Among these were measures set by the Great Powers to protect the national minorities and international commercial traffic across Romanian territory, as well as the payment by Romania of a portion of Austria-Hungary's war reparations. The Romanian delegation protested and refused to accept such terms, promising to grant the national minorities equal rights with the Romanian people and to take steps to facilitate transit traffic. According to the American historian Sherwin D. Spector, Brătianu succeeded in demonstrating that Romania could remain the perpetual object of machinations by the Great Powers, who would try to use it as a pawn.

Dissatisfied with the Allies' attitude, Brătianu left Paris on 2 July and resigned. He was succeeded by a cabinet led by General Artur Văitoianu. Discussions on the terms of the treaty with Austria continued, with Romania following the same policy of defending its national dignity and sovereignty and refusing to sign a humiliating treaty. A resolution passed by the new parliament elected in November 1919 affirmed the delegation's position. On the strength of this resolution, the new government led by Vaida-Voievod continued to insist on obtaining modifications to the treaty that would recognize the union of Bukovina with Romania, and be more in accordance with the right of peoples to exercise self-determination and form independent sovereign states. Further, "in accordance with justice and equity," the government sought the renunciation by Austria of any right or title to territories inhabited by different nationalities which now formed a part of the national states of Yugoslavia, Czechoslovakia, and Romania. Subsequently, by the Treaty of Sèvres, the boundaries between Bukovina and Galicia were set in accord with the treaty of Saint-Germain and in keeping with the ethnic situation; the union with Romania of the territories inhabited by a majority of Romanians also was recognized.

The Treaty of Trianon, between Hungary and the Allied and associated powers, regulated the most important matters of economy, legal, military, and territorial relations between the "successor" states. It also necessitated prolonged and laborious activity by a commission of experts. Vast territories inhabited by numerous non-Magyar peoples and forcibly incorporated into Hungary over the course of time had united with their natural homelands or had constituted themselves independent national states. The boundaries set by the Treaty of Trianon were researched *in situ* by a border commission composed of representatives of France, Great Britain, Italy, the United States, Romania, and Hungary. For twelve months the commission studied documentation that was as complete as it was varied; this was the basis for the "equitable and practical" drawing of the frontiers. In the end the commission made no proposals for modification, considering the boundaries set in the treaty to be well-founded.

The letter of transmission, signed by Alexandre Millérand, president of France and president of the Supreme Council, accompanying the copy of the treaty sent to the Hungarian delegation to the peace conference, emphasized that the authors had made a profoundly serious effort to understand the Central European situation, to weigh impartially the demands of the nationalities and Hungary's rights. The "will of the peoples," as expressed in October and December of 1918, when the dual monarchy collapsed and the long-oppressed peoples joined their kinsmen, was taken into account; these events constituted for the peace conference "so much more evidence concerning the feelings of the formerly subjugated nationalities." It was noted that the decisions incorporated into the treaty were made "after examining documents of all kinds that might be cited in support of the Hungarian position." In any case, according to Ch. Saymour, one of the experts best acquainted with the facts, the judgments by the authors of the Treaty of Trianon leaned in favor of Hungary, not Romania. "With few exceptions, the frontiers that were adopted are in conformity with the ethnic distribution of the population. Where the ethnic criterion was doubtful, it appears that the balance swung slightly in favor of the old dominant nationalities, the Germans and the Hungarians."

Article 45 of the treaty recognized the international legal validity of the union of Transylvania with Romania, stipulating, "Hungary renounced in favor of Romania all her rights and titles to the territories of the old Austro-Hungarian monarchy situated beyond the frontiers of Hungary as fixed in Art. 27, Para. 2, and as recognized by this treaty and by other treaties that have been concluded for the purpose of settling current problems having to do with the question of Romania." Article 45 in fact constituted the recognition and confirmation of the historic deed that was accomplished 1 December 1918 by the Great Assembly of Alba Iulia. The treaty meant international recognition of the justice of the Romanian people's national independence and unity. As one of its signers, the well-known Romanian politician and diplomat Nicolae Titulescu, put the matter, the treaty represented the consecration of an order of justice. Joseph Rudinsky evaluated it as "a work called for by historical justice as an obvious prerequisite for the proper functioning of the mechanism of peace."

Conference recognition of the union of Bessarabia with Romania took place on 28 October 1920, following discussions between representatives of Romania and Soviet Russia and an exchange of telegrams and letters between Alexandru Vaida-Voievod and the Soviet Commissar for Foreign Affairs Chicherin.

The nature of the peace treaties of 1919 and 1920 is sometimes disputed. It has been maintained that since they were the consequence of an imperialist war, the treaties themselves must be imperialist as well. But even the war, for all that it was in general an imperialistic venture, was in certain cases a war of national defense and national unification. Serbia, for example, was invaded by Austro-Hungarian armies and threatened with dismemberment; similarly, Romania sought neither to invade nor to conquer foreign territories, but only to liberate Romanian territories from foreign domination and to unite them in a single state within the ethnic boundaries of the Romanian people. The peace was necessarily two-sided. While the victorious Great Powers used the peace conference to expand their territories at

The Central Committee of the Romanian National Party in Transylvania, 1892.

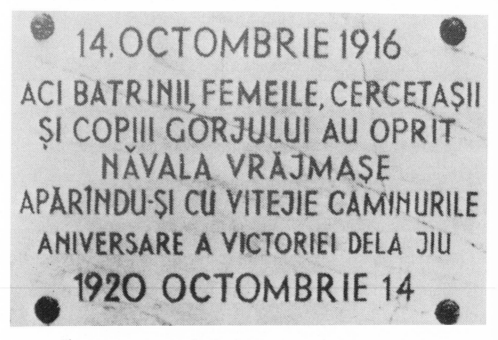

14. OCTOMBRIE 1916

ACI BATRINII, FEMEILE, CERCETAȘII
ȘI COPIII GORJULUI AU OPRIT
NĂVALA VRĂJMAȘE
APĂRÎNDU-ȘI CU VITEJIE CĂMINURILE
ANIVERSARE A VICTORIEI DELA JIU
1920 OCTOMBRIE 14

Plaque commemorating battles fought by the Romanian army in World War I.

the expense of the vanquished, some treaties did deal with the righting of historic wrongs, acknowledged the liberation of territories and populations from foreign domination, and recognized national states that had been unified or constituted by the will of their own people. To attack them would be to attack the very principle of self-determination of peoples and to deny the right of peoples and nations to decide their own destiny.

Epilogue

The establishment and recognition of the unified Romanian national state had consequences of incontestable significance for the country's internal development and external relationships. Unification meant, first of all, a noticeable increase in the country's production capabilities and its economic potential, since increased agricultural and mineral wealth opened the way for better organization of its factories and workshops. The removal of political and administrative barriers between the Romanian provinces gave a powerful boost to the economy; national markets developed, and trade between all parts of the country intensified.

The destruction wrought by the war was perhaps the heaviest in the history of the country. More than a million people died, and material damages amounted to over seventy-two thousand million lei. The economic losses, however, were recouped within the surprisingly short period of three years. A series of urgent measures were taken in order to eliminate the deficit in the balance of payments and balance the national budget, to bring inflation under control, to reconstruct the transportation system and other means of communication, and to develop foreign trade. The oil industry, severely damaged in the war, was reactivated and produced over 800 tons of oil in 1924. Coal production underwent a similar growth, from 2.3 million tons to 2.776 tons, and gold production increased from 706 kilograms to 1,311 kilograms. Output in the metallurgical, wood, chemical, and textile industries grew by 185 percent, 205 percent, 189 percent, and 241 percent respectively. Meanwhile, the number of factories was augmented 42 percent, the capital invested in industry 37 percent, and the number of workers 38 percent. Transylvania alone contributed about 48 percent of the country's total output in mining and metallurgy.

To satisfy the peasantry, which had borne such a heavy burden of sacrifice, agrarian reform gradually was effected. It was the most thoroughgoing reform in eastern and central Europe. Private estates and state lands—about 6 million hectares—were distributed among the peasants without regard to nationality, among the families of war dead and wounded, and among poor families who had fewer than five hectares. By improving the economic situation of a significant part of the peasantry, land reform also accelerated economic development. In 1924 the agricultural output had reached prewar levels, and livestock had actually increased, from 4.5 to 5.3 million cattle, from 1.48 to 1.84 million horses, from 2.5 to 3.1 million hogs, and from 8.7 to 13.6 million sheep.

As a result of the important strides made in all branches of the economy after the formation of Greater Romania, the budget was rebalanced in 1922 to 1923. Foreign trade, aided most significantly by increased exports of oil, grain, and wood, shot from 1,714 million lei in 1922 to 5,078 million lei in 1923.

The unification of the Romanian national state also created better conditions for the development of its political life. Although dominated by the wealthy, bourgeois, and landowning classes, the 1923 constitution and electoral laws, for all their limitations, made true progress toward a more democratic society. Male citizens were granted full political rights at the age of twenty-five, including both such fundamental rights as freedom of the individual, of movement, of work, worship, and property, and such secondary rights as freedom of the press, of education, and of association.

Romanian culture flourished in all provinces: the nation's (and, indeed, the world's) heritage was enriched by new and significant works. Romanian culture and scholarship made important advances, narrowing or in some fields even closing the gap between Romania and more developed countries. Primary education was made compulsory, while the flourishing economy created a rich network of vocational schools. Several new institutions of higher education were founded on modern principles. The scholar Emmanuel de Martonne, who was thoroughly familiar with Romania and the Romanian people, proclaimed his admiration for the cultural and educational achievements in the first decade following unification. "You have developed research with a brilliance that does honor to Romanian science," he wrote. New academic departments and new laboratories had

The Central Romanian National Council, November 1918.

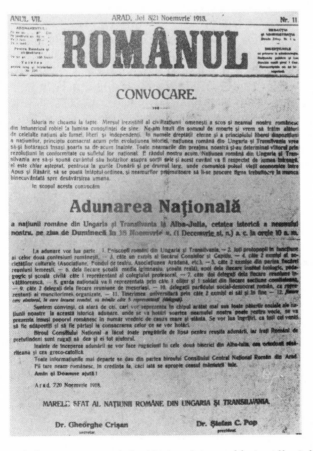

Notice of the convening of the National Assembly in Alba Iulia.

been created, and the renown of Romanian scholars too numerous to mention spread beyond the borders of the country.

Although internal factors played the decisive role in the achievement of unification of the national state, the process could nevertheless not have been fully completed without international support, especially on the part of the European peoples and the Americans, all of whom favored the final goal. The Romanian people's struggle for unification, in its final stage from 1859–1918, was vigorously supported by Romanian emigrants, and by expressions of progressive public opinion in several European countries and on other continents. Romania's unification movement worked closely with the general European movement of subjugated peoples, both giving and receiving strength as it did so.

Now, after centuries of exploitation and oppression, Romanian citizens of all nationalities strive year by year, day by day, to increase the cultural and material potential of their country. With equal rights assured for all, the inhabitants of Romania are linked by bonds of work and aspiration and have multiplied their efforts to consolidate their achievement and to assure that the Romanian nation will flourish—and that it will flourish in close cooperation with all the nations of the world, on the basis of general human principles of freedom and justice, independence and sovereignty. These are the essence of all the remarkable transformations in the life of the Romanian people, which today, free and independent, is forging its own history and a glorious future.

Bibliography

Introduction

Conea, I. "Transilvania, inimă a pămîntului românesc" [Transylvania, heart of the Romanian land]. In *Geopolitica și Geoistoria*, vol. 1. 1941.

Lupaș, I. *La Transylvanie, coeur de la vie roumaine.* Bucharest, 1942.

Mehedinți, S. *Ce este Transilvania?* [What is Transylvania?]. In *Opere complete*, vol. 2, p. 2. Bucharest, 1940.

———. *Der Zusammenhang der rumänischen Landschaft mit dem rumänischen Volke.* Jena and Leipzig, 1936.

Morariu, T. "Locul Transilvaniei în cadrul unitar al teritoriului României" [The place of Transylvania within the unitary territory of Romania]. In *Unitate și continuitate în istoria poporului român*, edited by D. Berciu. Bucharest, 1968.

Pascu, Șt. "Geographische und ethno-demographische Basis Siebenbürgens und der Bukowina." In *Habsburgische Monarchie, 1848–1918*, vol. 3. Vienna, 1977.

Tufescu, V. *România. Natură. Om. Economie* [Romania: nature, men, economy]. Bucharest, 1974.

Vâlsan, G. "Transilvania în cadrul unitar al pămîntului și statului român" [Transylvania within the unitary frame of the Romanian land and state]. In *Transilvania, Banatul, Crișana, și Maramureșul*, vol. 1. Bucharest, 1929.

Chapter 1

Alexandrescu, A. D. "Die Bronzeschwerter aus Rumänien." *Dacia* 10 (1966).

Bader, T. *Epoca bronzului în Nord-Vestul Transilvaniei. Cultura pretracică și tracică* [The bronze age in northwest Transylvania: pre-Thracian and Thracian culture]. Bucharest, 1978.

Berciu, D. *Arta traco-getică* [Thraco-Getic art]. Bucharest, 1969.

———. *Contribuții la problema neoliticului în România în lumina noilor cercetări* [Contributions to the questions of the neolithic period in Romania in the light of new research]. Bucharest, 1961.

———. *Zorile istoriei în Carpați și la Dunăre* [The dawn of history in the Carpatho-Danubian territory]. Bucharest, 1966.

Bichir, Gh. *Cultura carpică* [Carpathian culture]. Bucharest, 1973.

Bodor, A. "Contribuții la problema agriculturii în Dacia înainte de cucerirea romană. Problema obștilor la daci" [Contributions to the question of agriculture in Dacia before the Roman conquest: the problem of the peasant Dacian communities]. *Studii și cercetări de istorie veche* 7, nos. 3–4 (1955); 8, nos. 1–4 (1957).

Crişan, I. H. *Burebista şi epoca sa* [Burebista and his time]. 2d ed. Bucharest, 1977.

———. *Statul geto-dac* [The Geto-Dacian state]. Bucharest, 1977.

Daicoviciu, C. *La Transylvanie dans l'antiquité*. Bucharest, 1945.

——— –. *Dacii* [The Dacians]. Bucharest, 1972.

Dumitrescu, Vl. *Arta neolitică in România* [Neolithic art in Romania]. Bucharest, 1968.

———. *L'arte preistorica in Romania fino all'inizio dell'eta del fero*. Florence, 1972.

Florescu, R. *L'art des Daces*. Bucharest, 1968.

Glodariu, I., and Iaroslavschi, E. *Civilizaţia fierului la daci* [The Dacian iron civilization]. Cluj-Napoca, 1979.

Kendrick, M. S. *Pietrele dacilor vorbesc* [The Dacian stones speak]. Bucharest, 1978.

Macrea, M., et alia. *Cetăţi dacice din sudul Transilvaniei* [Dacian strongholds in the south of Transylvania]. Bucharest, 1966.

Nicolaescu, P. C. *Oamenii din vîrsta veche a pietrei (epoca paleolitică în România)* [The men of the middle stone age (the paleolithic age in Romania)]. Bucharest, 1965.

Pârvan, V. *Getica. O preistorie a Daciei* [Getica: a prehistory of Dacia]. Bucharest, 1926.

———. *Dacia. Civilizaţiile antice din ţările carpato-danubiene* [Dacia: the ancient civilizations in the Carpatho-Danubian lands]. 4th ed. Bucharest, 1967.

Păunescu, Al. *Evoluţia uneltelor şi armelor de piatră cioplită descoperite pe teritoriul României* [The evolution of cut stone weapons and tools discovered on Romanian territory]. Bucharest, 1970.

Petrescu-Dîmboviţa, M. *Depozitele de bronzuri din România* [Bronze hoards in Romania]. Bucharest, 1977.

———. *Scurtă istorie a Daciei preromane* [A short history of pre-Roman Dacia]. Iaşi, 1978.

Protase, D. *Riturile funerare la daci şi daco-romani* [The funeral practices of the Dacians and Daco-Romans]. Bucharest, 1971.

Russu, I. I. *Die Sprache der Thrako-Daker*. Bucharest, 1969.

Vlassa, N. *Neoliticul Transilvaniei* [The Transylvanian neolithic]. Cluj-Napoca, 1976.

Vulpe, R. *Studia Thracologica* [Thracian studies]. Bucharest, 1976.

Chapter 2

Biró, J. *Kollegiümok a roman Daciában* [Colleges in Roman Dacia]. Szeged, 1963.

Christescu, V. *Istoria militară a Daciei romane* [The military history of Roman Dacia]. Bucharest, 1937.

———. *Viaţa economică a Daciei romane* [The economic life of Roman Dacia]. Piteşti, 1929.

Macrea, M. *Viaţa in Dacia romană* [Life in Roman Dacia]. Bucharest, 1969.

Paribeni, R. *Optimus Princeps*. Messina, 1926.

Protase, D. *Autohtonii în Dacia romană* [The autochtonous population in Roman Dacia]. Bucharest, 1980.

Stein, A. *Die Reichsbeamten von Dazien*. Budapest, 1944.

Tudor, D. *Istoria sclavajului în Dacia Romană* [The history of slavery in Roman Dacia]. Bucharest, 1957.

———. *Oltenia romană* [Roman Oltenia]. 3d ed. Bucharest, 1968.
———. *Oraşe, tîrguri, şi sate în Dacia Romană* [Towns, boroughs, and villages in Roman Dacia]. Bucharest, 1968.

Chapter 3

Bârzu, L. *Continuitatea populaţiei autohtone în Transilvania în secolele IV-V* [The continuity of the autochthonous population in Transylvania in the fourth and fifth centuries]. Bucharest, 1973.
Comşa, M. "Sur le caractère de l'organisation social-économique et politique sur le territoire de la Roumanie durant la période du passage à la féodalité." *Nouvelles études d'histoire* 4 (1970).
———. *Cultura materială veche românească. Aşezările din secolele VIII-X de la Bucov-Ploieşti.* [Ancient Romanian material culture: settlements from the eighth to the tenth centuries in Bucov-Ploieşti]. Bucharest, 1978
Constantinescu, M., and Pascu, Şt., eds. *The Autochthonous People and the Migratory Populations.* Bucharest, 1975.
Horedt, K. *Contribuţii la istoria Transilvaniei în secolele IV-XIII* [Contributions to the history of Transylvania in the fourth to the thirteenth centuries]. Bucharest, 1958.
———. *Untersuchungen zur Frühgeschichte Siebenbürgens.* Bucharest, 1958.
Nestor, I. "L'établissement des Slaves en Roumanie." *Dacia* 5 (1961):429–48.
Protase, D. *Problema continuităţii în Dacia în lumina arheologiei şi numismaticii* [The question of continuity in Dacia in the light of archeology and numismatics]. Bucharest, 1966.
Russu, I. I. *Etnogeneza românilor* [The Romanians' birth as a people]. Bucharest, 1981.
Zaharia, E. *Contribuţii la problema culturii daco-romane în sec. VI-VII* [Contributions to the question of Daco-Roman culture in the sixth and seventh centuries]. Bucharest, 1978.

Chapter 4

Columbeanu, S. *Cnezate şi voievodate româneşti* [Romanian knezates and voivodates]. Bucharest, 1973.
Comşa, M. *Cultura materială veche românească. Aşezările din sec. VIII-X de la Bucov-Ploieşti* [Ancient Romanian material culture: settlements from the eighth to the tenth centuries in Bucov-Ploieşti]. Bucharest, 1978.
Condurachi, E., and Ştefan, Gh. "La Romanité orientale." *Nouvelles études d'histoire* 3 (1970).
Daicoviciu, C., and Pascu, Şt. *Din istoria Transilvaniei* [Aspects of the history of Transylvania]. Bucharest, 1963.
Diaconu, P. *Les Coumans au Bas-Danube aux XIᵉ-XIIᵉ siècles.* Bucharest, 1978.
———. *Les Pétchénègues.* Bucharest, 1970.
Giurescu, C. C. *The Formation of the Romanian People.* Bucharest, 1972.
Moga, I. *Voivodatul Transilvaniei. Fapte şi interpretări istorice (sec. XIII-XIV)* [The voivodate of Transylvania: facts and historical interpretations (thirteenth to fourteenth centuries)]. Cluj, 1945.
Nägler, T. *Die Ansiedlungen der Siebenbürger Sachsen.* Bucharest, 1979.
Niedermaier, P. *Siebenbürgische Städte.* Bucharest, 1979.

Panaitescu, P. P. *Introducere în istoria culturii românești* [Introduction to the history of Romanian culture]. Bucharest, 1969.

Pascu, Șt. *Meșteșugurile din Transilvania pînă în sec. XVI* [Trades in Transylvania before the sixteenth century]. Bucharest, 1954.

———. "Die mittelalterlichen Dorfsiedlungen in Siebenbürgen (bis 1400)." *Nouvelles études d'histoire* 2 (1960):135–48.

———; Ionașcu, I.; and Cihodariu, C. *Istoria medie a României* [The medieval history of Romania]. Vol. 1. Bucharest, 1966.

Petrovici, E. *La population de la Transylvanie au XIe siècle*. Bucharest, 1944.

Ștefan, Gh. *Formarea poporului român și a limbii sale* [The formation of the Romanian people and their language]. Bucharest, 1973.

Székely, Z. "Contribuții la problema stabilirii secuilor în sudul Transilvaniei" [Contributions to the question of the settlement of the Szeklers in southeastern Transylvania]. *Crisia* 4 (1974): 89–99.

Tagliavini, R. *Originea limbilor neolatine* [The origin of the neo-Latin languages]. Bucharest, 1976.

Theodorescu, R. *Bizanț, Balcani, Occident la începuturile culturii românești (sec. X-XIV)* [Byzantium, the Balkans and the West at the beginning of Romanian culture]. Bucharest, 1974.

Chapter 5

Anghel, Gh. *Cetăți medievale din Transilvania* [Medieval Transylvanian fortresses]. Bucharest, 1972.

Binder, P. "Contribuții la studiul dezvoltării feudalismului în Maramureș și în nordul Transilvaniei" [Contributions to the study of the development of feudalism in Maramureș and northern Transylvania]. *Studii și articole de istorie* 10 (1967): 27–61.

Columbeanu, S., and Velescu, O. "Registrul de la Oradea—un important document transilvănean din secolul XIII" (The Register of Oradea—an important thirteenth-century Transylvanian document]. *Studii și articole de istorie* 3 (1961):25–56.

Dragomir, S., and Belu, S. "Contribuții la istoria așezărilor românești din Munții Apuseni (sec. XIII-XIV)" [Contributions to the history of the Romanian settlements in the Bihor Mountains (thirteenth to sixteenth centuries)]. *Cumidava* 2 (1968):53–77.

Göllner, C. *Siebenbürgische Städte im Mittelalter*. Bucharest, 1971.

Lazea, E. "Agricultura în Transilvania în sec. XIV" [Agriculture in Transylvania in the fourteenth century]. *Studii* 2 (1904): 249–75.

Pascu, Șt. *Meșteșugurile din Transilvania pînă în sec. XVI* [Trades in Transylvania before the sixteenth century]. Bucharest, 1954.

———. "Die mittelalterlichen Dorfsiedlungen in Siebenbürgen (bis 1400)." *Nouvelles études d'histoire* 2 (1960):135–48.

———. "Premisele unității politice a românilor (sec. XII–XVI)" [Premises of the political unity of the Romanians (twelfth to sixteenth centuries)]. *Apulum* 7 (1969):41–73.

Popa, R. *Țara Maramureșului în sec. XIV* [Țara Maramureșului in the fourteenth century]. Bucharest, 1970.

Trâpcea, T. "Despre unele cătăți medievale din Banat" [On some medieval fortresses in the Banat]. *Studii de istoria Banatului* 1 (1969):23–82.

Vătășianu, V. *Istoria artei feudale în țările române* [The history of feudal art in the Romanian principalities]. Vol. 1. Bucharest, 1959.

Chapter 6

Albu, N. *Istoria învăţămîntului românesc din Transilvania pînă la 1800* [The history of Romanian education in Transylvania before 1800]. Blaj, 1944.

Arion, Gh. *Sculptura gotică din Transilvania* [Gothic sculpture in Transylvania]. Cluj, 1974.

Dan, M. *Un stegar al luptei antiotomane, Iancu de Hunedoara* [A standard-bearer of the anti-Ottoman struggle, Iancu of Hunedoara]. Bucharest, 1974.

Demény, L. *Az 1437–38–as bábolnai népi felkelés* [The popular uprising of Bobîlna in the years 1437–38]. Bucharest, 1860.

Drăguţ, V. *Pictura murală în Transilvania (sec. XIV-XV)* [Mural painting in Transylvania (fourteenth to fifteenth centuries)]. Bucharest, 1970.

Ionescu, Gr. *Istoria arhitecturii în România* [The history of architecture in Romania]. Vol. 1. Bucharest, 1965.

Jakó, S. *Philobiblon transilvan* [Transylvanian philobiblon]. Bucharest, 1971.

Mureşan, C. *Iancu de Hunedoara.* 2d ed. Bucharest, 1968.

Pascu, Şt. *Bobîlna.* 2d ed. Bucharest, 1963.

————. "Les institutions centrales des pays roumains à l'époque féodale." *Bulletin de la Faculté de lettres et philosophie de Strasbourg* 45, no. 5 (1967):389–404.

————. *Răscoalele ţărăneşti în Transilvania* [The peasant uprisings in Transylvania]. Vol. 1. *Epoca voivodatului* [The voivodate period]. Cluj, 1947.

————. *La révolte populaire de Transylvanie des années 1437–1438.* Bucharest, 1964.

————. *Rolul cnezilor din Transilvania în lupta antiotomană a lui Iancu de Hunedoara* [The part played by the Transylvanian knezi in the anti-Ottoman struggle led by Iancu of Hunedoara]. Cluj, 1957.

————, ed. *Istoria învăţămîntului din România* [The history of Romanian education]. Vol. 1. Bucharest, 1979.

Chapter 7

Albu, C. *Umanistul Nicolaus Olahus* [Nicolaus Olahus the humanist]. Bucharest, 1968.

Birăescu, T. *Banatul sub turci* [The Banat under the Turks]. Timişoara, 1934.

Capesius, B. *Sie förderten den Lauf der Dinge. Deutsche Humanisten auf dem Boden Siebenbürgens.* Bucharest, 1967.

Decei, A. "Aspecte economice şi sociale din viaţa Banatului în epoca otomană" [Economic and social aspects of life in the Banat during the Ottoman period]. In *Studii cu privire la istoria Banatului,* vol. 2. Timişoara, 1974.

Dumitrescu-Buşulenga, Z. *Valori şi echivalenţe umanistice* [Humanistic values and equivalences]. Bucharest, 1973.

Duţu, Al. *Les livres de sagesse dans la culture roumaine. Introduction à l'histoire des mentalités sud-est européennes.* Bucharest, 1971.

————. *Umaniştii români şi cultura europeană* [The Romanian humanists and European culture]. Bucharest, 1974.

Goldenberg, S. *Clujul în sec. XVI. Producţia şi schimbul de mărfuri* [Cluj in the sixteenth century: the production and exchange of wares]. Bucharest, 1958.

Heltai, Gáspár. *Gáspár Heltai válogatott munkái* [Selected works of Gáspár Heltai]. Edited by E. Székely. Bucharest, 1957.

Imreh, Şt. "Contribuţii la studiul agriculturii transilvănene (1570–1610)" [Contributions to the study of Transylvanian agriculture (1570–1610)]. *Acta Musei Napocensis* 9 (1969):189–209.

Iroaie, P. *Umanismo romano.* Trapani, 1967.

Juhász, I. *A reformáció az erdélyi románok között* [The reformation among the Transylvanian Romanians]. Cluj, 1940.

Magyari, A. *A parasztság helyzete, Habsburg-ellenes és antifeudális harca a XVII-ik szźad fordulóján* [The situation of the peasantry and its struggle against the Habsburgs and feudalism by the turn of the seventeenth century]. Cluj, 1972.

Nistor, I. *Domnia lui Mihai Viteazul în Transilvania. 1 nov. 1599–19 aug. 1601* [The reign of Michael the Brave in Transylvania, 1 Nov. 1599–19 Aug. 1601]. Bucharest, 1946.

Nussbächer, G. *Johannes Honterus. Sein Leben und Werk.* Bucharest, 1976.

Panaitescu, P. P. *Introducere în istoria culturii românești* [Introduction to the history of Romanian culture]. Bucharest, 1969.

——. *Mihai Viteazul* [Michael the Brave]. Bucharest, 1936.

Pascu, Şt. "Collèges et académies dans les pays roumains du moyen âge." *Revue roumaine d'histoire* 5, no. 6 (1966):925–36.

——. *L'humanisme et la culture roumaine ancienne.* Cluj, 1971.

——. *Mihai Viteazul. Unirea şi centralizarea ţărilor române* [Michael the Brave: the unification and centralization of the Romanian principalities]. Bucharest, 1973.

——. *Mişcările tărăneşti prilejuite de intrarea lui Mihai Viteazul în Transilvania* [Peasant uprisings occasioned by Michael the Brave's arrival in Transylvania]. Bucharest, 1956.

Prodan, D. *Iobăgia în Transilvania în sec. XVI* [Serfdom in Transylvania in the sixteenth century]. 2 vols. Bucharest, 1962, 1968.

Sebestyén, G., and Sebestyén, V. *Arhitectura renaşterii în Transilvania* [Renaissance architecture in Transylvania]. Bucharest, 1963.

Chapter 8

Blaga, L. *Gîndirea românească în Transilvania în secolul al XVIII-lea* [Romanian thought in Transylvania in the eighteenth century]. Bucharest, 1966.

Catoşman, P. "Contribuţii la istoria scoalelor românești din Banat" [Contributions to the history of the Romanian schools in the Banat]. *Mitropolia Banatului* 6, nos. 7–12 (1956); 7, nos. 1–12 (1957); 8, nos. 1–3 (1958).

Csetri, E., and Imreh, Şt. "Stratificarea socială a populaţiei din Transilvania la sfîrşitul orînduirii feudale" [The social stratification of the Transylvanian population by the end of the feudal period]. In *Populaţie şi societate*, vol. 1, pp. 139–238. Cluj, 1975.

Decei, A. "Memoriul (Supplex libellus) lui I. Inochentie Micu Klein către regina Maria Tereza, din anul 1744" [The memorial (Supplex libellus) of Inochentie Micu Klein to empress Maria Theresa in 1744]. *Anuarul Institutului de Istorie din Cluj* 10 (1967):178–235,

Dragomir, S. *Istoria dezrobirii religioase a românilor din Ardeal în sec. XVIII* [The history of the religious emancipation of the Transylvanian Romanians in the eighteenth century]. 2 vols. Sibiu, 1920, 1930.

Duţu, Al. *Coordonate ale culturii românşti în sec. XVIII (1700–1821)* [Coordinates of Romanian culture in the eighteenth century (1700–1821)]. Bucharest, 1969.

Göllner, C. *Regimentele grăniceresti din Transilvania 1784–1851* [The frontier guard regiments of Transylvania, 1784–1851]. Bucharest, 1973.

Imreh, I.; Benkö, S.; and Csetri, E. *Tanulmányok az erdélyi kapitalizmus*

Kezdeteiröl [Studies on the beginning of capitalism in Transylvania]. Bucharest, 1956.

Jakó, S. *Philobiblon transilvan* [Transylvanian philobiblon]. Bucharest, 1977.

Neamțu, Al. "Organizarea și exploatarea ocnelor de sare din Transilvania în sec. XVIII" [The organization and exploitation of Transylvanian salt pits in the eighteenth century]. *Anuarul Institutului de Istorie din Cluj* 16 (1973):43–75.

———. "Tehnica minieră din Transilvania în sec. XVIII" [Mining technique in Transylvania in the eighteenth century]. *Anuarul Institutului de Istorie din Cluj* 14 (1971):8–104.

Păclișanu, Z. "Statistique des Roumains de Transylvanie au XVIIᵉ siècle." *Revue de Transylvanie* 1 (1934).

Pascu, Șt. *Istoria Transilvaniei* [History of Transylvania]. Pt. 3. Blaj, 1944.

Prodan, D. *La théorie de l'immigration des roumains des principautés roumaines en Transylvanie au XVIIIᵉ siècle. Étude critique.* Sibiu, 1948.

Surdu, B. "Contribuții la problema nașterii manufacturilor din Transilvania în secolul al XVIII-lea" [Contributions to the question of the establishment of Transylvanian manufactures in the eighteenth century]. *Anuarul Institutului de Istorie din Cluj* 7 (1964):216–45.

Țintă, A. *Colonizările habsburgice în Banat, 1716–1740* [Habsburg colonization in the Banat]. Timișoara, 1972.

Chapter 9

Benkö, S. *Sorsformáló értelem. Müvelödéstörténeti dolgozatok* [The reason of existence: studies on the history of culture]. Bucharest, 1971.

Densușianu, N. *Revoluțiunea lui Horea în Transilvania și Ungaria, 1784–85* [Horea's revolt in Transylvania and Hungary, 1784–85]. Bucharest, 1884.

Edroiu, N. *Răsunetul european al răscoalei lui Horea* [The European echo of Horea's uprising]. Cluj, 1976.

Ghișe, E., and Teodor, P. *Fragmentarium illuminist* [Enlightenment fragmentarium]. Cluj, 1972.

Giurgiu, N. "Populația Transilvaniei la sfîrșitul secolului al XVIII-lea și începutul secolului al XIX-lea" [The population of Transylvania at the end of the eighteenth century and the beginning of the nineteenth century]. In *Populație și societate*, vol. 1, pp. 97–138. Cluj, 1975.

Imreh, I. *Erdélyi hétköznapok, 1750–1850* [Everyday life in Transylvania, 1750–1850]. Bucharest, 1979.

———; Benkö, S.; and Csetri, E. *Tanulmányok az erdélyi kapitalizmus Kezdeteiröl* [Studies on the beginning of capitalism in Transylvania]. Bucharest, 1956.

Jancsó, E. *Erdélyi jakobinusok* [The Transylvanian jacobins]. Cluj, 1947.

Lübhord, Fr. *Menschen und Zeiten. Aufsätz und Studien.* Bucharest, 1970.

Lungu, I. *Școala Ardeleană* [The Transylvanian school]. Bucharest, 1978.

Lupaș, I. *Contribuții la istoria politică a românilor ardeleni, 1780–92* [Contributions to the political history of the Transylvanian Romanians, 1780–92]. Bucharest, 1928.

———. *Răscoala țăranilor din Transilvania la 1784* [The Transylvanian peasants' rebellion of 1784]. Cluj, 1934.

Munteanu, R. *Contribuția Școlii ardelene la culturalizarea maselor* [The contribution of the Transylvanian school to the enlightenment of the masses]. Bucharest, 1962.

Păclișanu, Z. *Luptele politice ale românilor ardeleni din 1790–92* [The political struggle of the Transylvanian Romanians between 1790 and 1792]. Bucharest, 1923.

Pascu, Şt. "The Publication of Sources Concerning Horea's Revolt." *Romanian Studies* 1 (1970):149–72.

——. *Les sources et les recherches de démographie historique en Roumanie.* Liège, 1965.

Popovici, D. *La littérature roumaine à l'epoque des Lumières.* Sibiu, 1945.

Prodan, D. "Desfiinţarea şerbiei în Transilvania (1785)" [The abolition of serfdom in Transylvania (1785). *Studii şi materiale de istorie medie* 4 (1974):9–68.

——. *Răscoala lui Horea* [Horea's rebellion]. 2 vols. Bucharest, 1978.

——. "*Supplex Libellus Valachorum,*" or the Political Struggle of the Romanians in Transylvania during the Eighteenth Century. Bucharest, 1971.

Protopopescu, L. *Contribuţii la istoria învăţămîntului din Transilvania 1774–1805* [Contributions to the history of education in Transylvania 1774–1805]. Bucharest, 1966.

Răduţiu, A., and Gyémánt, L. "*Supplex Libellus Valachorum*" *în variantele româneşti de la Schei* [The Supplex Libellus Valachorum in Romanian translations from Schei]. Cluj, 1975.

Ranca, I. "Aspects de l'affirmation de la conscience nationale du peuple roumain pendant l'insurrection de Horea." *Revue roumaine d'histoire* 7, no. 6 (1968):271–97.

Teodor, P. ed. *Enlightenment and Romanian Society.* Cluj-Napoca, 1980.

Chapter 10

Bodea, C. *The Romanians' Struggle for Unification, 1834–1849.* Bucharest, 1970.

Cândea, V. "Les Lumières et la naissance de la conscience nationale chez les Roumains." In *Les Lumières et la formation de la conscience nationale chez les peuples du sud-est européen.* Bucharest, 1970.

Cheresteşiu, V. *Adunarea naţională de la Blaj* [The national assembly of Blaj]. Bucharest, 1966.

Demény, Lajos, ed. *1848. Arcok, eszmék, tettek* [1848. Aspects, ideas, facts]. Bucharest 1974.

Dragomir, S. *Avram Iancu.* Bucharest, 1965.

——. *Istoria revoluţiei românilor din Transilvania* [The history of the revolution of the Transylvanian Romanians]. Pt. 1. Cluj, 1949.

Duţu, Al. "Les racines de la conscience nationale chez les Roumains." In *Le Developpement de la conscience nationale en Europe orientale.* Paris, 1961.

Egyed, A. "A jobbágyfelszabadítás az 1848–az kolozsvári országgyülésen" [The abolition of serfdom by the 1848 diet]. In *1848. Arcok, eszmék, tettek,* pp. 84–103. Bucharest, 1974.

Florea, Z. *Natiunea română şi socialismul* [The Romanian nation and socialism]. Bucharest, 1974.

Göllner, C. *Die Siebenbürger Sachsen in der Revolutionsjahren 1848–1849.* Bucharest, 1967.

Kovács, J. *Adatok az 1848 utáni erdélyi tőkés mezögazdaságról.* [Facts about Transylvanian capitalist agriculture after 1848]. Bucharest, 1957.

Kroner, M. *Stephan Ludwig Roth.* Cluj, 1974.

Marica, G., et alia. *Ideologia generaţiei române de la 1848 din Transilvania* [The ideology of the 1848 Romanian generation in Transylvania]. Bucharest, 1968.

Pascu, St. *Avram Iancu. Viaţa şi faptele unui erou şi martir* [Avram Iancu: the life and feats of a hero and martyr]. Bucharest, 1972.

——. "The Constitution of the South East European Nations—Expression of

Bibliography

Social Modernization." *Studia Universitatis "Babeş-Bolyai."* *Historia,* 1979, p. 1–23.
——. *Formarea naţiunii române* [The formation of the Romanian nation]. Bucharest, 1959.
Revoluţia de la 1848 în ţările române [The revolution of 1848 in the Romanian principalities]. Bucharest, 1974.
Stănescu, E. "Roumanie. Histoire d'un mot chez les Roumains aux XVIIe-XIXe siècles." *Balkan Studies* 1 (1969):69–94.
Suciu, I. D. *Revoluţia de la 1848–1849 în Banat* [The revolution of 1848–1849 in the Banat]. Bucharest, 1968.
Teodor, P. *Avram Iancu în memorialistică* [Avram Iancu in memoirs]. Cluj, 1972.
Ursu, H. *Avram Iancu.* Bucharest, 1966.

Chapter 11

Károlyi, D. "Mişcarea antihabsburgică din Transilvania sub conducerea lui Makk Gál (1849–1854)" [The anti-Habsburg movement in Transylvania under the leadership of Makk Gál (1849–1854)]. *Studii* 8, no. 4 (1955):67–85.
Kovás, I. *Adatok az 1848 utáni erdélyi tőkés mezögazdaságról* [Facts about Transylvanian capitalist agriculture after 1848]. Bucharest, 1957.
——. "Despre politica agrară a guvernului transilvănean în perioada 1849–1850" [On the agrarian policy of the Transylvanian government in the period 1849–1850]. *Acta Musei Napocensis* 8 (1971):645–59.
——. "Mişcări ţărăneşti în Munţii Apuseni şi împrejurimi între anii 1849–1859" [Peasant movements in the Bihor Mountains and surroundings between the years 1849 and 1854]. *Studii şi articole de istorie modernă* 1 (1957):139–60.
Pascu, Şt. "Ecoul unirii Ţării Româneşti şi Moldovei în Transilvania" [The echo of the unification of Ţara Românească and Moldavia in Transylvania]. In *Studii privind Unirea Principatelor,* edited by Andrei Oţetea, pp. 451–66, Bucharest, 1960.
Retegan, S. *Dieta românească din 1863* [The Romanian diet of 1863]. Cluj, 1979.
——. "Eforturi şi realizări politice ale românilor din Transilvania în anii premergători dualismului" [Political efforts and achievements of the Transylvanian Romanians in the years before the dualism]. In *Românii din Transilvania împotriva dualismului austro-ungar,* edited by Şt. Pascu, pp. 38–83. Cluj, 1978.
——. "Răzvrătirea moţilor din 1852. Rolul lui Avram Iancu" [The revolt of the Romanians from the Bihor Mountains region in 1852: the role of Avram Iancu]. *Anuarul Institutului de Istorie din Cluj* 15 (1972):239–62.
——. "Structura social-economică a burgheziei româneşti din Transilvania în anii regimului liberal (1860–1867)" [The social and economic structure of the Romanian bourgeoisie in the years of the liberal regime (1860–1867)]. *Acta Musei Napocensis* 8 (1971): pp. 274–96.
Stan, A. "Legături economice ale Ţării Româneşti cu Transilvania (1848–1859)" [Economic relations between Ţara Românească and Transylvania (1848–1859)]. *Studii şi materiale de istorie modernă* 4 (1953):111–76.
Suciu, D. "Acţiuni politice româneşti împotriva suprimării autonomiei Transilvaniei între 1848–1867" [Romanian political actions against the abolition of Transylvanian autonomy between 1848 and 1867]. In *Românii din Transilvania împotriva dualismului austro-ungar,* pp. 84–117. Cluj, 1978.

Chapter 12

Abrudan, P. "Ajutorul bănesc și material al Transilvănenilor în sprijinul Războiului pentru cucerirea Independenței de stat a României" [The support in money and goods given by the Transilvanians to the Romanian war of state independence]. *Revista de istorie* 30 (1977), no. 1, pp. 23–46; no. 2, pp. 279–300.

Bodea, C., and Kovács, I. "Les Roumains de la monarchie des Habsbourgs et le compromis de 1867." *Revue roumaine d'histoire* 7, no. 3 (1967):359–70.

Bologa, V. L. *Ajutorul românilor ardeleni pentru răniții Războiului Independenții* [The support given by the Transylvanian Romanians to the wounded of the war of independence]. Sibiu, 1941.

Brașovul și Războiul de Independență [The town of Brașov and the war of independence]. Brașov, 1977.

Ceaușescu, I. *România în războiul de independență* [Romania in the war of independence]. Bucharest, 1977.

———; Mocanu, V.; and Călin, I. *Drum de glorii. Pagini din eroismul armatei române în războiul nostru pentru indepență* [The way of glory: aspects of the heroism of the Romanian army in our war for independence]. Craiova, 1977.

Cicală, I. *Mișcarea muncitorească și socialistă din Transilvania, 1901–1921* [The socialist and working-class movement in Transylvania, 1901–1921]. Bucharest, 1979.

Coman, I., ed. *România în Războiul de Independență* [Romania in the war of independence]. Bucharest, 1977.

Csucsuja, Șt. "Manifestări ale solidarității maselor populare maghiare cu războiul pentru independența României" [Manifestations of the solidarity of the Hungarians with the war of independence of România]. *Revista de istorie* 30, no. 5 (1977):811–27.

Deac, A. *Mișcarea muncitorească din Transilvania* [The working-class movement in Transylvania]. Bucharest, 1962.

Diculescu, Vl. "The Romanians of Transylvania and the 1877–1878 War." *Revue des études sud-est européennes* 15, no. 5 (1977):3–23.

Egyed, A. *A parasztság Erdélyben a századfordulon* [Transylvanian peasantry at the turn of the nineteenth century]. Bucharest, 1975.

———. *Falu, város, civilizáció, 1848–1914* [Village, town, civilization, 1848–1914]. Bucharest, 1981.

———. "Istoricul asociațiilor muncitorești din Transilvania între anii 1868–1872" [The history of the workers' associations in Transylvania between 1868 and 1872]. *Studii* 9, no. 6 (1959):27–50.

———. "Unele caracteristici ale dezvoltării industriei în Transilvania la sfîrșitul sec. al XIX-lea" [Some characteristics of industrial development in Transylvania by the end of the nineteenth century]. *Acta Musei Napocensis* 5 (1968):251–64.

———; Vajda, L.; and Cicală, I. *Munkás és parasztmozgalmak Erdélyben* [Workers' and peasants' movements in Transylvania]. Bucharest, 1962.

Gyémánt, L., and Gündisch, K. *Das Echo des Unabhängigkeitskrieges von 1877 in Siebenbürgen.* Cluj, 1977.

Kroner, M. "Die Stellung der Siebenbürger Sachsen zu dem Unabhängigkeitskrieg Rumäniens von 1877–1878." *Revue roumaine d'histoire* 16, no. 2 (1977):297–308.

Maior, L. *Transilvania și Războiul pentru Independență* [Transylvania and the war of independence]. Cluj, 1977.

Moroianu, G. *Les luttes des Roumains transylvains pour la liberté et l'opinion européenne.* Paris, 1933.

Netea, V. *Istoria Memorandului* [The history of the memorandum]. Bucharest, 1946.

————. *Lupta românilor din Transilvania pentru libertate națională* (1848–81) [The struggle of the Romanians in Transylvania for national liberty (1848–81)]. Bucharest, 1974.

Olteanu, C. *Masele populare și războiul de independență* [The masses and the war of independence]. Bucharest, 1977.

Retegan, S. "Pronunciamentul de la Blaj (1868)" [The pronunciamentum of Blaj (1868)]. *Anuarul Institutului de Istorie din Cluj* 9 (1966):127–42.

Suciu, I. D. "Solidaritatea românilor bănățeni cu Războiul de Independență [The solidarity of the Romanians of the Banat with the war of independence]. *Revista de istorie* 30, no. 3 (1977):397–412.

Vajda, L. "Despre situația economică și social-politică a Transilvaniei în primii ani ai sec. al XX-lea" [On the economic, social, and political situation in Transylvania in the early nineteenth century]. *Studii și materiale de istorie modernă* 1 (1957):215–349.

Chapter 13

Armbruster, A., and Jaeger, H. "Über die Einstellung der deutschen Bevölkerung Siebenbürgens und des Banats zur Vereinigung von 1918." *Revue roumaine d'histoire* 7, no. 6 (1968):1087–97.

Bihorul și Unirea [The Bihor region and the union]. Oradea, 1978.

Ciobanu, P. *Unirea Banatului și încorporarea Timișoarei la România Mare* [The union of the Banat and the incorporation of Timișoara into Greater Romania]. Timișoara, 1934.

Ciobanu, Șt. *Unirea Basarabiei cu România* [Bessarabia's union with Romania]. Bucharest, 1928.

Cloțel, I. *Frămîntările unui an* [The unrest of a year]. Sibiu, 1919.

Constantinescu, M., and Pascu, Șt., eds. *Unification of the Romanian State. The Union of Transylvania with Old Romania.* Bucharest, 1970.

Cupșa, I. *Armata româna în campaniile din anii 1916–1917* [The Romanian army in the campaigns of 1916 and 1917]. Bucharest, 1967.

Deac, A. *Caracterul participării României la primul război mondial* [The nature of Romania's participation in the first world war]. Bucharest, 1974.

Gheorghiu, I., and Nuțu, C. *Adunarea Națională de la Alba Iulia. 1 Decembrie 1918* [The national assembly of Alba Iulia. 1 December 1918]. Bucharest, 1968.

Giannini, A. "L'unità nazionale delle Romania alle Conferenza delle Pace." In *Studi sulla Romania*, pp. 17–25. Naples, 1923.

Guillemont, M. *L'unité roumaine.* Paris, 1919.

Hăgan, Tr., et alia. *Maramureșul și Unirea* [The Maramureș region and the union]. Baia Mare, 1968.

Hurmuzache, Șt., and Adam, I. "Consiliile naționale române în lupta pentru Unirea Transilvaniei cu România" [The Romanian councils in their struggle for the union of Transylvania with Old Romania]. *Revista Arhivelor* 11, no. 2 (1968) p. 133–51.

Kirițescu, C. *La Roumanie dans la guerre mondiale* (1916–19). Bucharest, 1927.

Kovács, I. "La presse hongroise au sujet de l'Assemblé nationale d'Alba Iulia du 1er decembre 1918." *Revue roumaine d'histoire* 7, no. 6 (1968):1075–85.

Leeper, A.W. *The Justice of Romania's Cause,* New York, 1917.

Netea, V. *O zi din istoria Transilvaniei* [A day in the history of Transylvania]. Bucharest, 1970.

Nistor, I. *Unirea Bucovinei, 28 noiembrie 1918* [Bukovina's Union, 28 November 1918]. Bucharest, 1928.

Păcățianu, T. V. *Jertfele românilor din Ardeal, Banat, Crișana, Sătmar, și Mara-*

mureş aduse în războiul mondial din 1914–18 [The sacrifices of the Romanians of Transylvania, the Banat, Crişana, Sătmar, and Maramureş in the world war of 1914 to 1918]. Sibiu, 1925.

Pascu,, St. *Marea Adunare Naţională de la Alba Iulia* [The Great National Assembly of Alba Iulia]. Cluj, 1968.

——. "The National Unity of the Romanians and the Breaking of the Austro-Hungarian Empire." *Austrian History Yearbook* 4 (1969): 83–105.

Popescu, E. "Ecoul Unirii Transilvaniei cu Vechea Românie în presa de dincoace de Carpaţi" [The echo of the union of Transylvania with Old Romania in the press across the Carpathians]. In *Unitate şi continuitate în istoria poporului român*, edited by D. Berciu, pp. 417–28. Bucharest, 1968.

Popescu-Puţuri, I., and Deac, A., eds. *1918. Unirea Transilvaniei cu România* [1918: the union of Transylvania with Old Romania]. 3d ed. Bucharest, 1978.

Porţeanu, Al. "L'apport du mouvement ouvrier et socialiste de Transylvanie au parachèvement de l'unité de l'état national roumain." *Revue roumaine d'histoire* 7, no. 6 (1968):1007–36.

Romania 1918. L'unione della Transilvania con Romania. Rome, 1973.

Stoica, V. *In America pentru cauza românească* [In America for the Romanian cause]. Bucharest, 1926.

Suciu, I.D. "La lutte des Roumains du Banat pour la réalisation de l'unité de l'état." *Revue roumaine d'histoire* 7, no. 6 (1968):980–1005.

Toderaşcu, C. "Evoluţia voluntariatului în anii 1916–18" [The evolution of the volunteer corps between 1916 and 1918]. In *Oastea cea Mare* [The great army], pp. 219–48. Centrul de studii şi cercetări de istorie şi teorie militară. Bucharest, 1972.

Chapter 14

Agrigoroaiei, P. "Unirea din 1918—începutul unei noi etape în dezvoltarea istorică a României" [Union of 1918—beginning of a new phase in the historical development of Romania]. *Anuarul Institutului de istorie şi arheologie din Iaşi* 15 (1978): 257–76.

Axenciuc, V. "Unificarea organismului economiei naţionale şi refacerea economică postbelică a României" [Unification of the structure of the national economy and the economic recovery of Romania after the war]. *Revista de istorie* 30, no. 5 (1977): 931–47.

Brătianu, G. *Actiunea politică şi militară a României în 1919* [Romania's political and military activity in 1919]. Bucharest, 1940.

Cicală, I. "Urmările unirii Transilvaniei cu România" [The consequences of Transylvania's union with Romania]. *Anuarul Institutului de istorie şi arheologie din Cluj-Napoca* 21 (1978): 30–50.

Galea, A. "Unele aspecte ale activităţii Consiliului Dirigent în perioada 2 decembrie 1918–10 aprilie 1920" [Some aspects of the activity of the Administrative Council from 2 December 1918 to 10 April 1920]. *Ziridava* (1977):267–82.

Iancu, Gh. "Preocupări ale Consiliului Dirigent pentru reorganizarea activităţii industriale a Transilvaniei" [Strivings of the Administrative Council after the reorganization of industrial life in Transylvania]. *Marisia* 5 (1975):261–81.

——. "Consideraţii cu privire la rolul şi locul Consiliului Dirigent în primii ani după unire" [Considerations on the role and place of the Administrative Council during the first years after unification]. *Anuarul Institutului de istorie şi arheologie din Cluj-Napoca* 21 (1978):51–65.

Jura, E.; Mleşniţă, V., and Benke, Al. "Aspecte ale agriculturii României între cele două războaie mondiale" [Aspects of Romania's agriculture between the two world wars]. In *Studii de istorie a economiei şi gîndirii economice româneşti*, pp. 57–76. Cluj, 1958.

Lapedatu, Al. *Actes d'union des provinces de Bessarabie, Bucovine, Transylvanie, Banat avec la Roumanie.* Paris, 1919.

Moisiuc, V. "Tratatul de la Trianon—consacrare internaţională a legitimităţii unirii Transilvaniei cu România" [The Trianon treaty—international recognition of the legitimate union of Transylvania with Romania]. *Analele Institutului de studii social-politice* 22, no. 3 (1976): 44–57.

Muşat, M., and Ardeleanu, I. *La vie politique en Roumanie, 1918–1921.* Bucharest, 1977.

Şandru, D. *Reforma agrară din 1921 în România* [Agrarian reform in Romania in 1921]. Bucharest, 1975.

Seişanu, R. *Principiul Naţionalităţilor. Originile, evoluţia, şi elementele constitutive ale naţionalităţii* [The principle of nationalities: the origins, evolution, and constitutive elements of the nationality]. Bucharest, 1935.

Sofronie, G. *Principiul naţionalităţilor în tratatele de pace din 1919–1920* [The principle of the nationalities in the peace treaties of 1919–1920]. Bucharest, 1936.

Tilea, V. *Acţiunea diplomatică a României nov. 1919–martie 1920* [The diplomatic activity of Romania, November 1919–March 1920]. Sibiu, 1925.

Index

Ştefan Pascu is an internationally recognized authority on Romanian history. A fellow of the Romanian Academy, he is president of its Historical Sciences Division and is also the director of the Institute of History and Archeology in Cluj-Napoca. Formerly dean of the faculty of history and philosophy and rector of the University of Cluj-Napoca, he currently serves as president of the National Committee of Romanian Historians, the International Committee of Historical Demography, and the Society of Historical Sciences in Romania. Professor Pascu has published extensively in Romanian and other languages.

D. Robert Ladd is an American-born scholar who was living in Romania as a Fulbright fellow when he undertook this translation.

Paul E. Michelson has been an IREX-Fulbright researcher at the Institute of History in Bucharest and is a student of Romanian historiography. He teaches history at Huntington College.

The manuscript was edited by Sherwyn T. Carr. The book was designed by Jim Billingsley. The index was prepared by Faith Sheptoski.

The typeface for the text and display is Mergenthaler VIP Trump, based on a design by Georg Trump in 1954. The text is printed on 60 lb. Glatfelter paper and the book is bound in Holliston Mills' Roxite cloth over binder's boards.

Manufactured in the United States of America.